WJHC
Hold Tight!

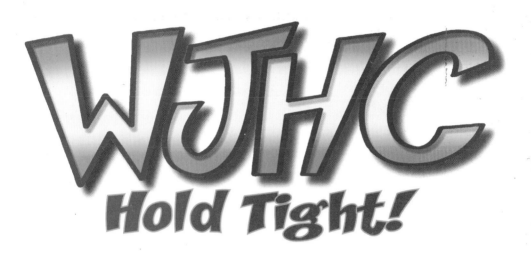

Writer
Jane Smith Fisher

Penciler
Joe Staton

Inker
Adam Dekraker

Colorist and Letterer
John Green

Editor
Iyna B. Caruso

Original Character Design
Kirsten Petersen

Book Design and Production
John Green

Creative Consultant
Alex Simmons

Print Coordination
Harold Buchholz

Inspiration
Andrew Fisher

Safety Net
Inez

WJHC was created by
Jane Smith Fisher

Wilson Place Comics, Inc.
P.O. Box 435
Oceanside, NY 11572

www.WJHC.com

ISBN: 0-9744235-1-3
PRINTED IN CANADA

For the rest of the Smith kids, Carole and Harrison, and Bea and Dave Smith (who I miss each and every day)

Meet the cast of WJHC

Janey Wells - Watch and learn. This girl's on a fast track to the top. When Janey's on a mission nothing can stand in her way.

Ciel (pronounced Seel) Chin-King - Now Ciel knows fashion. Just don't be fooled by her trendy girl looks. Great ideas pop out of this brightly colored mind.

Tara O'Toole - In every school there's someone who thinks they're just a little better than everyone else. Well Jackson Hill's someone is Tara O'Toole.

The Skate - "Way cool" is the only way to describe Jackson Hill's beatnik on blades. And wait 'til you see how this guy works a microphone.

Roland Drayton - You have to give this kid credit. He'll take on any challenge--even if he's the completely wrong one for the job.

Sandy Diaz - Meet Jackson Hill's electronics whiz--lifetime member of the Audio/Visual department. You know a guy like this will come in handy.

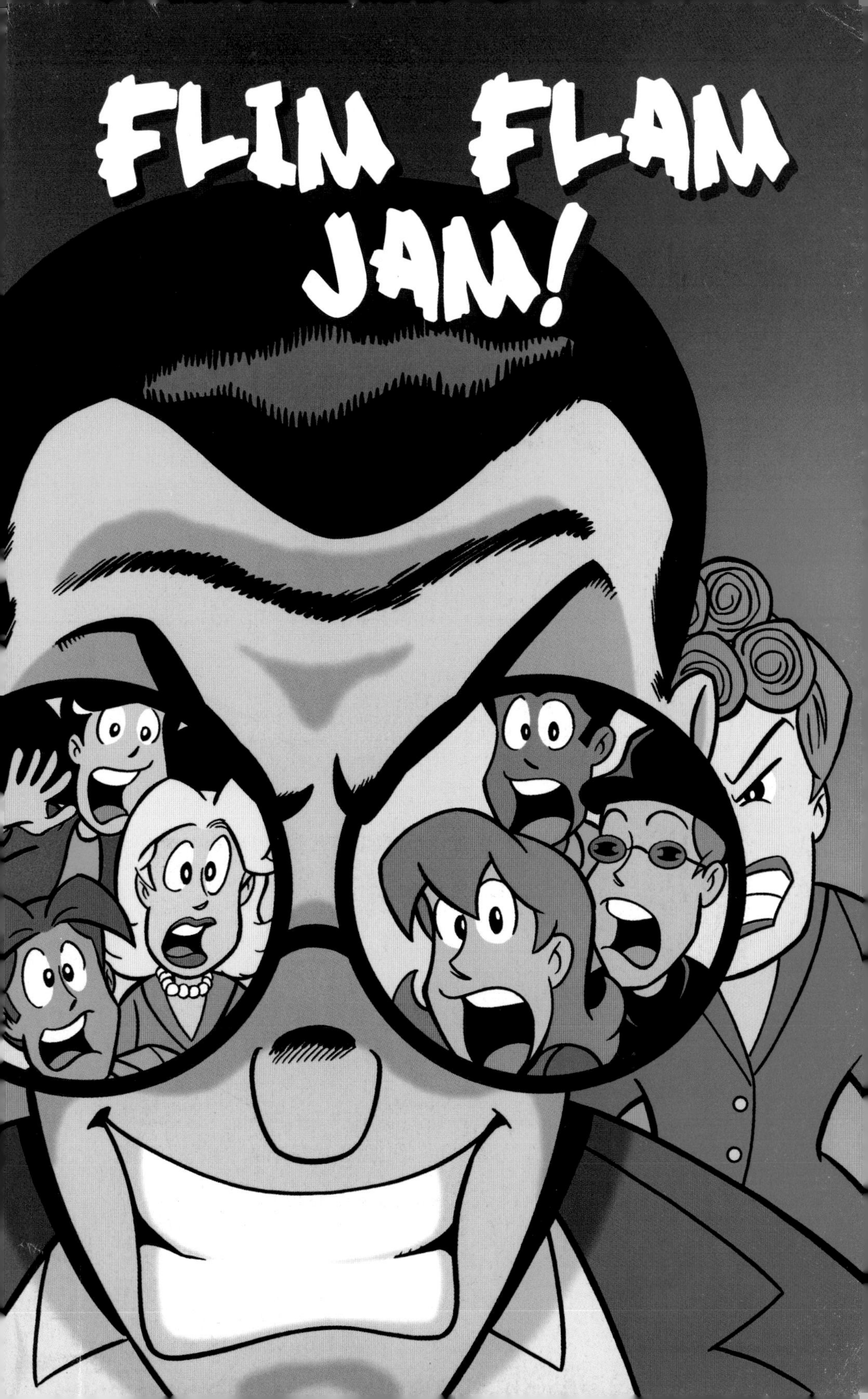
FLIM FLAM JAM!

Previously seen in WJHC...

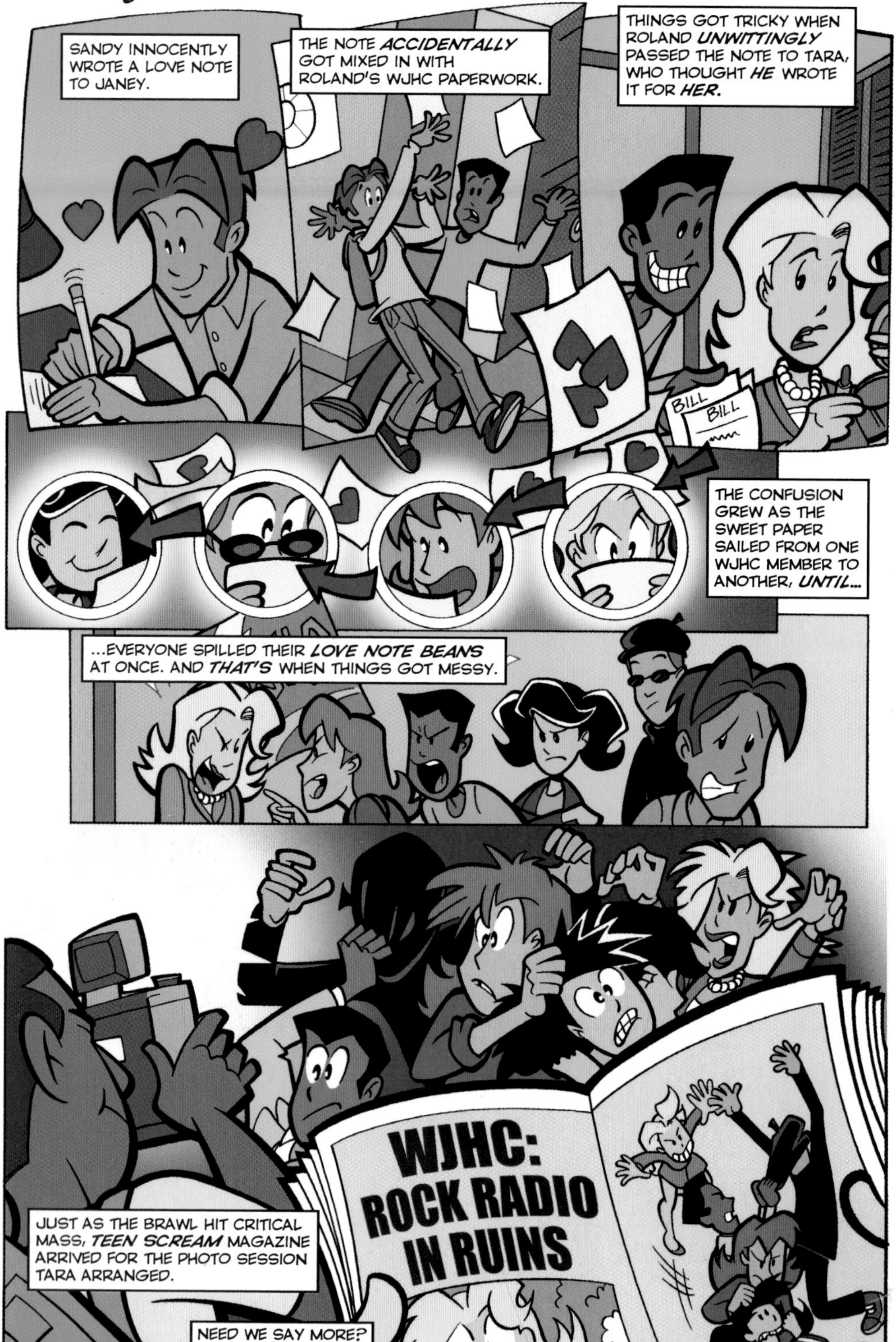

SANDY INNOCENTLY WROTE A LOVE NOTE TO JANEY.
THE NOTE ACCIDENTALLY GOT MIXED IN WITH ROLAND'S WJHC PAPERWORK.
THINGS GOT TRICKY WHEN ROLAND UNWITTINGLY PASSED THE NOTE TO TARA, WHO THOUGHT HE WROTE IT FOR HER.
BILL
BILL
THE CONFUSION GREW AS THE SWEET PAPER SAILED FROM ONE WJHC MEMBER TO ANOTHER, UNTIL...
...EVERYONE SPILLED THEIR LOVE NOTE BEANS AT ONCE. AND THAT'S WHEN THINGS GOT MESSY.
JUST AS THE BRAWL HIT CRITICAL MASS, TEEN SCREAM MAGAZINE ARRIVED FOR THE PHOTO SESSION TARA ARRANGED.
WJHC: ROCK RADIO IN RUINS
NEED WE SAY MORE?

OUR STORY CONTINUES ON A BRIGHT FRIDAY MORNING.

OOH LA LA, THAT *BRAD PITT*. WHAT A *HUNK*.

HUBBA, HUBBA!

MISS WILLOW.

WHA--!

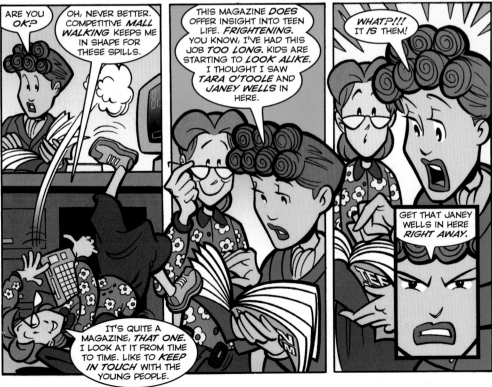

ARE YOU *OK?*

OH, NEVER BETTER. COMPETITIVE *MALL WALKING* KEEPS ME IN SHAPE FOR THESE SPILLS.

THIS MAGAZINE *DOES* OFFER INSIGHT INTO TEEN LIFE. *FRIGHTENING.* YOU KNOW, I'VE HAD THIS JOB *TOO LONG.* KIDS ARE STARTING TO *LOOK ALIKE.* I THOUGHT I SAW *TARA O'TOOLE* AND *JANEY WELLS* IN HERE.

WHAT?!!! IT *IS* THEM!

IT'S QUITE A MAGAZINE, *THAT ONE.* I LOOK AT IT FROM TIME TO TIME. LIKE TO *KEEP IN TOUCH* WITH THE YOUNG PEOPLE.

GET THAT JANEY WELLS IN HERE *RIGHT AWAY.*

7

HI, MRS. BORT. MISS WILLOW SAID YOU NEEDED TO SEE ME.

OH, NO! MRS. BORT SAW THE *TEEN SCREAM SPREAD*??!! I BETTER STAY CALM AND *ACT DUMB*.

SOOO... HOW'S JACKSON HILL HIGH TREATING YOU THESE DAYS?

VERY WELL UNTIL *THIS* MORNING.

THEN I SAW *THIS*.

K RADIO RUINS

OH, THOSE *PHOTOS*. TALK ABOUT *SENSATIONALISM*. I CAN EXPLAIN...

I THINK YOU *MISUNDERSTOOD* THE PURPOSE OF THIS MEETING, MISS WELLS. I'M NOT LOOKING FOR EXPLANATIONS.

MISS WILLOW, PLEASE SEND IN MR. STANGER.

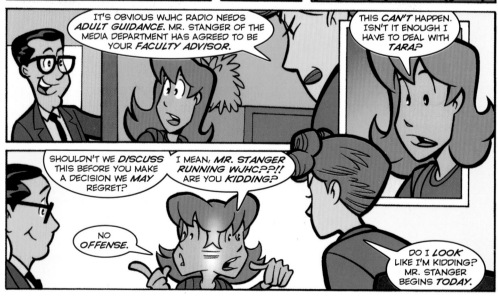

IT'S OBVIOUS WJHC RADIO NEEDS *ADULT GUIDANCE*. MR. STANGER OF THE MEDIA DEPARTMENT HAS AGREED TO BE YOUR *FACULTY ADVISOR*.

THIS *CAN'T* HAPPEN. ISN'T IT ENOUGH I HAVE TO DEAL WITH *TARA*?

SHOULDN'T WE *DISCUSS* THIS BEFORE YOU MAKE A DECISION WE *MAY* REGRET?

I MEAN, *MR. STANGER RUNNING WJHC*??!! ARE YOU *KIDDING*?

NO *OFFENSE*.

DO I *LOOK* LIKE I'M KIDDING? MR. STANGER BEGINS *TODAY*.

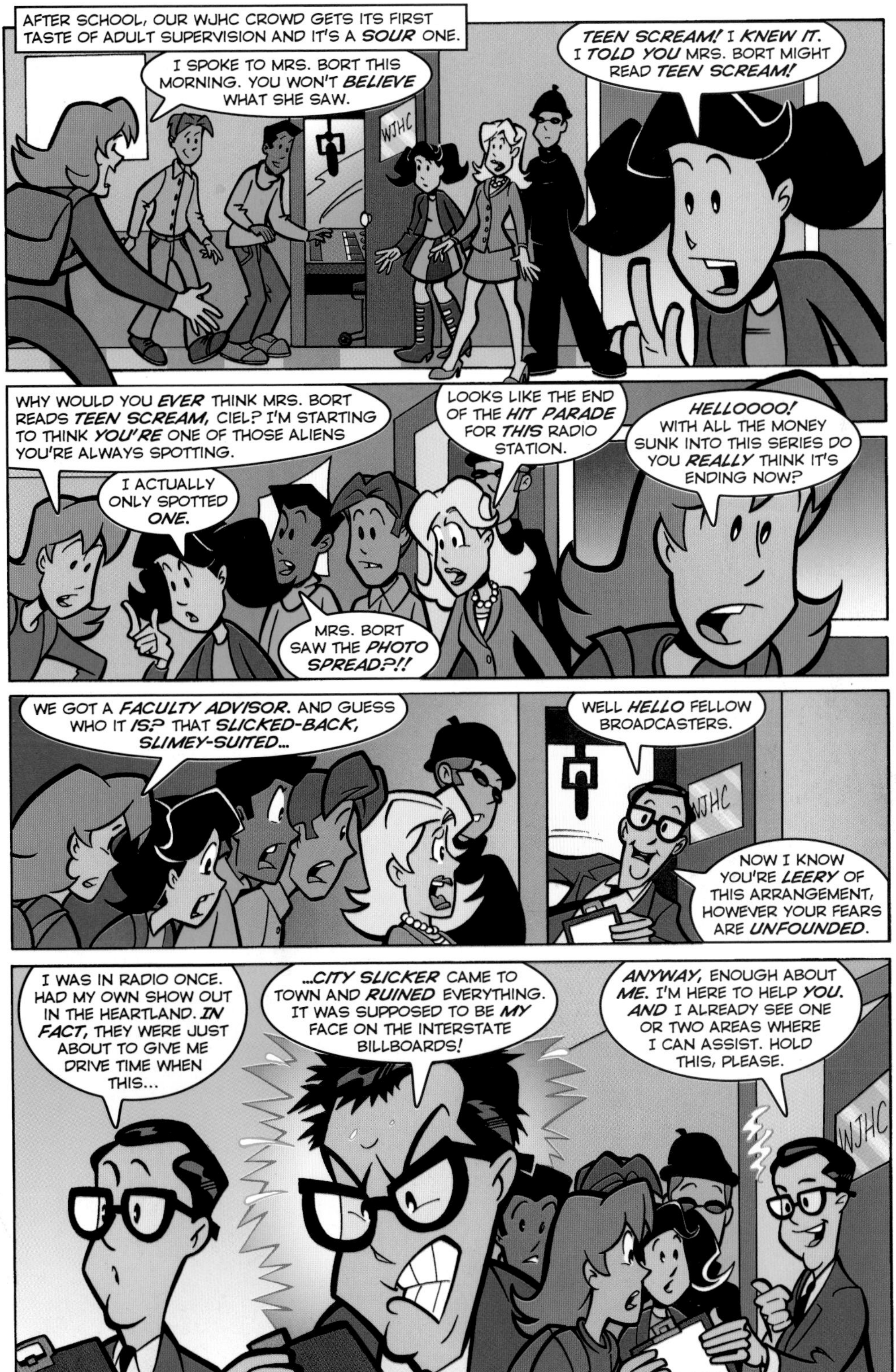

AFTER SCHOOL, OUR WJHC CROWD GETS ITS FIRST TASTE OF ADULT SUPERVISION AND IT'S A SOUR ONE.
I SPOKE TO MRS. BORT THIS MORNING. YOU WON'T BELIEVE WHAT SHE SAW.
WJHC
TEEN SCREAM! I KNEW IT. I TOLD YOU MRS. BORT MIGHT READ TEEN SCREAM!
WHY WOULD YOU EVER THINK MRS. BORT READS TEEN SCREAM, CIEL? I'M STARTING TO THINK YOU'RE ONE OF THOSE ALIENS YOU'RE ALWAYS SPOTTING.
I ACTUALLY ONLY SPOTTED ONE.
MRS. BORT SAW THE PHOTO SPREAD?!!
LOOKS LIKE THE END OF THE HIT PARADE FOR THIS RADIO STATION.
HELLOOOO! WITH ALL THE MONEY SUNK INTO THIS SERIES DO YOU REALLY THINK IT'S ENDING NOW?
WE GOT A FACULTY ADVISOR. AND GUESS WHO IT IS? THAT SLICKED-BACK, SLIMEY-SUITED...
WELL HELLO FELLOW BROADCASTERS.
WJHC
NOW I KNOW YOU'RE LEERY OF THIS ARRANGEMENT, HOWEVER YOUR FEARS ARE UNFOUNDED.
I WAS IN RADIO ONCE. HAD MY OWN SHOW OUT IN THE HEARTLAND. IN FACT, THEY WERE JUST ABOUT TO GIVE ME DRIVE TIME WHEN THIS...
...CITY SLICKER CAME TO TOWN AND RUINED EVERYTHING. IT WAS SUPPOSED TO BE MY FACE ON THE INTERSTATE BILLBOARDS!
ANYWAY, ENOUGH ABOUT ME. I'M HERE TO HELP YOU. AND I ALREADY SEE ONE OR TWO AREAS WHERE I CAN ASSIST. HOLD THIS, PLEASE.
WJHC

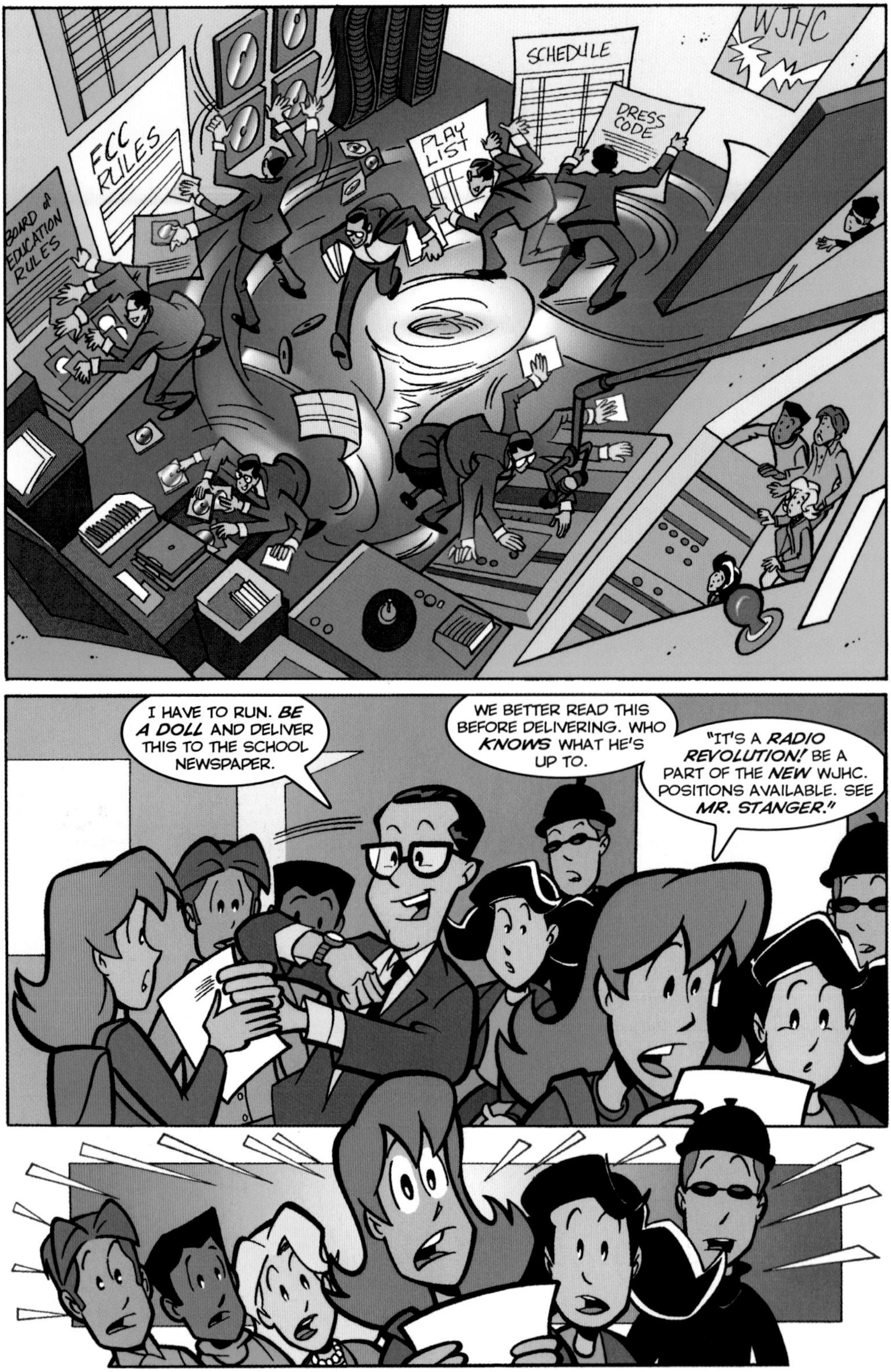

BOARD of EDUCATION RULES
FCC RULES
PLAY LIST
SCHEDULE
DRESS CODE
WJHC
I HAVE TO RUN. BE A DOLL AND DELIVER THIS TO THE SCHOOL NEWSPAPER.
WE BETTER READ THIS BEFORE DELIVERING. WHO KNOWS WHAT HE'S UP TO.
"IT'S A RADIO REVOLUTION! BE A PART OF THE NEW WJHC. POSITIONS AVAILABLE. SEE MR. STANGER."

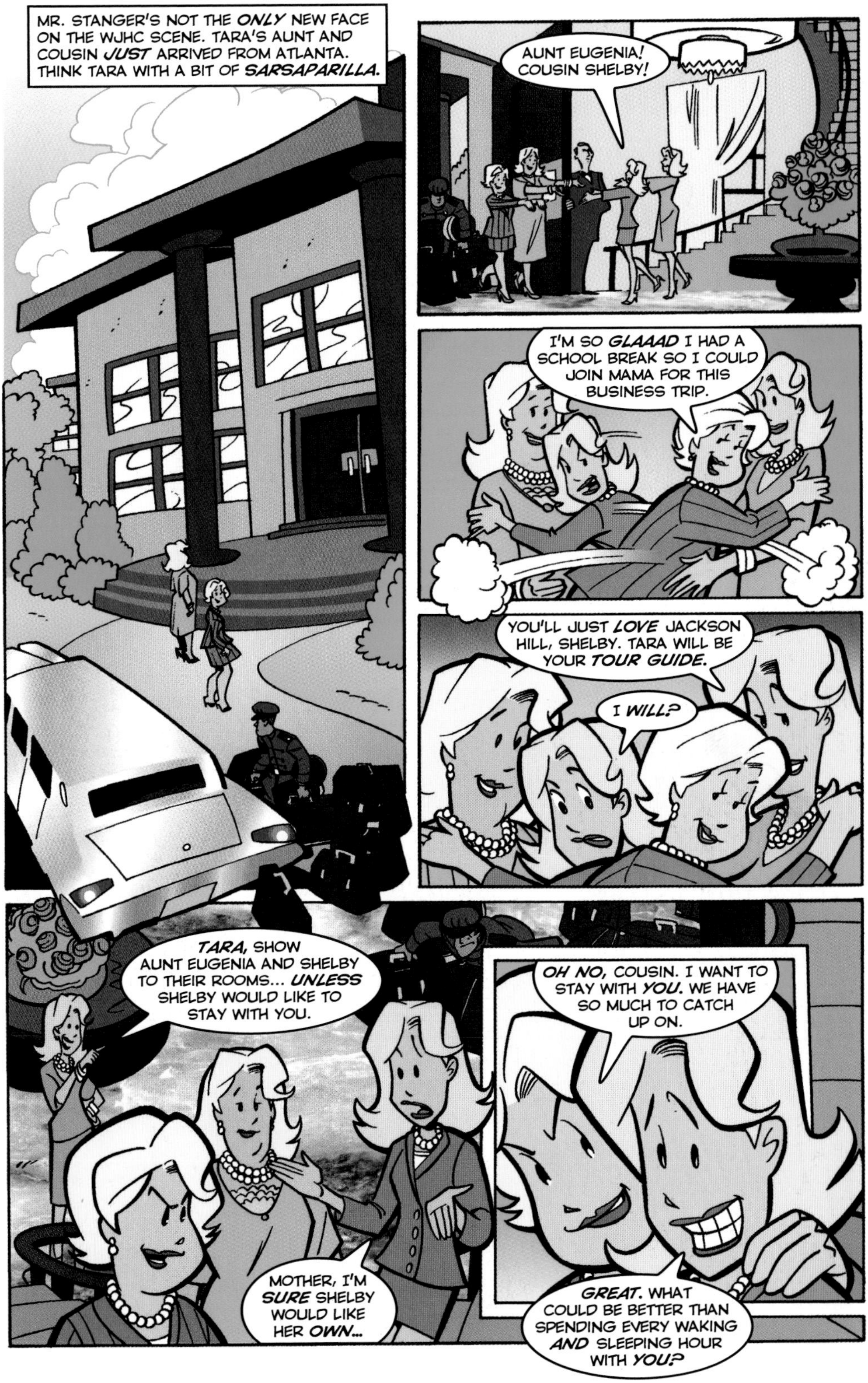
MR. STANGER'S NOT THE ONLY NEW FACE ON THE WJHC SCENE. TARA'S AUNT AND COUSIN JUST ARRIVED FROM ATLANTA. THINK TARA WITH A BIT OF SARSAPARILLA.
AUNT EUGENIA! COUSIN SHELBY!
I'M SO GLAAAD I HAD A SCHOOL BREAK SO I COULD JOIN MAMA FOR THIS BUSINESS TRIP.
YOU'LL JUST LOVE JACKSON HILL, SHELBY. TARA WILL BE YOUR TOUR GUIDE.
I WILL?
TARA, SHOW AUNT EUGENIA AND SHELBY TO THEIR ROOMS... UNLESS SHELBY WOULD LIKE TO STAY WITH YOU.
MOTHER, I'M SURE SHELBY WOULD LIKE HER OWN...
OH NO, COUSIN. I WANT TO STAY WITH YOU. WE HAVE SO MUCH TO CATCH UP ON.
GREAT. WHAT COULD BE BETTER THAN SPENDING EVERY WAKING AND SLEEPING HOUR WITH YOU?

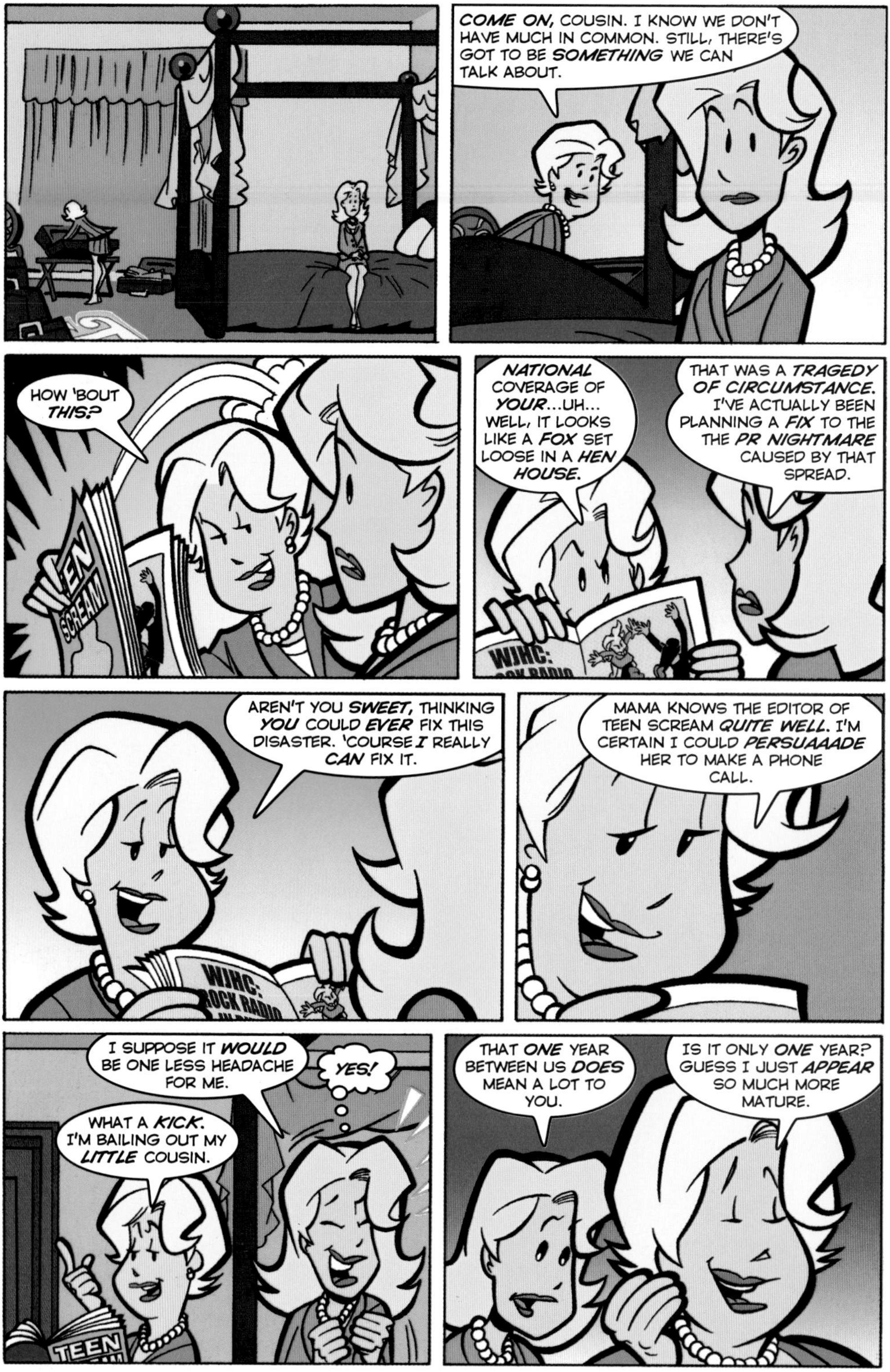
COME ON, COUSIN. I KNOW WE DON'T HAVE MUCH IN COMMON. STILL, THERE'S GOT TO BE SOMETHING WE CAN TALK ABOUT.
HOW 'BOUT THIS?
TEEN SCREAM
NATIONAL COVERAGE OF YOUR...UH... WELL, IT LOOKS LIKE A FOX SET LOOSE IN A HEN HOUSE.
THAT WAS A TRAGEDY OF CIRCUMSTANCE. I'VE ACTUALLY BEEN PLANNING A FIX TO THE THE PR NIGHTMARE CAUSED BY THAT SPREAD.
WJHC:
AREN'T YOU SWEET, THINKING YOU COULD EVER FIX THIS DISASTER. 'COURSE I REALLY CAN FIX IT.
WJHC: ROCK RADIO
MAMA KNOWS THE EDITOR OF TEEN SCREAM QUITE WELL. I'M CERTAIN I COULD PERSUAAADE HER TO MAKE A PHONE CALL.
I SUPPOSE IT WOULD BE ONE LESS HEADACHE FOR ME.
YES!
WHAT A KICK. I'M BAILING OUT MY LITTLE COUSIN.
TEEN
THAT ONE YEAR BETWEEN US DOES MEAN A LOT TO YOU.
IS IT ONLY ONE YEAR? GUESS I JUST APPEAR SO MUCH MORE MATURE.

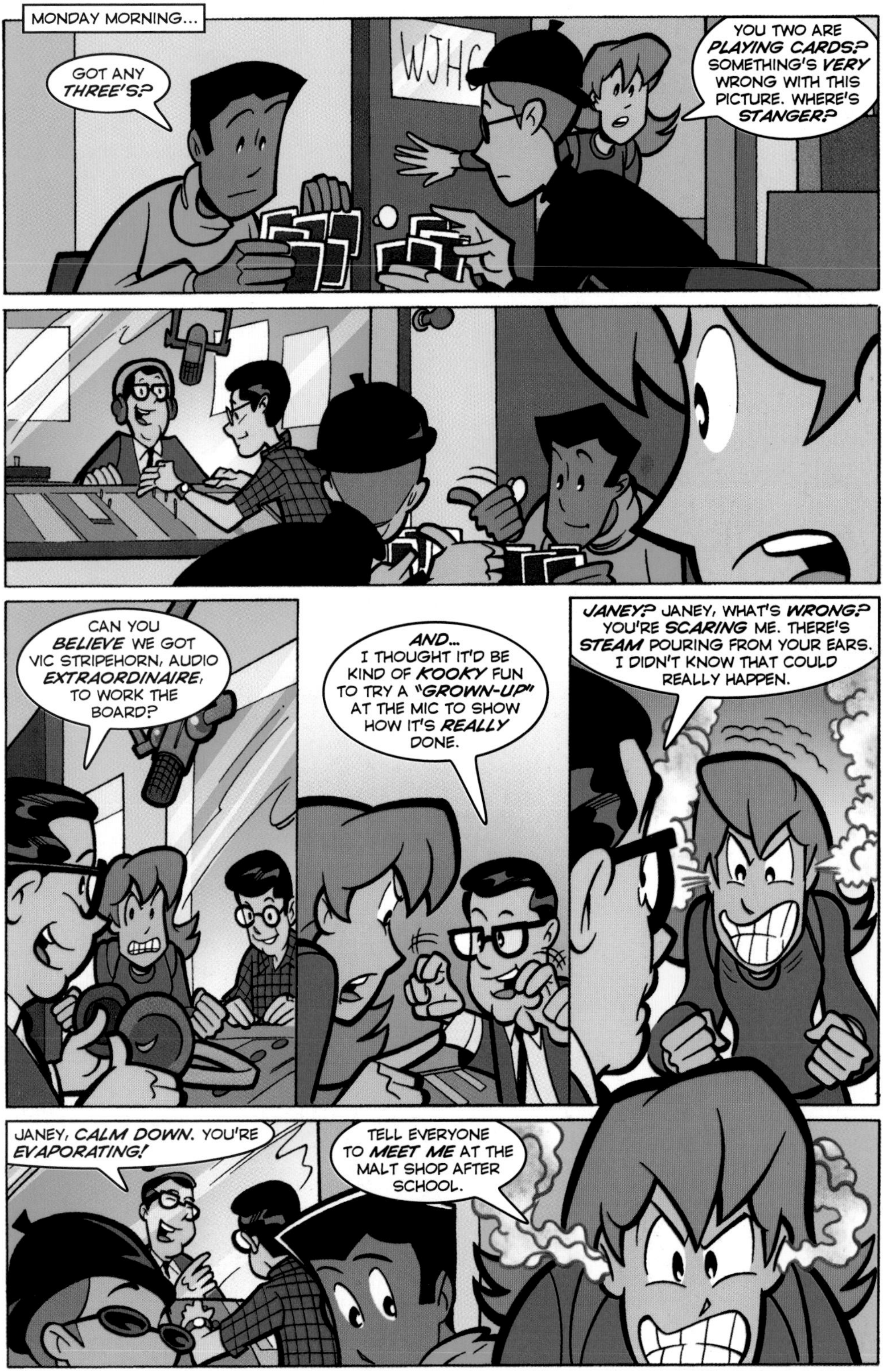
MONDAY MORNING...
GOT ANY THREE'S?
WJHC
YOU TWO ARE PLAYING CARDS? SOMETHING'S VERY WRONG WITH THIS PICTURE. WHERE'S STANGER?
CAN YOU BELIEVE WE GOT VIC STRIPEHORN, AUDIO EXTRAORDINAIRE, TO WORK THE BOARD?
AND... I THOUGHT IT'D BE KIND OF KOOKY FUN TO TRY A "GROWN-UP" AT THE MIC TO SHOW HOW IT'S REALLY DONE.
JANEY? JANEY, WHAT'S WRONG? YOU'RE SCARING ME. THERE'S STEAM POURING FROM YOUR EARS. I DIDN'T KNOW THAT COULD REALLY HAPPEN.
JANEY, CALM DOWN. YOU'RE EVAPORATING!
TELL EVERYONE TO MEET ME AT THE MALT SHOP AFTER SCHOOL.

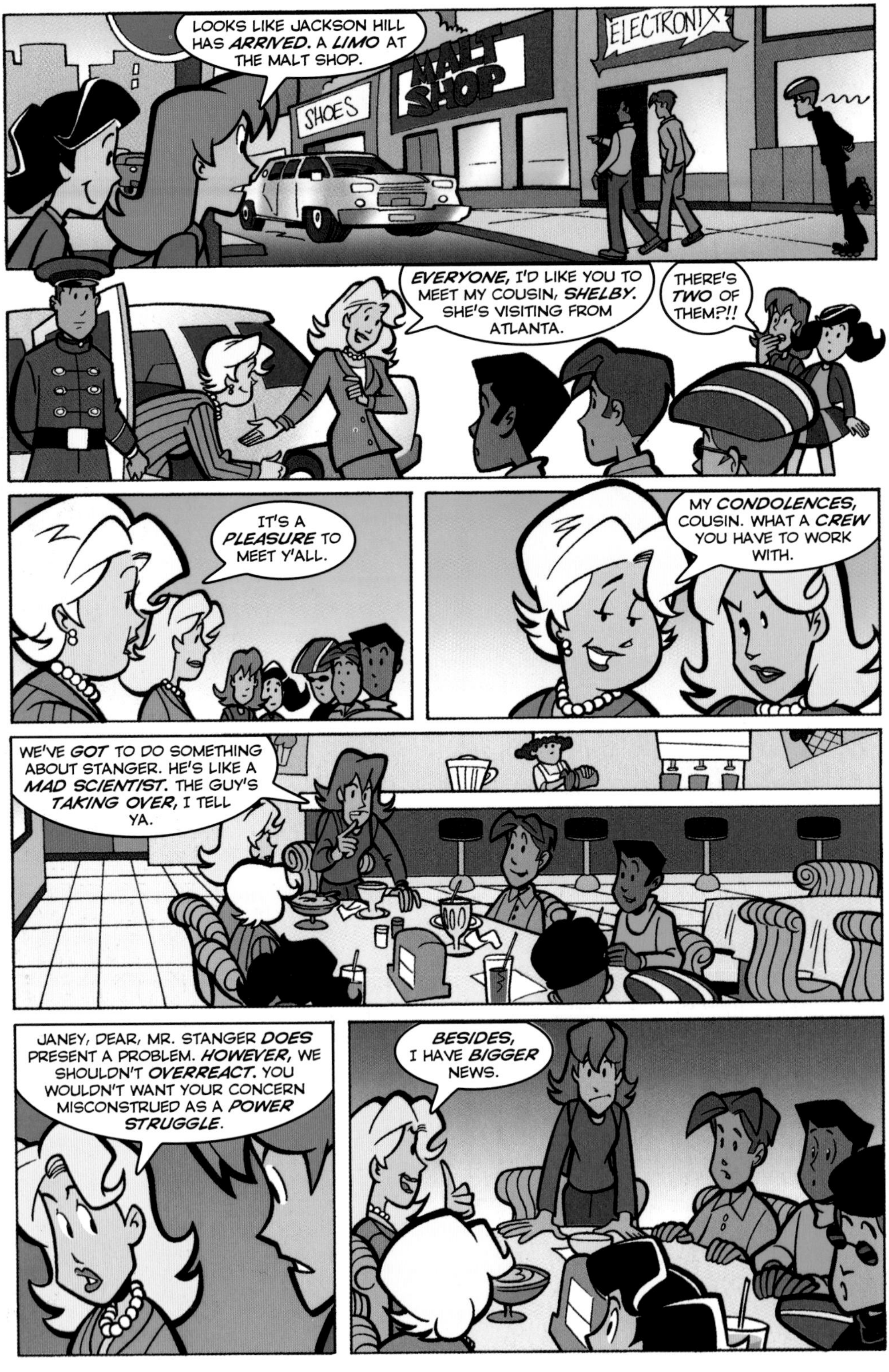
LOOKS LIKE JACKSON HILL HAS ARRIVED. A LIMO AT THE MALT SHOP.
MALT SHOP
SHOES
ELECTRONIX
EVERYONE, I'D LIKE YOU TO MEET MY COUSIN, SHELBY. SHE'S VISITING FROM ATLANTA.
THERE'S TWO OF THEM?!!
IT'S A PLEASURE TO MEET Y'ALL.
MY CONDOLENCES, COUSIN. WHAT A CREW YOU HAVE TO WORK WITH.
WE'VE GOT TO DO SOMETHING ABOUT STANGER. HE'S LIKE A MAD SCIENTIST. THE GUY'S TAKING OVER, I TELL YA.
JANEY, DEAR, MR. STANGER DOES PRESENT A PROBLEM. HOWEVER, WE SHOULDN'T OVERREACT. YOU WOULDN'T WANT YOUR CONCERN MISCONSTRUED AS A POWER STRUGGLE.
BESIDES, I HAVE BIGGER NEWS.

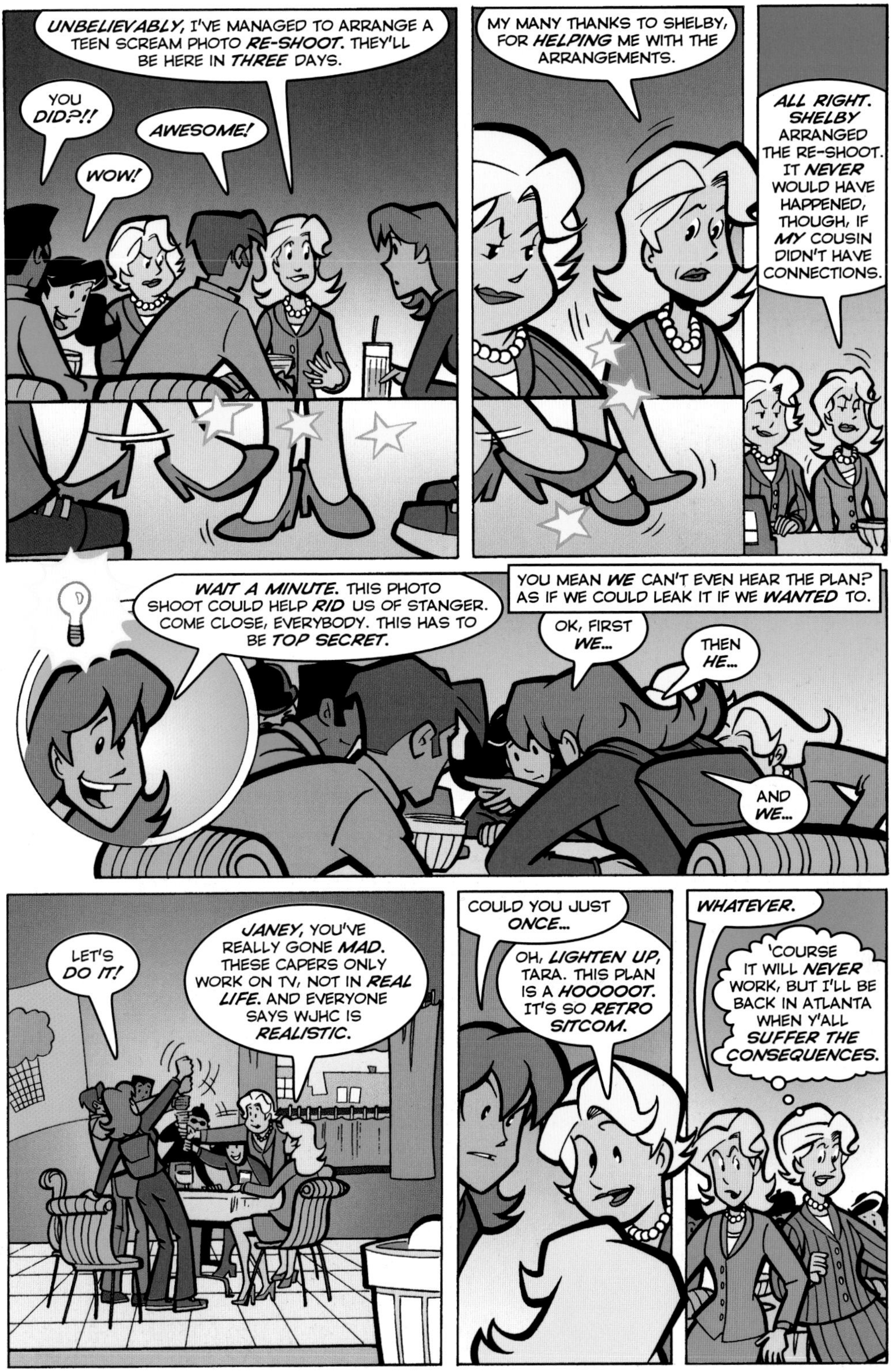
UNBELIEVABLY, I'VE MANAGED TO ARRANGE A TEEN SCREAM PHOTO RE-SHOOT. THEY'LL BE HERE IN THREE DAYS.
YOU DID?!!
AWESOME!
WOW!
MY MANY THANKS TO SHELBY, FOR HELPING ME WITH THE ARRANGEMENTS.
ALL RIGHT. SHELBY ARRANGED THE RE-SHOOT. IT NEVER WOULD HAVE HAPPENED, THOUGH, IF MY COUSIN DIDN'T HAVE CONNECTIONS.
WAIT A MINUTE. THIS PHOTO SHOOT COULD HELP RID US OF STANGER. COME CLOSE, EVERYBODY. THIS HAS TO BE TOP SECRET.
YOU MEAN WE CAN'T EVEN HEAR THE PLAN? AS IF WE COULD LEAK IT IF WE WANTED TO.
OK, FIRST WE...
THEN HE...
AND WE...
LET'S DO IT!
JANEY, YOU'VE REALLY GONE MAD. THESE CAPERS ONLY WORK ON TV, NOT IN REAL LIFE. AND EVERYONE SAYS WJHC IS REALISTIC.
COULD YOU JUST ONCE...
OH, LIGHTEN UP, TARA. THIS PLAN IS A HOOOOOT. IT'S SO RETRO SITCOM.
WHATEVER.
'COURSE IT WILL NEVER WORK, BUT I'LL BE BACK IN ATLANTA WHEN Y'ALL SUFFER THE CONSEQUENCES.

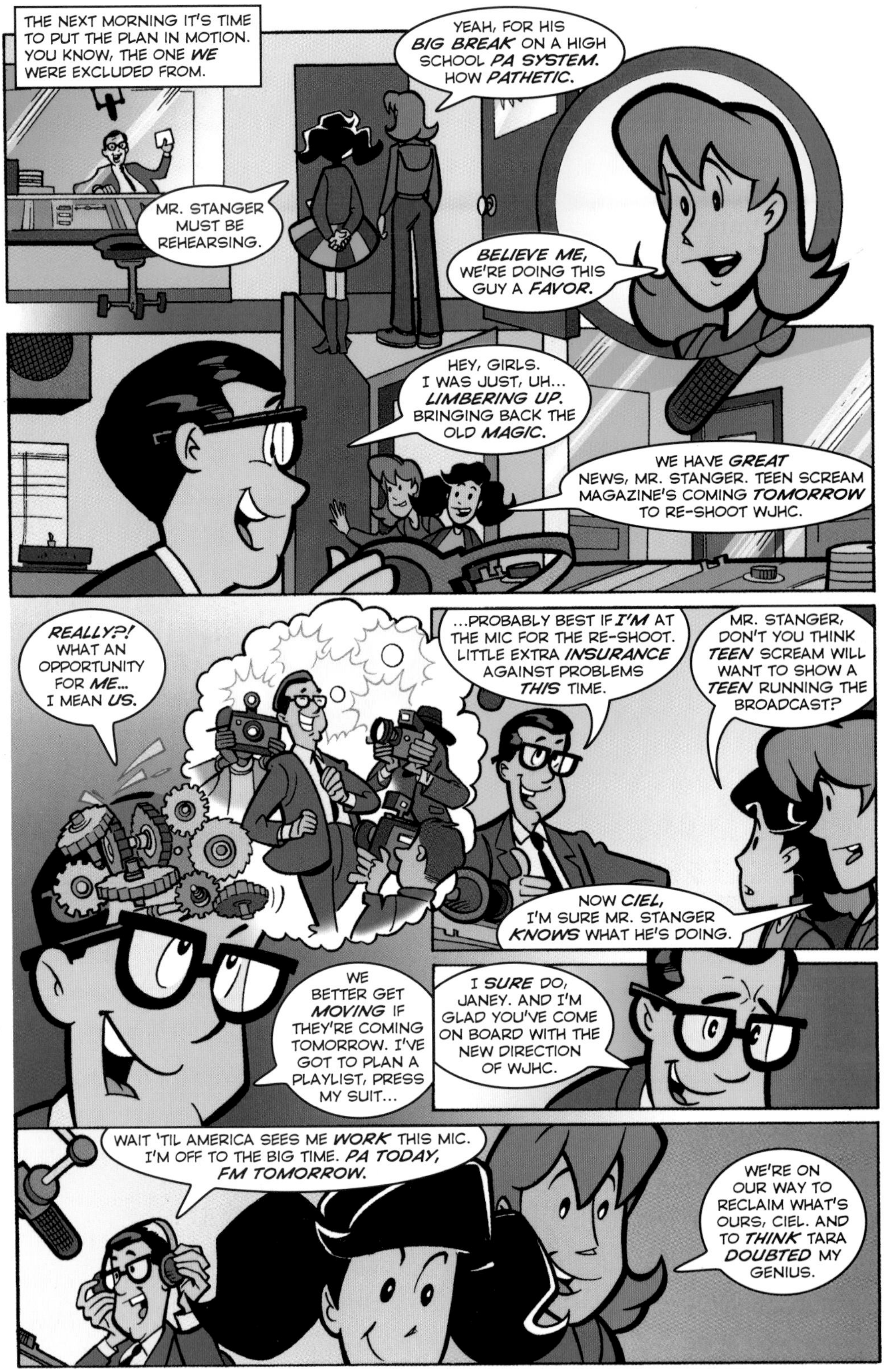
THE NEXT MORNING IT'S TIME TO PUT THE PLAN IN MOTION. YOU KNOW, THE ONE WE WERE EXCLUDED FROM.
YEAH, FOR HIS BIG BREAK ON A HIGH SCHOOL PA SYSTEM. HOW PATHETIC.
MR. STANGER MUST BE REHEARSING.
BELIEVE ME, WE'RE DOING THIS GUY A FAVOR.
HEY, GIRLS. I WAS JUST, UH... LIMBERING UP. BRINGING BACK THE OLD MAGIC.
WE HAVE GREAT NEWS, MR. STANGER. TEEN SCREAM MAGAZINE'S COMING TOMORROW TO RE-SHOOT WJHC.
REALLY?! WHAT AN OPPORTUNITY FOR ME... I MEAN US.
...PROBABLY BEST IF I'M AT THE MIC FOR THE RE-SHOOT. LITTLE EXTRA INSURANCE AGAINST PROBLEMS THIS TIME.
MR. STANGER, DON'T YOU THINK TEEN SCREAM WILL WANT TO SHOW A TEEN RUNNING THE BROADCAST?
NOW CIEL, I'M SURE MR. STANGER KNOWS WHAT HE'S DOING.
I SURE DO, JANEY. AND I'M GLAD YOU'VE COME ON BOARD WITH THE NEW DIRECTION OF WJHC.
WE BETTER GET MOVING IF THEY'RE COMING TOMORROW. I'VE GOT TO PLAN A PLAYLIST, PRESS MY SUIT...
WAIT 'TIL AMERICA SEES ME WORK THIS MIC. I'M OFF TO THE BIG TIME. PA TODAY, FM TOMORROW.
WE'RE ON OUR WAY TO RECLAIM WHAT'S OURS, CIEL. AND TO THINK TARA DOUBTED MY GENIUS.

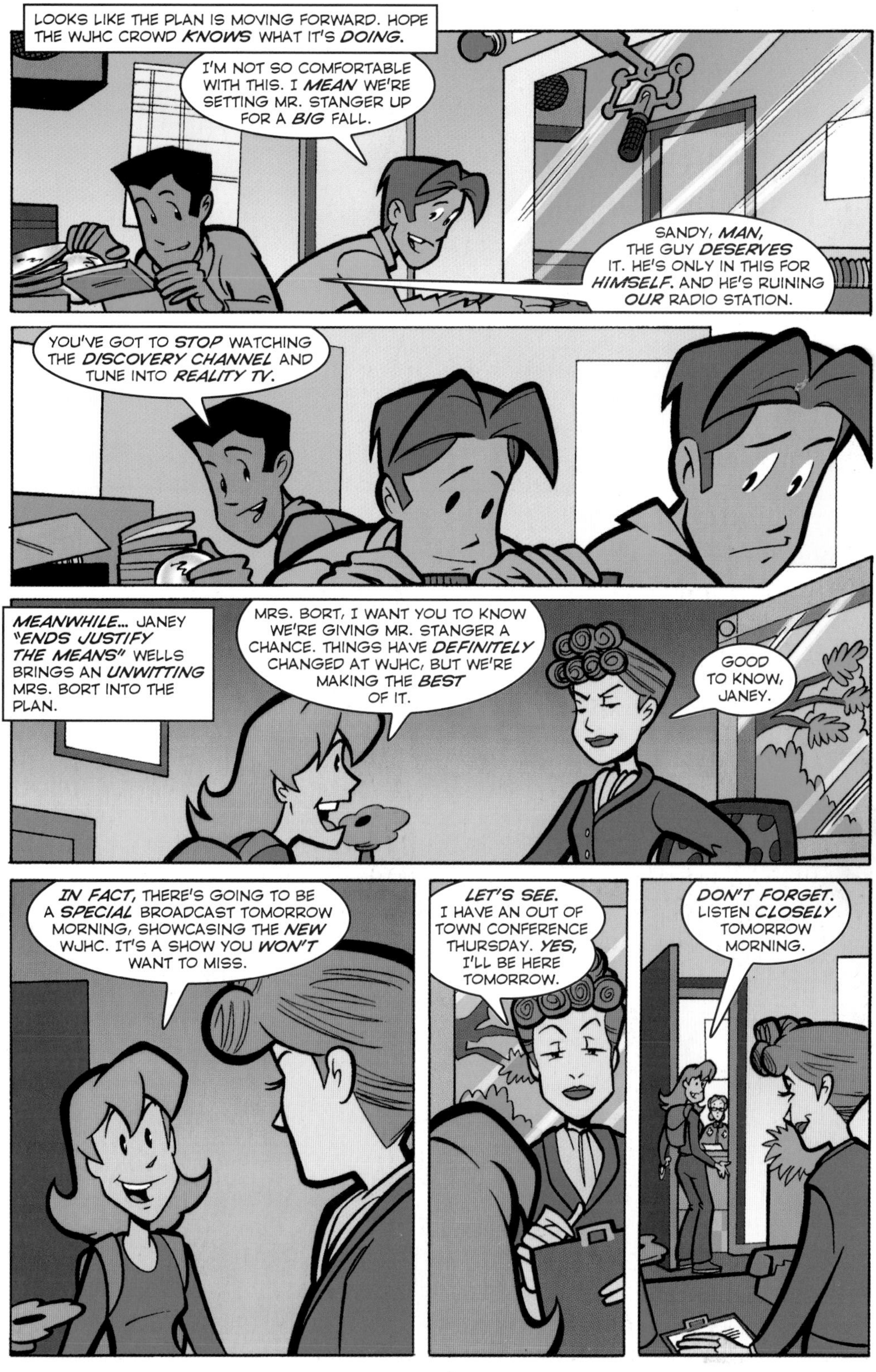
LOOKS LIKE THE PLAN IS MOVING FORWARD. HOPE THE WJHC CROWD KNOWS WHAT IT'S DOING.
I'M NOT SO COMFORTABLE WITH THIS. I MEAN WE'RE SETTING MR. STANGER UP FOR A BIG FALL.
SANDY, MAN, THE GUY DESERVES IT. HE'S ONLY IN THIS FOR HIMSELF. AND HE'S RUINING OUR RADIO STATION.
YOU'VE GOT TO STOP WATCHING THE DISCOVERY CHANNEL AND TUNE INTO REALITY TV.
MEANWHILE... JANEY "ENDS JUSTIFY THE MEANS" WELLS BRINGS AN UNWITTING MRS. BORT INTO THE PLAN.
MRS. BORT, I WANT YOU TO KNOW WE'RE GIVING MR. STANGER A CHANCE. THINGS HAVE DEFINITELY CHANGED AT WJHC, BUT WE'RE MAKING THE BEST OF IT.
GOOD TO KNOW, JANEY.
IN FACT, THERE'S GOING TO BE A SPECIAL BROADCAST TOMORROW MORNING, SHOWCASING THE NEW WJHC. IT'S A SHOW YOU WON'T WANT TO MISS.
LET'S SEE. I HAVE AN OUT OF TOWN CONFERENCE THURSDAY. YES, I'LL BE HERE TOMORROW.
DON'T FORGET. LISTEN CLOSELY TOMORROW MORNING.

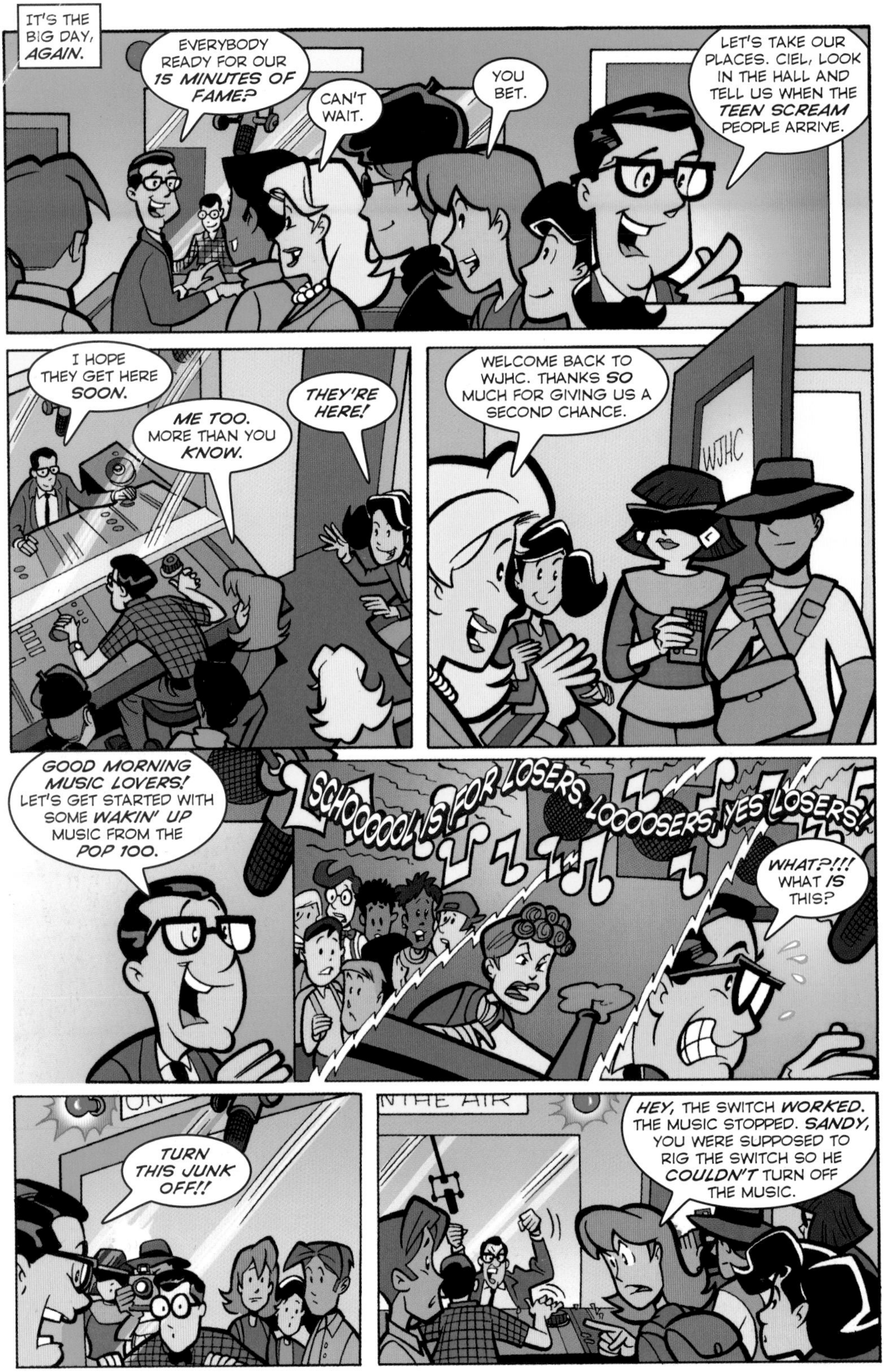
IT'S THE BIG DAY, AGAIN.
EVERYBODY READY FOR OUR 15 MINUTES OF FAME?
CAN'T WAIT.
YOU BET.
LET'S TAKE OUR PLACES. CIEL, LOOK IN THE HALL AND TELL US WHEN THE TEEN SCREAM PEOPLE ARRIVE.
I HOPE THEY GET HERE SOON.
ME TOO. MORE THAN YOU KNOW.
THEY'RE HERE!
WELCOME BACK TO WJHC. THANKS SO MUCH FOR GIVING US A SECOND CHANCE.
WJHC
GOOD MORNING MUSIC LOVERS! LET'S GET STARTED WITH SOME WAKIN' UP MUSIC FROM THE POP 100.
SCHOOOOOL IS FOR LOSERS. LOOOOSERS, YES LOSERS!
WHAT?!!! WHAT IS THIS?
TURN THIS JUNK OFF!!
HEY, THE SWITCH WORKED. THE MUSIC STOPPED. SANDY, YOU WERE SUPPOSED TO RIG THE SWITCH SO HE COULDN'T TURN OFF THE MUSIC.

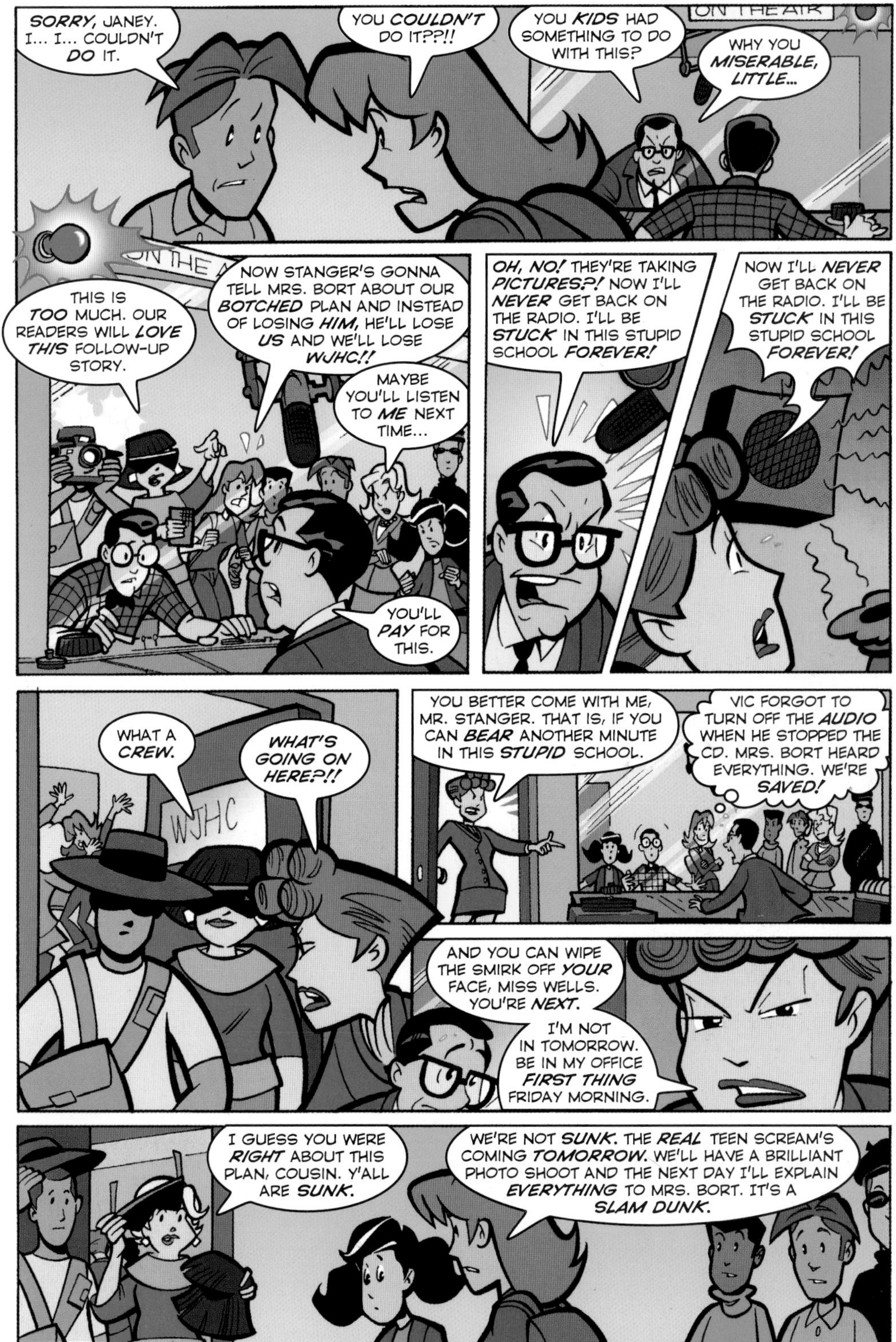
SORRY, JANEY. I... I... COULDN'T DO IT.
YOU COULDN'T DO IT??!!
YOU KIDS HAD SOMETHING TO DO WITH THIS?
WHY YOU MISERABLE, LITTLE...
THIS IS TOO MUCH. OUR READERS WILL LOVE THIS FOLLOW-UP STORY.
NOW STANGER'S GONNA TELL MRS. BORT ABOUT OUR BOTCHED PLAN AND INSTEAD OF LOSING HIM, HE'LL LOSE US AND WE'LL LOSE WJHC!!
MAYBE YOU'LL LISTEN TO ME NEXT TIME...
YOU'LL PAY FOR THIS.
OH, NO! THEY'RE TAKING PICTURES?! NOW I'LL NEVER GET BACK ON THE RADIO. I'LL BE STUCK IN THIS STUPID SCHOOL FOREVER!
NOW I'LL NEVER GET BACK ON THE RADIO. I'LL BE STUCK IN THIS STUPID SCHOOL FOREVER!
WHAT A CREW.
WJHC
WHAT'S GOING ON HERE?!!
YOU BETTER COME WITH ME, MR. STANGER. THAT IS, IF YOU CAN BEAR ANOTHER MINUTE IN THIS STUPID SCHOOL.
VIC FORGOT TO TURN OFF THE AUDIO WHEN HE STOPPED THE CD. MRS. BORT HEARD EVERYTHING. WE'RE SAVED!
AND YOU CAN WIPE THE SMIRK OFF YOUR FACE, MISS WELLS. YOU'RE NEXT.
I'M NOT IN TOMORROW. BE IN MY OFFICE FIRST THING FRIDAY MORNING.
I GUESS YOU WERE RIGHT ABOUT THIS PLAN, COUSIN. Y'ALL ARE SUNK.
WE'RE NOT SUNK. THE REAL TEEN SCREAM'S COMING TOMORROW. WE'LL HAVE A BRILLIANT PHOTO SHOOT AND THE NEXT DAY I'LL EXPLAIN EVERYTHING TO MRS. BORT. IT'S A SLAM DUNK.

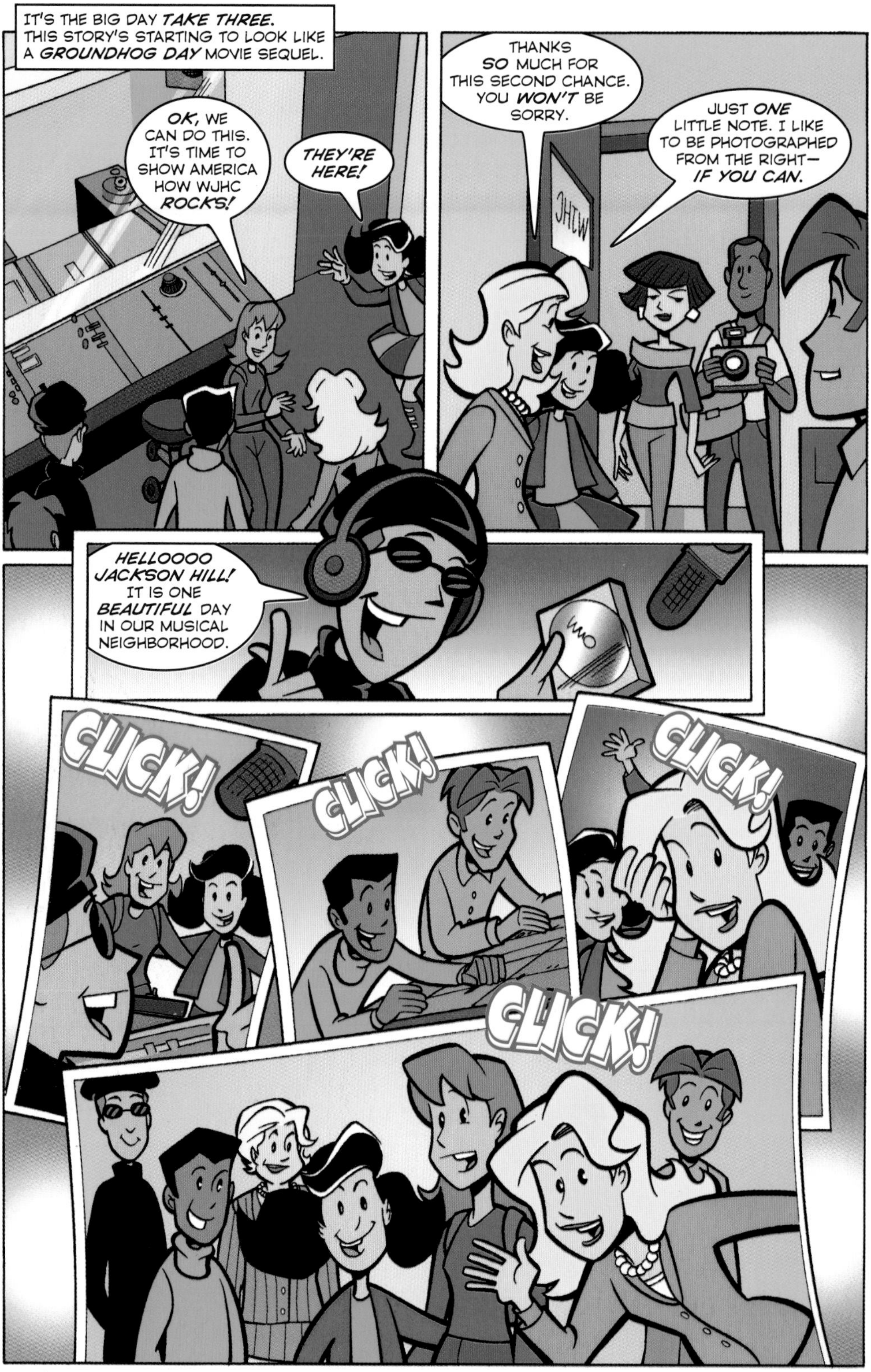
IT'S THE BIG DAY TAKE THREE. THIS STORY'S STARTING TO LOOK LIKE A GROUNDHOG DAY MOVIE SEQUEL.
OK, WE CAN DO THIS. IT'S TIME TO SHOW AMERICA HOW WJHC ROCKS!
THEY'RE HERE!
THANKS SO MUCH FOR THIS SECOND CHANCE. YOU WON'T BE SORRY.
JUST ONE LITTLE NOTE. I LIKE TO BE PHOTOGRAPHED FROM THE RIGHT— IF YOU CAN.
WJHC
HELLOOOO JACKSON HILL! IT IS ONE BEAUTIFUL DAY IN OUR MUSICAL NEIGHBORHOOD.
CLICK!
CLICK!
CLICK!
CLICK!

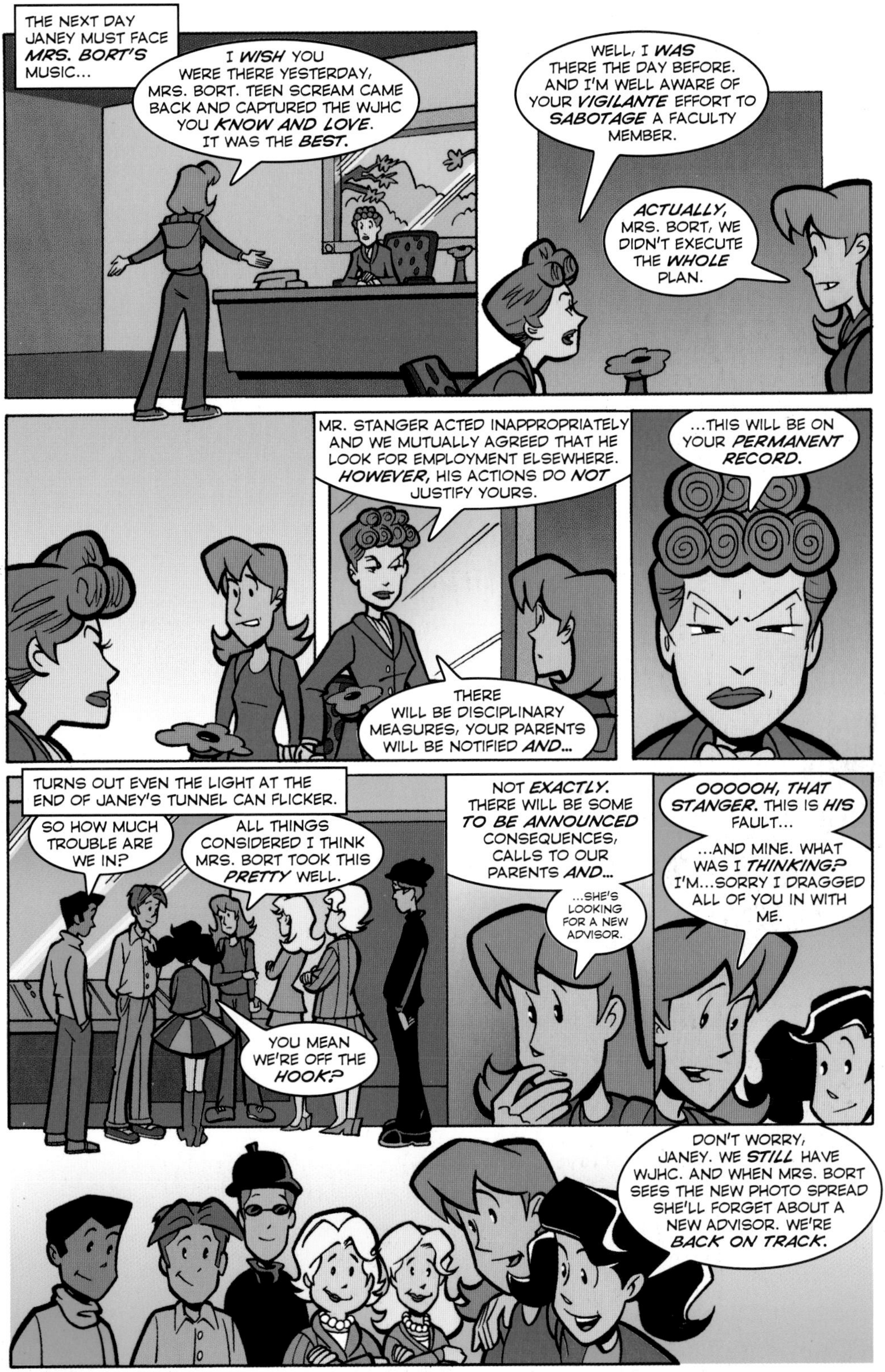

THE NEXT DAY JANEY MUST FACE MRS. BORT'S MUSIC...
I WISH YOU WERE THERE YESTERDAY, MRS. BORT. TEEN SCREAM CAME BACK AND CAPTURED THE WJHC YOU KNOW AND LOVE. IT WAS THE BEST.
WELL, I WAS THERE THE DAY BEFORE. AND I'M WELL AWARE OF YOUR VIGILANTE EFFORT TO SABOTAGE A FACULTY MEMBER.
ACTUALLY, MRS. BORT, WE DIDN'T EXECUTE THE WHOLE PLAN.
MR. STANGER ACTED INAPPROPRIATELY AND WE MUTUALLY AGREED THAT HE LOOK FOR EMPLOYMENT ELSEWHERE. HOWEVER, HIS ACTIONS DO NOT JUSTIFY YOURS.
THERE WILL BE DISCIPLINARY MEASURES, YOUR PARENTS WILL BE NOTIFIED AND...
...THIS WILL BE ON YOUR PERMANENT RECORD.
TURNS OUT EVEN THE LIGHT AT THE END OF JANEY'S TUNNEL CAN FLICKER.
SO HOW MUCH TROUBLE ARE WE IN?
ALL THINGS CONSIDERED I THINK MRS. BORT TOOK THIS PRETTY WELL.
YOU MEAN WE'RE OFF THE HOOK?
NOT EXACTLY. THERE WILL BE SOME TO BE ANNOUNCED CONSEQUENCES, CALLS TO OUR PARENTS AND...
...SHE'S LOOKING FOR A NEW ADVISOR.
OOOOOH, THAT STANGER. THIS IS HIS FAULT...
...AND MINE. WHAT WAS I THINKING? I'M...SORRY I DRAGGED ALL OF YOU IN WITH ME.
DON'T WORRY, JANEY. WE STILL HAVE WJHC. AND WHEN MRS. BORT SEES THE NEW PHOTO SPREAD SHE'LL FORGET ABOUT A NEW ADVISOR. WE'RE BACK ON TRACK.

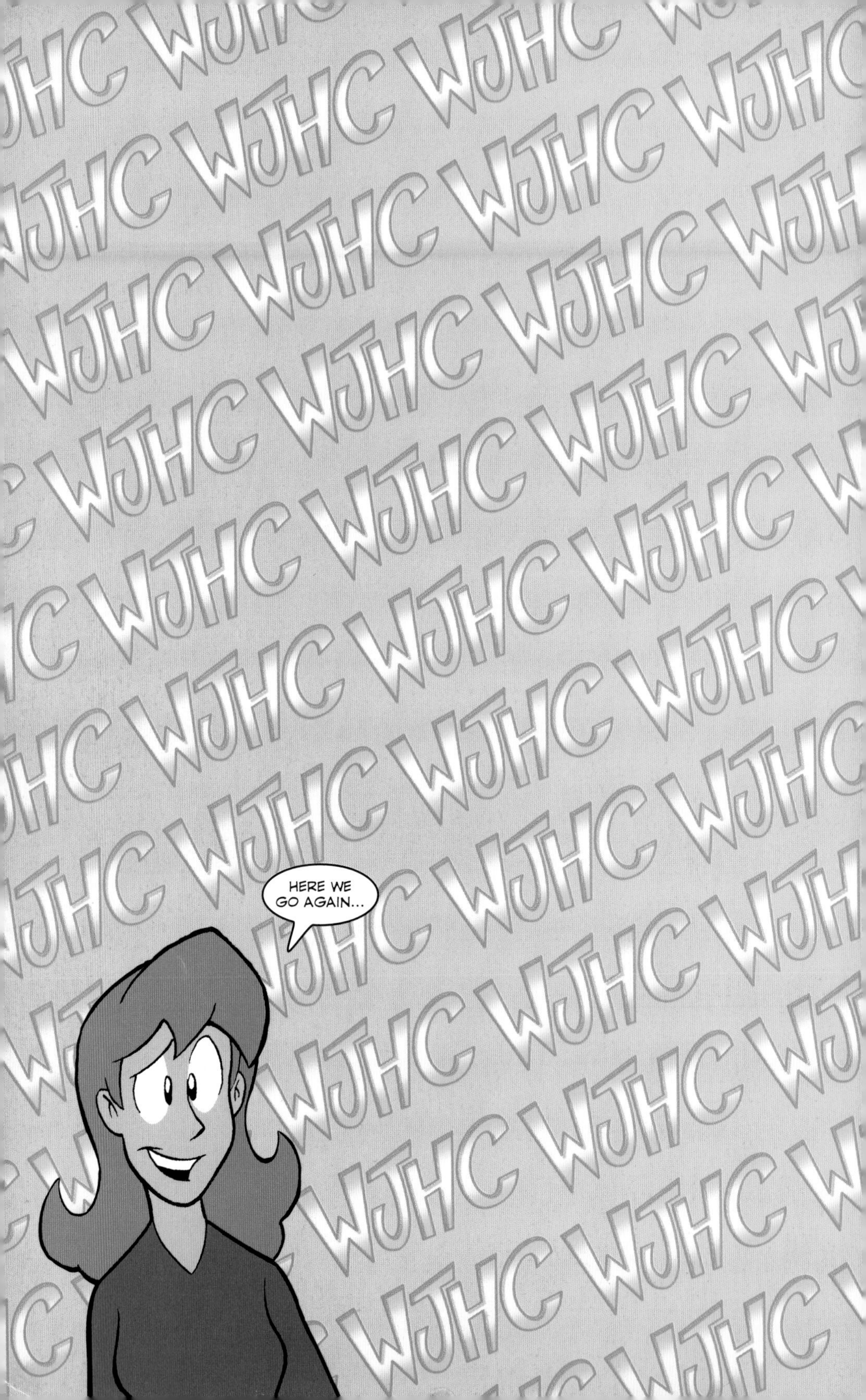
HERE WE GO AGAIN...

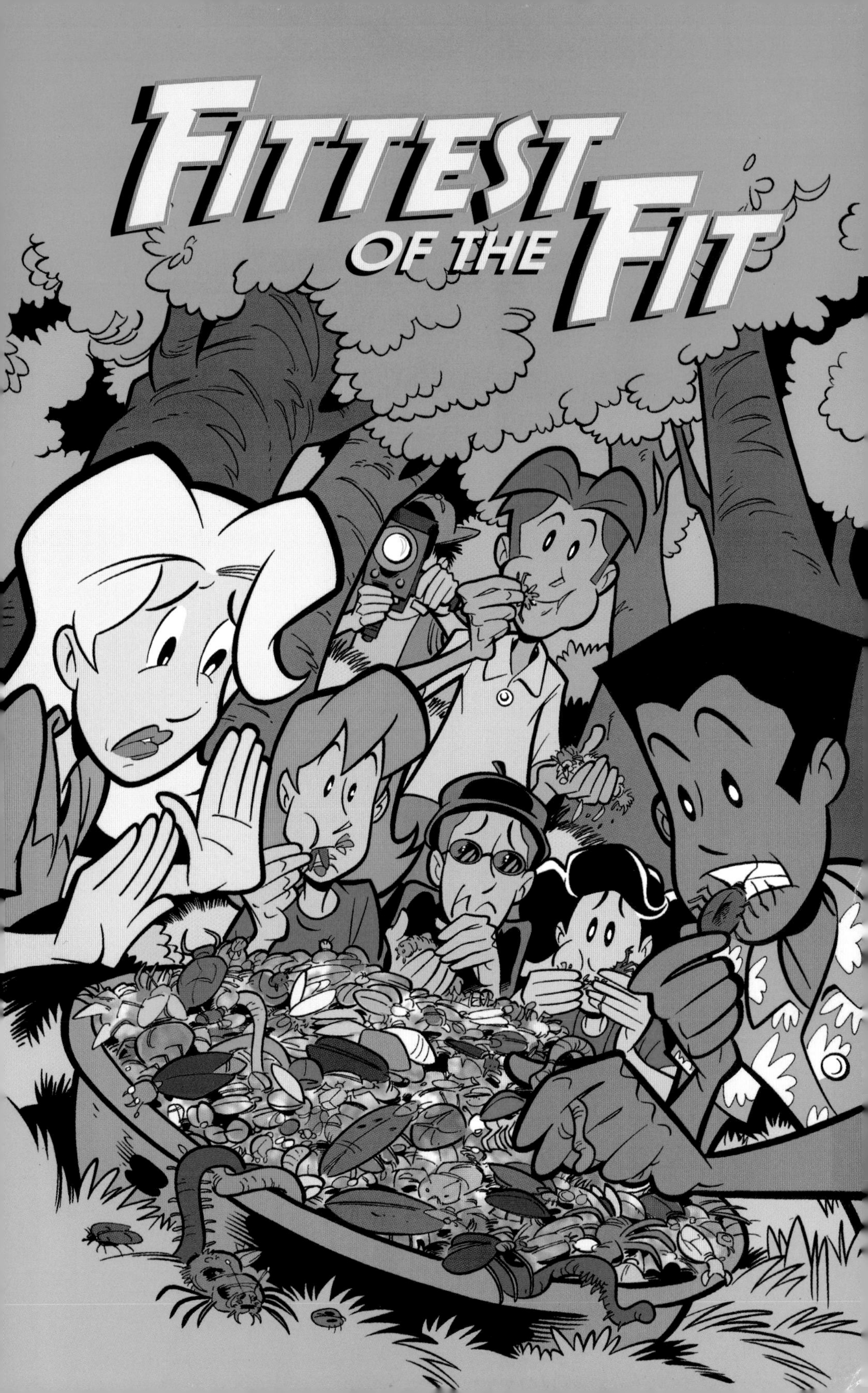
FITTEST OF THE FIT

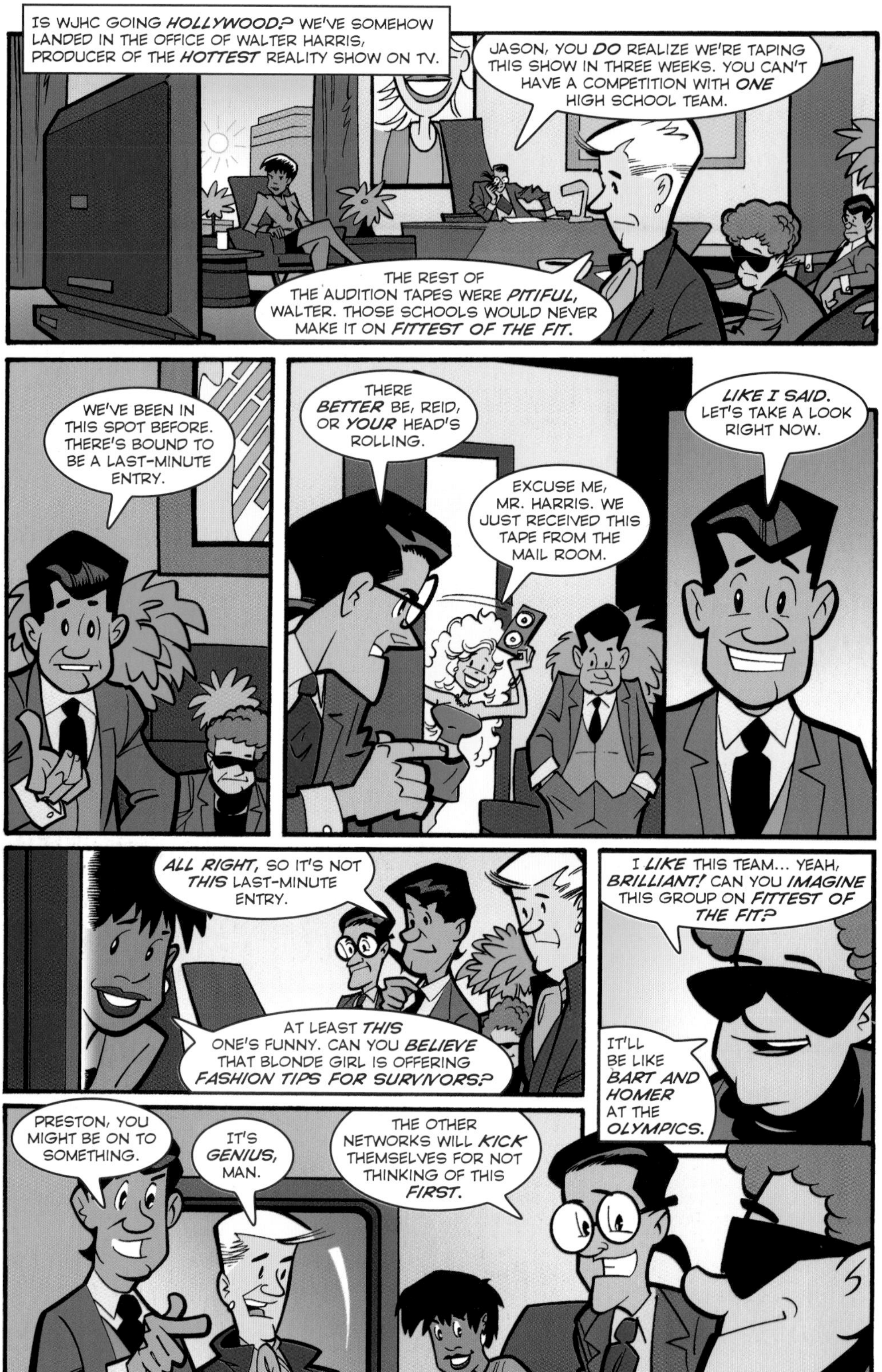
IS WJHC GOING HOLLYWOOD? WE'VE SOMEHOW LANDED IN THE OFFICE OF WALTER HARRIS, PRODUCER OF THE HOTTEST REALITY SHOW ON TV.
JASON, YOU DO REALIZE WE'RE TAPING THIS SHOW IN THREE WEEKS. YOU CAN'T HAVE A COMPETITION WITH ONE HIGH SCHOOL TEAM.
THE REST OF THE AUDITION TAPES WERE PITIFUL, WALTER. THOSE SCHOOLS WOULD NEVER MAKE IT ON FITTEST OF THE FIT.
WE'VE BEEN IN THIS SPOT BEFORE. THERE'S BOUND TO BE A LAST-MINUTE ENTRY.
THERE BETTER BE, REID, OR YOUR HEAD'S ROLLING.
EXCUSE ME, MR. HARRIS. WE JUST RECEIVED THIS TAPE FROM THE MAIL ROOM.
LIKE I SAID. LET'S TAKE A LOOK RIGHT NOW.
ALL RIGHT, SO IT'S NOT THIS LAST-MINUTE ENTRY.
AT LEAST THIS ONE'S FUNNY. CAN YOU BELIEVE THAT BLONDE GIRL IS OFFERING FASHION TIPS FOR SURVIVORS?
I LIKE THIS TEAM... YEAH, BRILLIANT! CAN YOU IMAGINE THIS GROUP ON FITTEST OF THE FIT?
IT'LL BE LIKE BART AND HOMER AT THE OLYMPICS.
PRESTON, YOU MIGHT BE ON TO SOMETHING.
IT'S GENIUS, MAN.
THE OTHER NETWORKS WILL KICK THEMSELVES FOR NOT THINKING OF THIS FIRST.

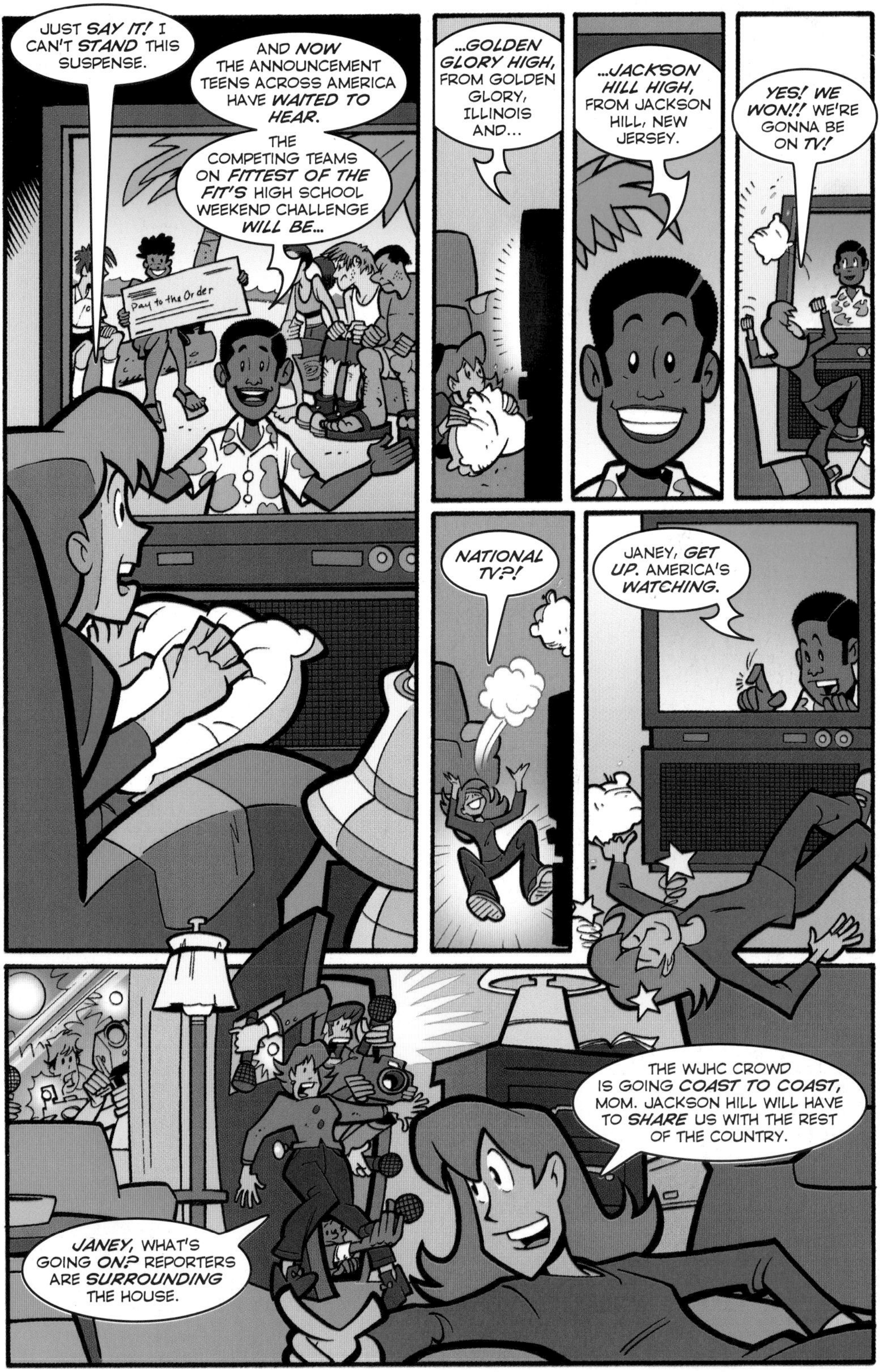
JUST SAY IT! I CAN'T STAND THIS SUSPENSE.
AND NOW THE ANNOUNCEMENT TEENS ACROSS AMERICA HAVE WAITED TO HEAR.
THE COMPETING TEAMS ON FITTEST OF THE FIT'S HIGH SCHOOL WEEKEND CHALLENGE WILL BE...
Pay to the Order
...GOLDEN GLORY HIGH, FROM GOLDEN GLORY, ILLINOIS AND...
...JACKSON HILL HIGH, FROM JACKSON HILL, NEW JERSEY.
YES! WE WON!! WE'RE GONNA BE ON TV!
NATIONAL TV?!
JANEY, GET UP. AMERICA'S WATCHING.
THE WJHC CROWD IS GOING COAST TO COAST, MOM. JACKSON HILL WILL HAVE TO SHARE US WITH THE REST OF THE COUNTRY.
JANEY, WHAT'S GOING ON? REPORTERS ARE SURROUNDING THE HOUSE.

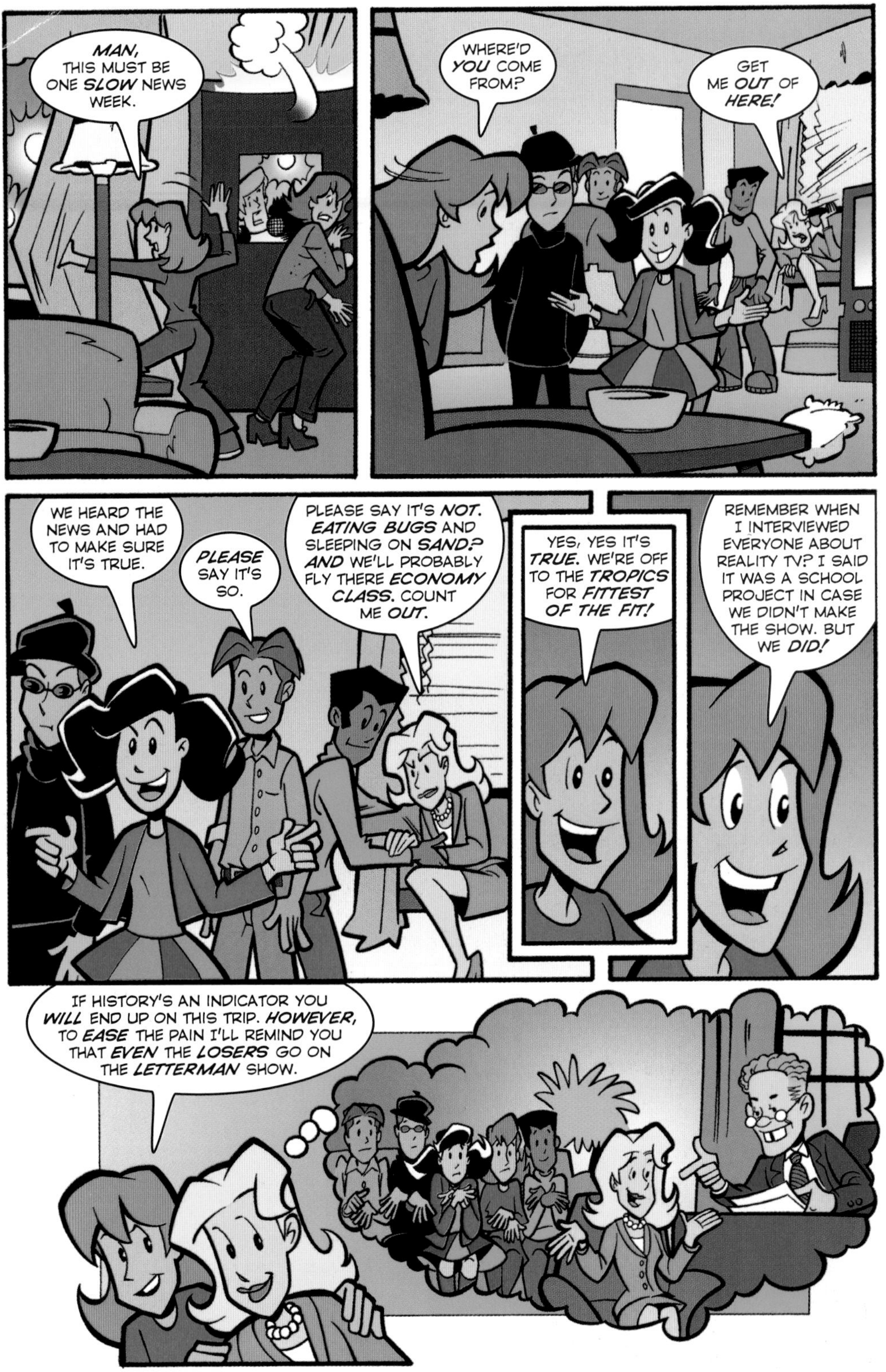

MAN, THIS MUST BE ONE SLOW NEWS WEEK.
WHERE'D YOU COME FROM?
GET ME OUT OF HERE!
WE HEARD THE NEWS AND HAD TO MAKE SURE IT'S TRUE.
PLEASE SAY IT'S SO.
PLEASE SAY IT'S NOT. EATING BUGS AND SLEEPING ON SAND? AND WE'LL PROBABLY FLY THERE ECONOMY CLASS. COUNT ME OUT.
YES, YES IT'S TRUE. WE'RE OFF TO THE TROPICS FOR FITTEST OF THE FIT!
REMEMBER WHEN I INTERVIEWED EVERYONE ABOUT REALITY TV? I SAID IT WAS A SCHOOL PROJECT IN CASE WE DIDN'T MAKE THE SHOW. BUT WE DID!
IF HISTORY'S AN INDICATOR YOU WILL END UP ON THIS TRIP. HOWEVER, TO EASE THE PAIN I'LL REMIND YOU THAT EVEN THE LOSERS GO ON THE LETTERMAN SHOW.

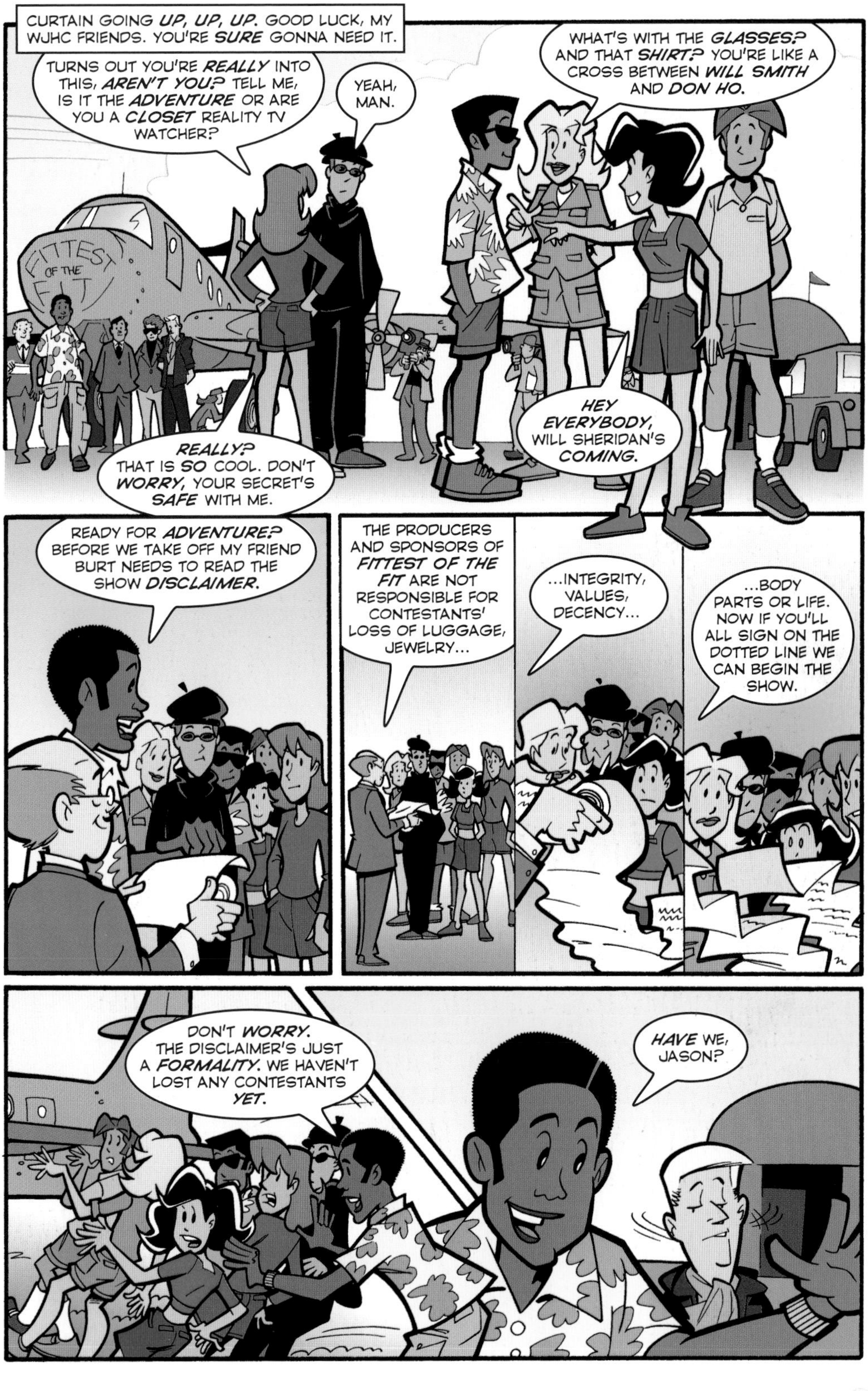
CURTAIN GOING UP, UP, UP. GOOD LUCK, MY WJHC FRIENDS. YOU'RE SURE GONNA NEED IT.
TURNS OUT YOU'RE REALLY INTO THIS, AREN'T YOU? TELL ME, IS IT THE ADVENTURE OR ARE YOU A CLOSET REALITY TV WATCHER?
YEAH, MAN.
REALLY? THAT IS SO COOL. DON'T WORRY, YOUR SECRET'S SAFE WITH ME.
WHAT'S WITH THE GLASSES? AND THAT SHIRT? YOU'RE LIKE A CROSS BETWEEN WILL SMITH AND DON HO.
HEY EVERYBODY, WILL SHERIDAN'S COMING.
FITTEST OF THE FIT
READY FOR ADVENTURE? BEFORE WE TAKE OFF MY FRIEND BURT NEEDS TO READ THE SHOW DISCLAIMER.
THE PRODUCERS AND SPONSORS OF FITTEST OF THE FIT ARE NOT RESPONSIBLE FOR CONTESTANTS' LOSS OF LUGGAGE, JEWELRY...
...INTEGRITY, VALUES, DECENCY...
...BODY PARTS OR LIFE. NOW IF YOU'LL ALL SIGN ON THE DOTTED LINE WE CAN BEGIN THE SHOW.
DON'T WORRY. THE DISCLAIMER'S JUST A FORMALITY. WE HAVEN'T LOST ANY CONTESTANTS YET.
HAVE WE, JASON?

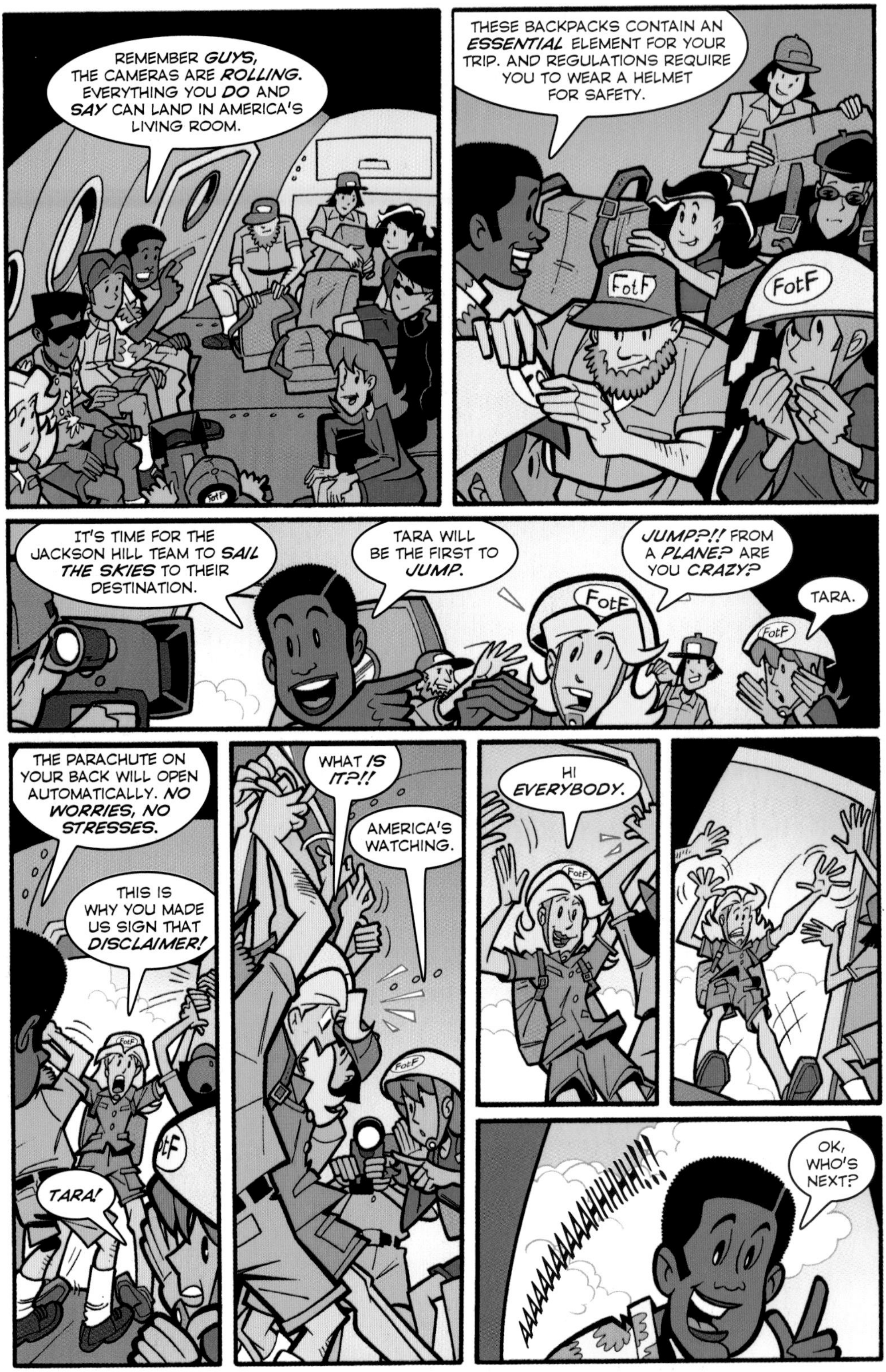
REMEMBER GUYS, THE CAMERAS ARE ROLLING. EVERYTHING YOU DO AND SAY CAN LAND IN AMERICA'S LIVING ROOM.
THESE BACKPACKS CONTAIN AN ESSENTIAL ELEMENT FOR YOUR TRIP. AND REGULATIONS REQUIRE YOU TO WEAR A HELMET FOR SAFETY.
FotF
FotF
IT'S TIME FOR THE JACKSON HILL TEAM TO SAIL THE SKIES TO THEIR DESTINATION.
TARA WILL BE THE FIRST TO JUMP.
JUMP?!! FROM A PLANE? ARE YOU CRAZY?
TARA.
THE PARACHUTE ON YOUR BACK WILL OPEN AUTOMATICALLY. NO WORRIES, NO STRESSES.
THIS IS WHY YOU MADE US SIGN THAT DISCLAIMER!
TARA!
WHAT IS IT?!!
AMERICA'S WATCHING.
HI EVERYBODY.
AAAAAAAAAAAHHHHHH!!!
OK, WHO'S NEXT?

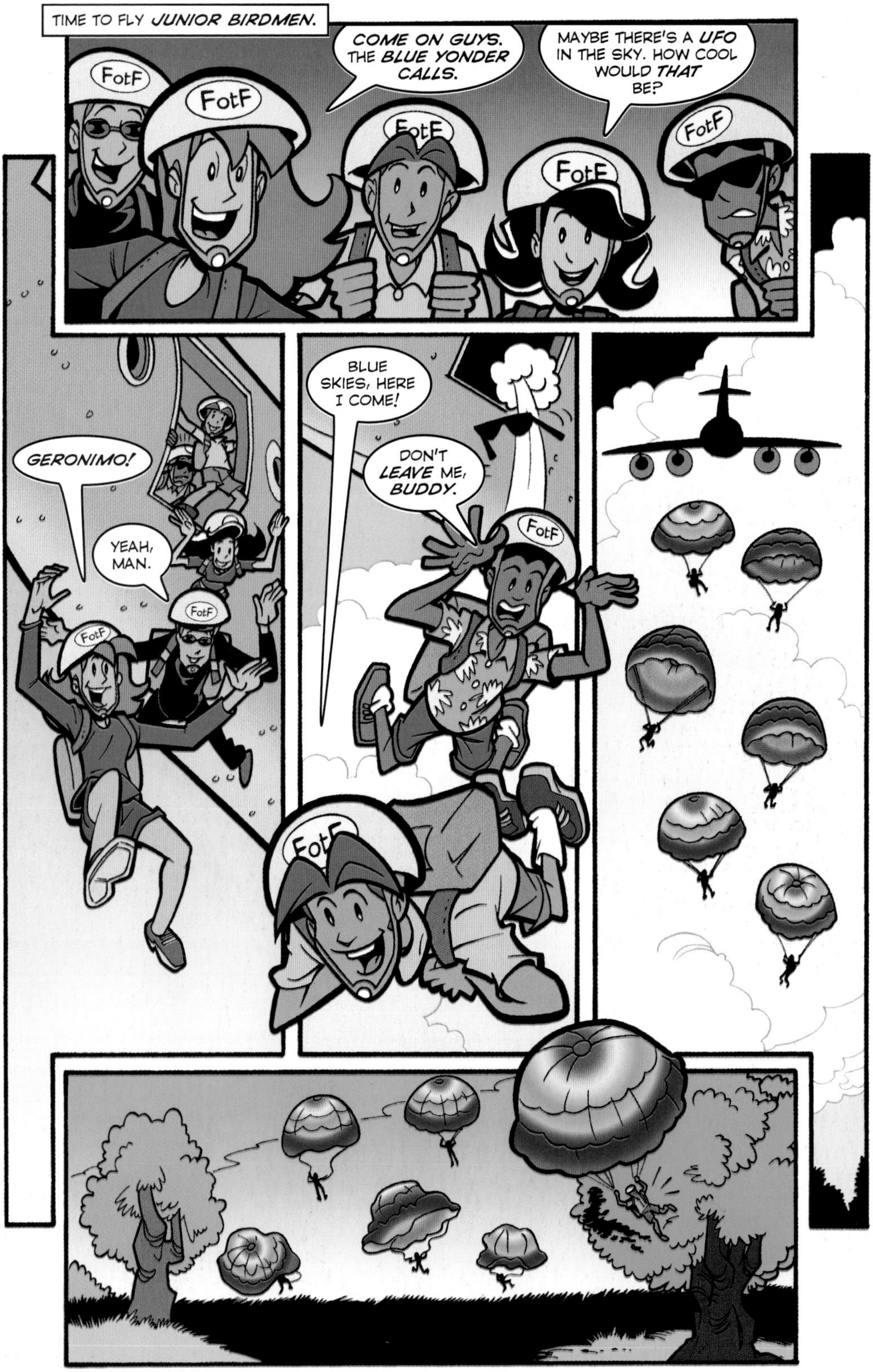
TIME TO FLY *JUNIOR BIRDMEN.*
COME ON GUYS. THE *BLUE YONDER CALLS.*
MAYBE THERE'S A *UFO* IN THE SKY. HOW COOL WOULD *THAT* BE?
FotF
GERONIMO!
YEAH, MAN.
BLUE SKIES, HERE I COME!
DON'T *LEAVE* ME, *BUDDY.*

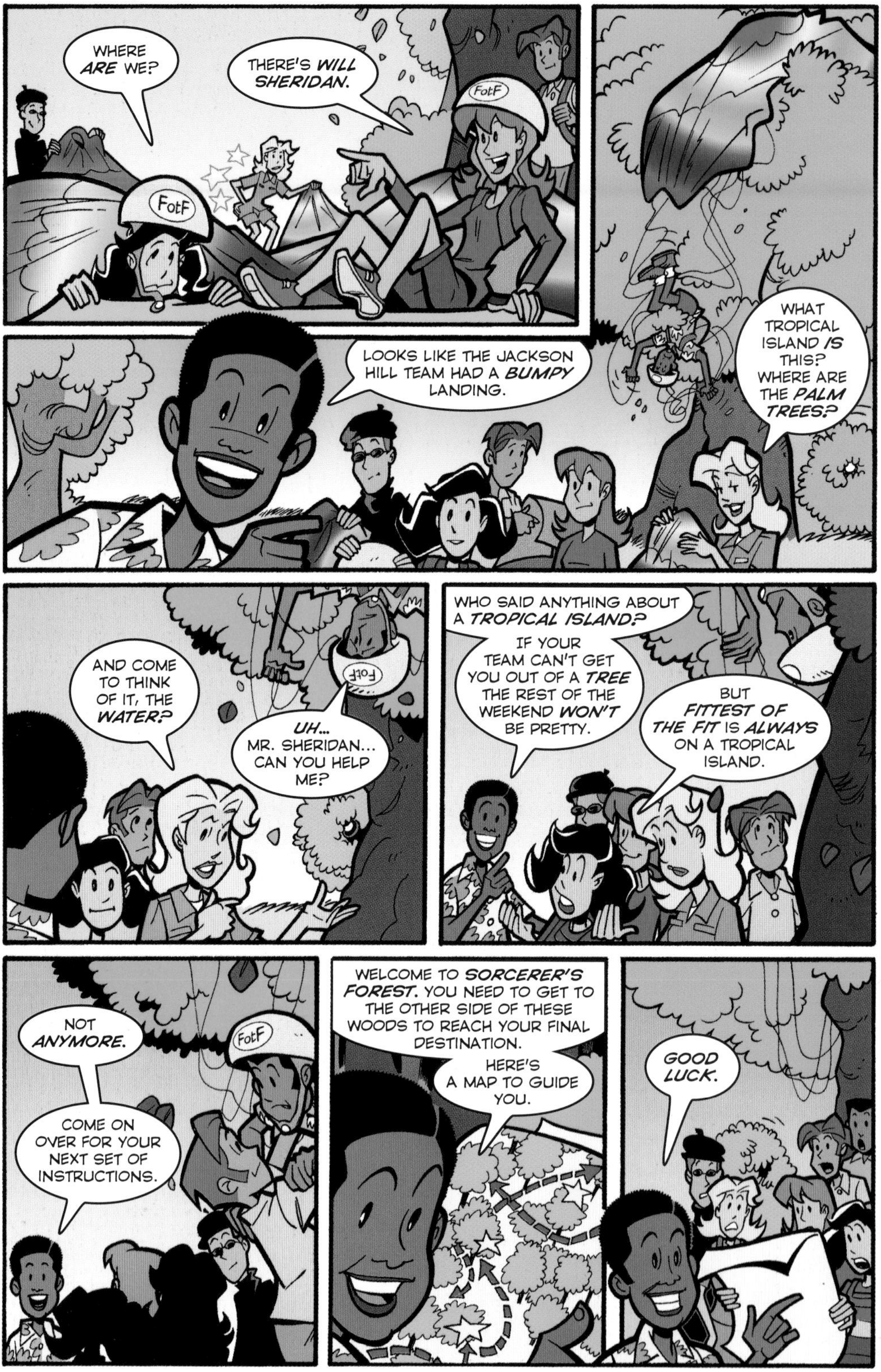
WHERE ARE WE?
THERE'S WILL SHERIDAN.
FotF
WHAT TROPICAL ISLAND IS THIS? WHERE ARE THE PALM TREES?
LOOKS LIKE THE JACKSON HILL TEAM HAD A BUMPY LANDING.
AND COME TO THINK OF IT, THE WATER?
UH... MR. SHERIDAN... CAN YOU HELP ME?
WHO SAID ANYTHING ABOUT A TROPICAL ISLAND?
IF YOUR TEAM CAN'T GET YOU OUT OF A TREE THE REST OF THE WEEKEND WON'T BE PRETTY.
BUT FITTEST OF THE FIT IS ALWAYS ON A TROPICAL ISLAND.
NOT ANYMORE.
COME ON OVER FOR YOUR NEXT SET OF INSTRUCTIONS.
WELCOME TO SORCERER'S FOREST. YOU NEED TO GET TO THE OTHER SIDE OF THESE WOODS TO REACH YOUR FINAL DESTINATION.
HERE'S A MAP TO GUIDE YOU.
GOOD LUCK.

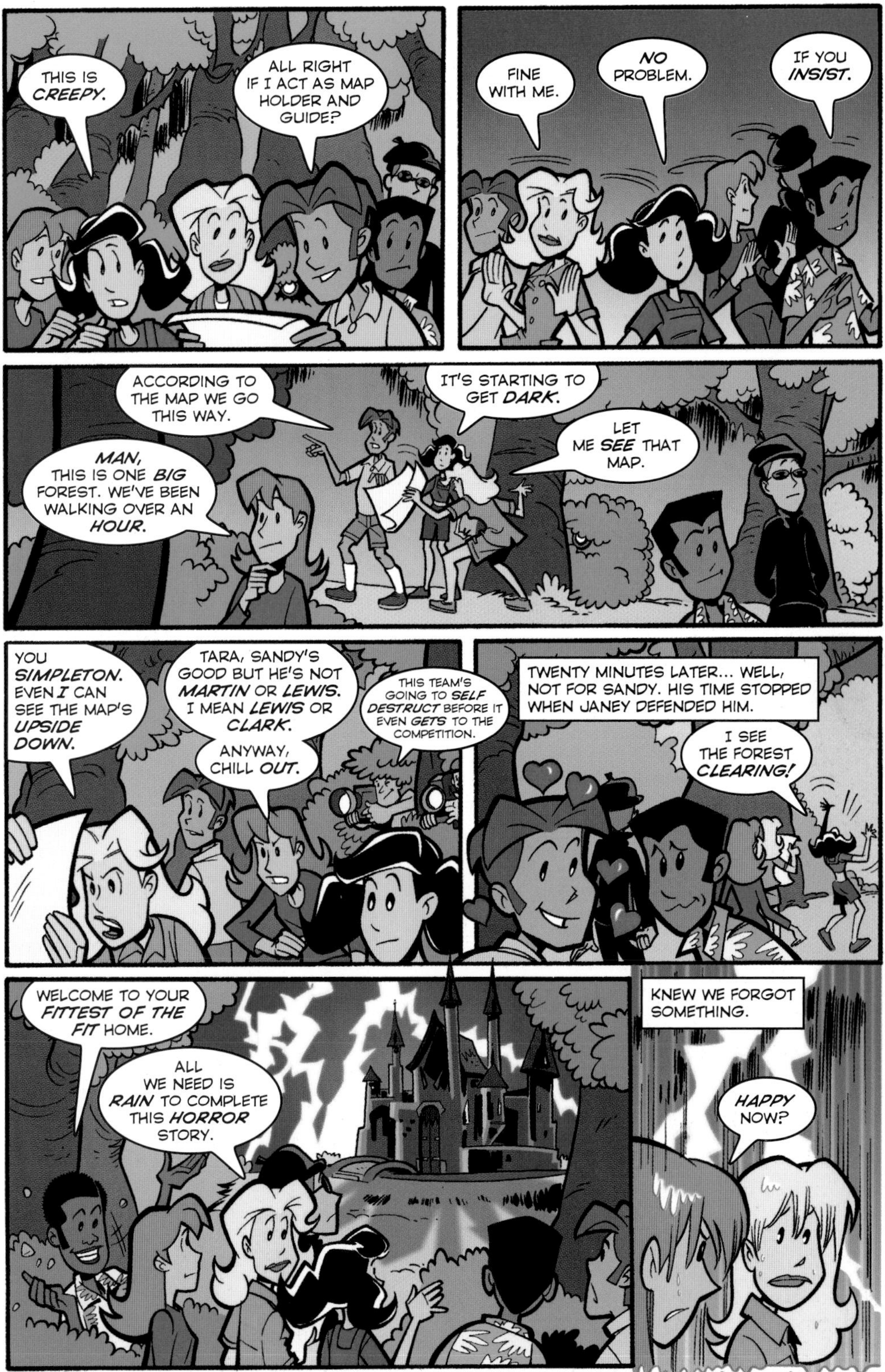
THIS IS CREEPY.
ALL RIGHT IF I ACT AS MAP HOLDER AND GUIDE?
FINE WITH ME.
NO PROBLEM.
IF YOU INSIST.
ACCORDING TO THE MAP WE GO THIS WAY.
IT'S STARTING TO GET DARK.
MAN, THIS IS ONE BIG FOREST. WE'VE BEEN WALKING OVER AN HOUR.
LET ME SEE THAT MAP.
YOU SIMPLETON. EVEN I CAN SEE THE MAP'S UPSIDE DOWN.
TARA, SANDY'S GOOD BUT HE'S NOT MARTIN OR LEWIS. I MEAN LEWIS OR CLARK.
ANYWAY, CHILL OUT.
THIS TEAM'S GOING TO SELF DESTRUCT BEFORE IT EVEN GETS TO THE COMPETITION.
TWENTY MINUTES LATER... WELL, NOT FOR SANDY. HIS TIME STOPPED WHEN JANEY DEFENDED HIM.
I SEE THE FOREST CLEARING!
WELCOME TO YOUR FITTEST OF THE FIT HOME.
ALL WE NEED IS RAIN TO COMPLETE THIS HORROR STORY.
KNEW WE FORGOT SOMETHING.
HAPPY NOW?

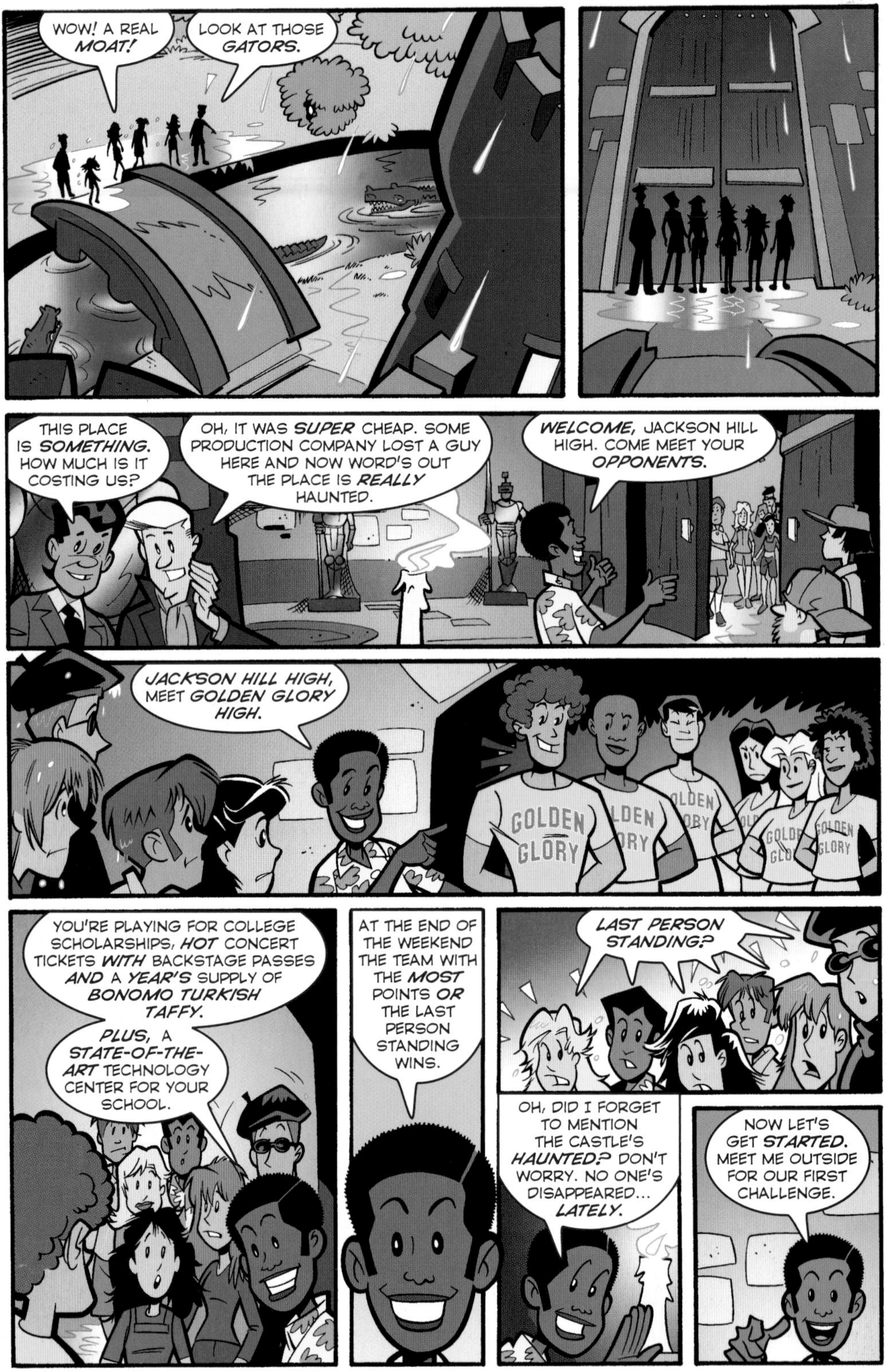
WOW! A REAL MOAT!
LOOK AT THOSE GATORS.
THIS PLACE IS SOMETHING. HOW MUCH IS IT COSTING US?
OH, IT WAS SUPER CHEAP. SOME PRODUCTION COMPANY LOST A GUY HERE AND NOW WORD'S OUT THE PLACE IS REALLY HAUNTED.
WELCOME, JACKSON HILL HIGH. COME MEET YOUR OPPONENTS.
JACKSON HILL HIGH, MEET GOLDEN GLORY HIGH.
GOLDEN GLORY
YOU'RE PLAYING FOR COLLEGE SCHOLARSHIPS, HOT CONCERT TICKETS WITH BACKSTAGE PASSES AND A YEAR'S SUPPLY OF BONOMO TURKISH TAFFY.
PLUS, A STATE-OF-THE-ART TECHNOLOGY CENTER FOR YOUR SCHOOL.
AT THE END OF THE WEEKEND THE TEAM WITH THE MOST POINTS OR THE LAST PERSON STANDING WINS.
LAST PERSON STANDING?
OH, DID I FORGET TO MENTION THE CASTLE'S HAUNTED? DON'T WORRY. NO ONE'S DISAPPEARED... LATELY.
NOW LET'S GET STARTED. MEET ME OUTSIDE FOR OUR FIRST CHALLENGE.

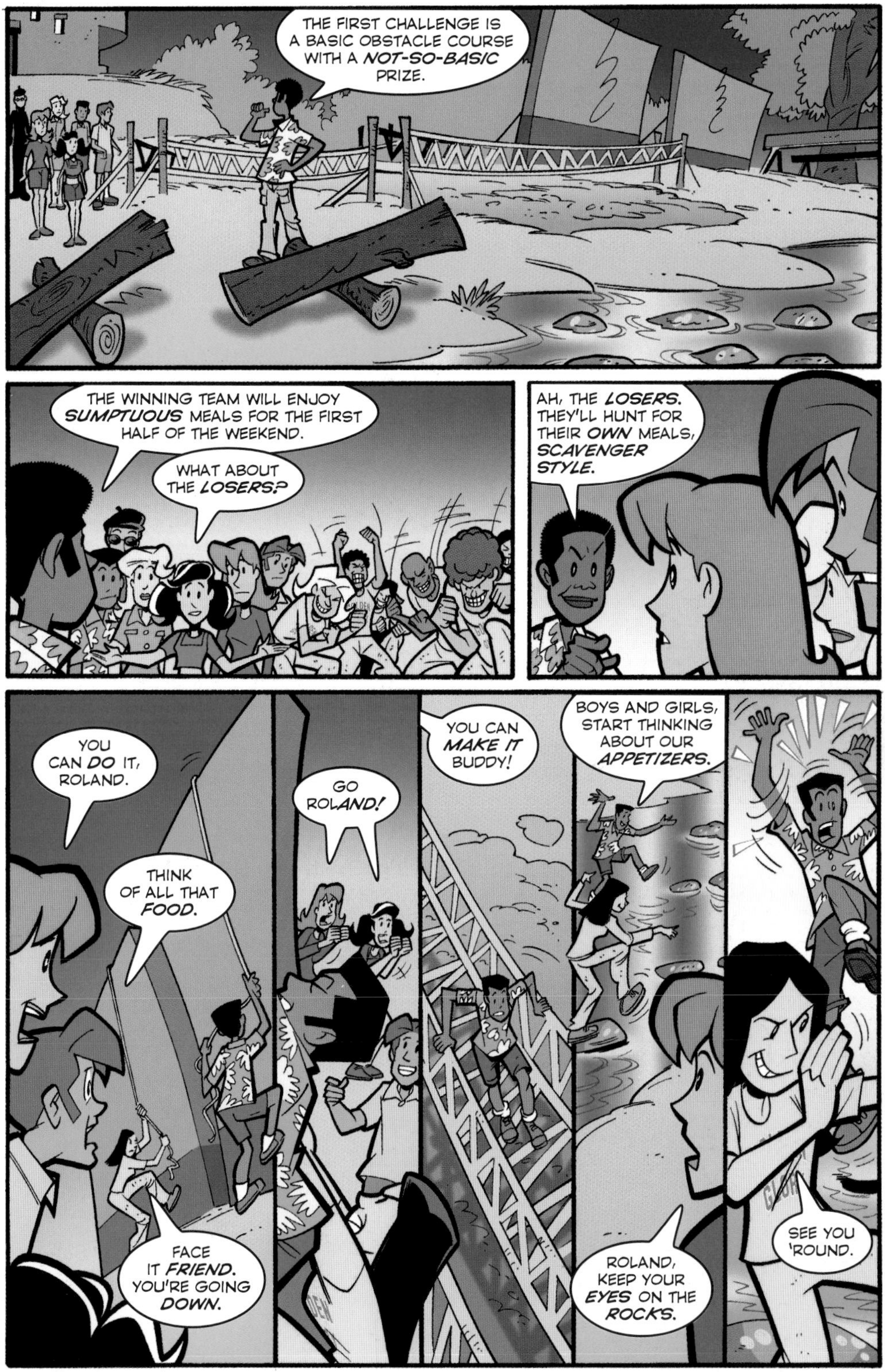
THE FIRST CHALLENGE IS A BASIC OBSTACLE COURSE WITH A NOT-SO-BASIC PRIZE.
THE WINNING TEAM WILL ENJOY SUMPTUOUS MEALS FOR THE FIRST HALF OF THE WEEKEND.
WHAT ABOUT THE LOSERS?
AH, THE LOSERS. THEY'LL HUNT FOR THEIR OWN MEALS, SCAVENGER STYLE.
YOU CAN DO IT, ROLAND.
THINK OF ALL THAT FOOD.
FACE IT FRIEND. YOU'RE GOING DOWN.
GO ROLAND!
YOU CAN MAKE IT BUDDY!
BOYS AND GIRLS, START THINKING ABOUT OUR APPETIZERS.
ROLAND, KEEP YOUR EYES ON THE ROCKS.
SEE YOU 'ROUND.

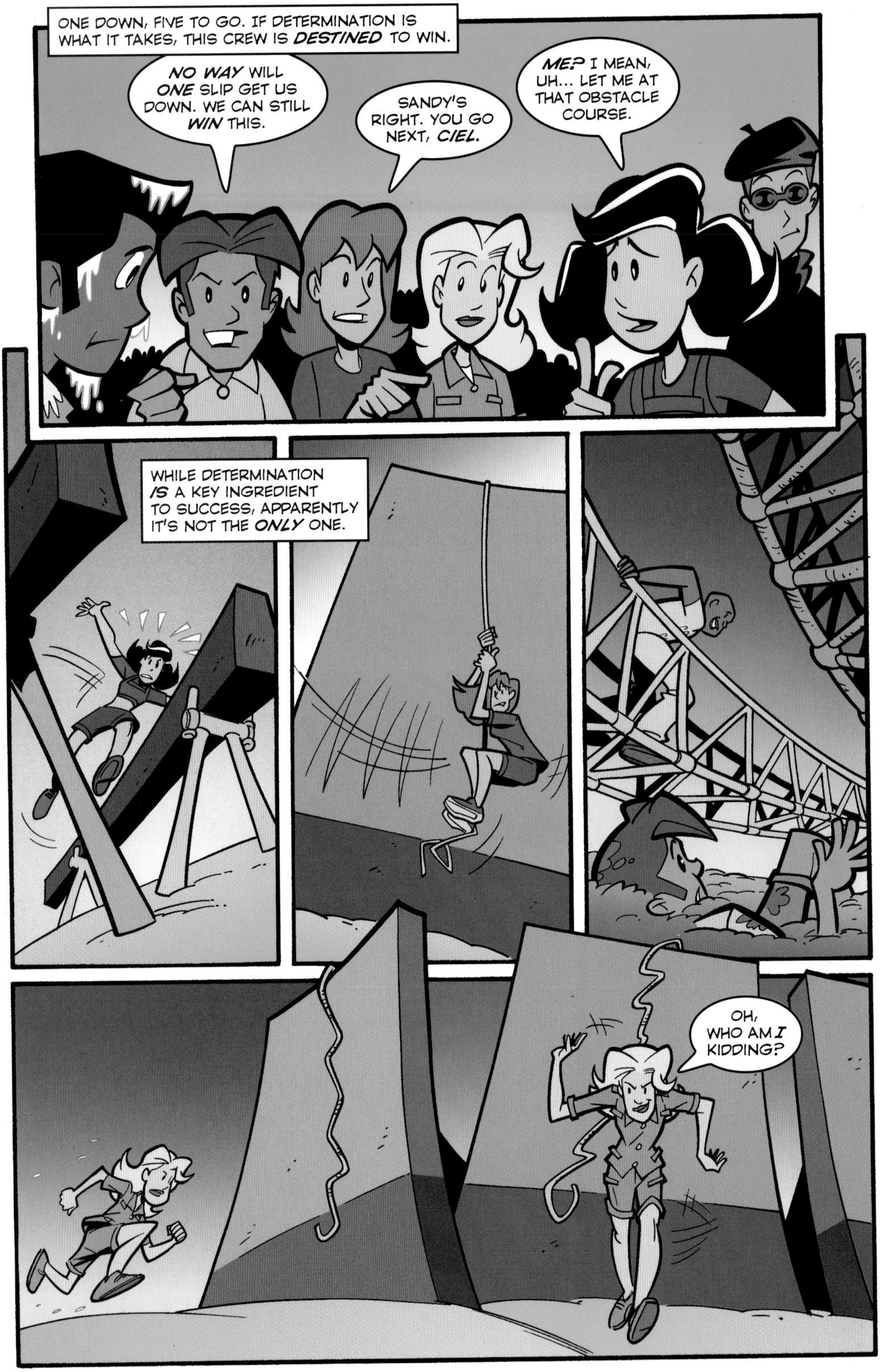
ONE DOWN, FIVE TO GO. IF DETERMINATION IS WHAT IT TAKES, THIS CREW IS DESTINED TO WIN.
NO WAY WILL ONE SLIP GET US DOWN. WE CAN STILL WIN THIS.
SANDY'S RIGHT. YOU GO NEXT, CIEL.
ME? I MEAN, UH... LET ME AT THAT OBSTACLE COURSE.
WHILE DETERMINATION IS A KEY INGREDIENT TO SUCCESS, APPARENTLY IT'S NOT THE ONLY ONE.
OH, WHO AM I KIDDING?

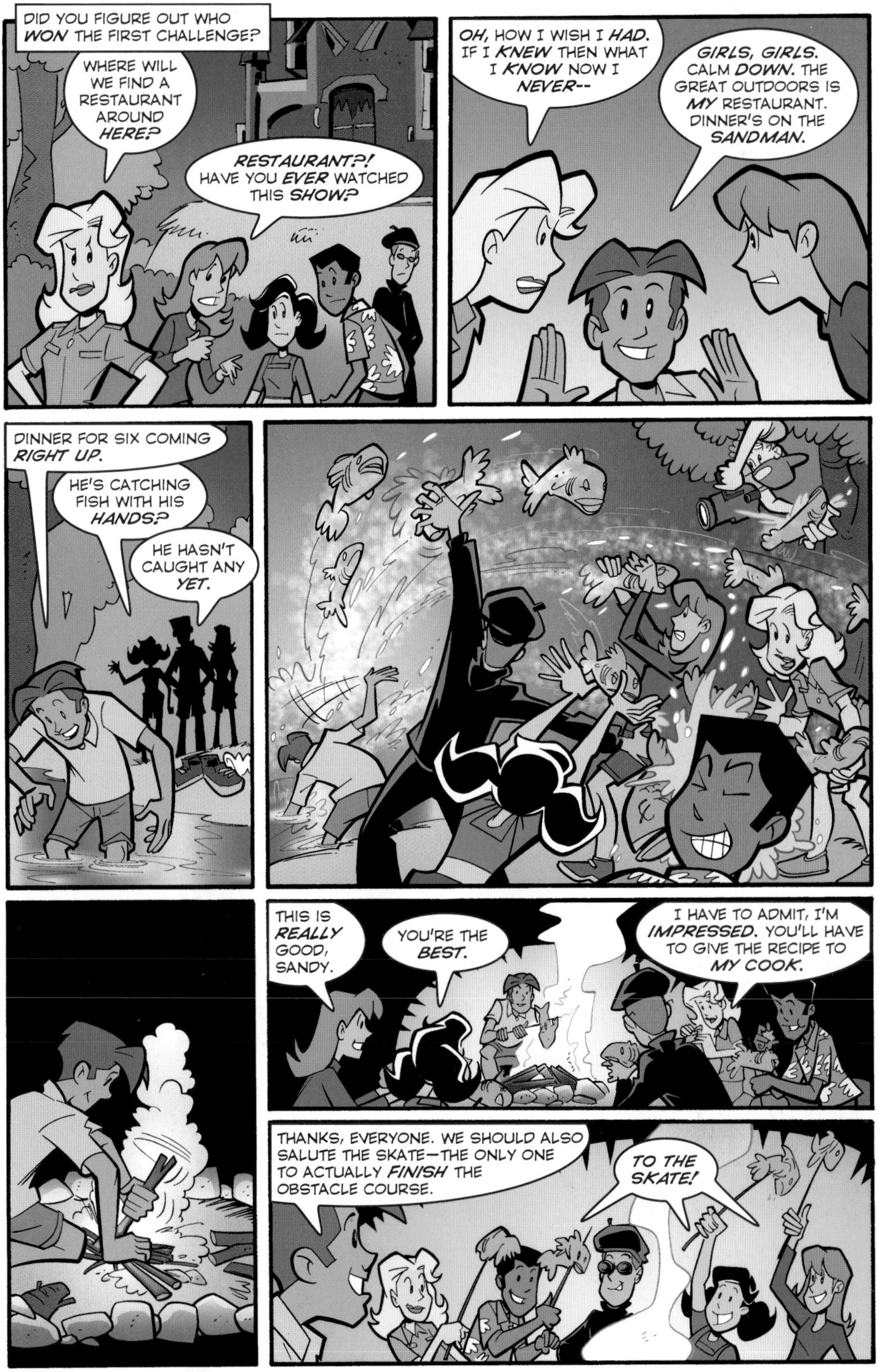
DID YOU FIGURE OUT WHO WON THE FIRST CHALLENGE?
WHERE WILL WE FIND A RESTAURANT AROUND HERE?
RESTAURANT?! HAVE YOU EVER WATCHED THIS SHOW?
OH, HOW I WISH I HAD. IF I KNEW THEN WHAT I KNOW NOW I NEVER--
GIRLS, GIRLS. CALM DOWN. THE GREAT OUTDOORS IS MY RESTAURANT. DINNER'S ON THE SANDMAN.
DINNER FOR SIX COMING RIGHT UP.
HE'S CATCHING FISH WITH HIS HANDS?
HE HASN'T CAUGHT ANY YET.
THIS IS REALLY GOOD, SANDY.
YOU'RE THE BEST.
I HAVE TO ADMIT, I'M IMPRESSED. YOU'LL HAVE TO GIVE THE RECIPE TO MY COOK.
THANKS, EVERYONE. WE SHOULD ALSO SALUTE THE SKATE—THE ONLY ONE TO ACTUALLY FINISH THE OBSTACLE COURSE.
TO THE SKATE!

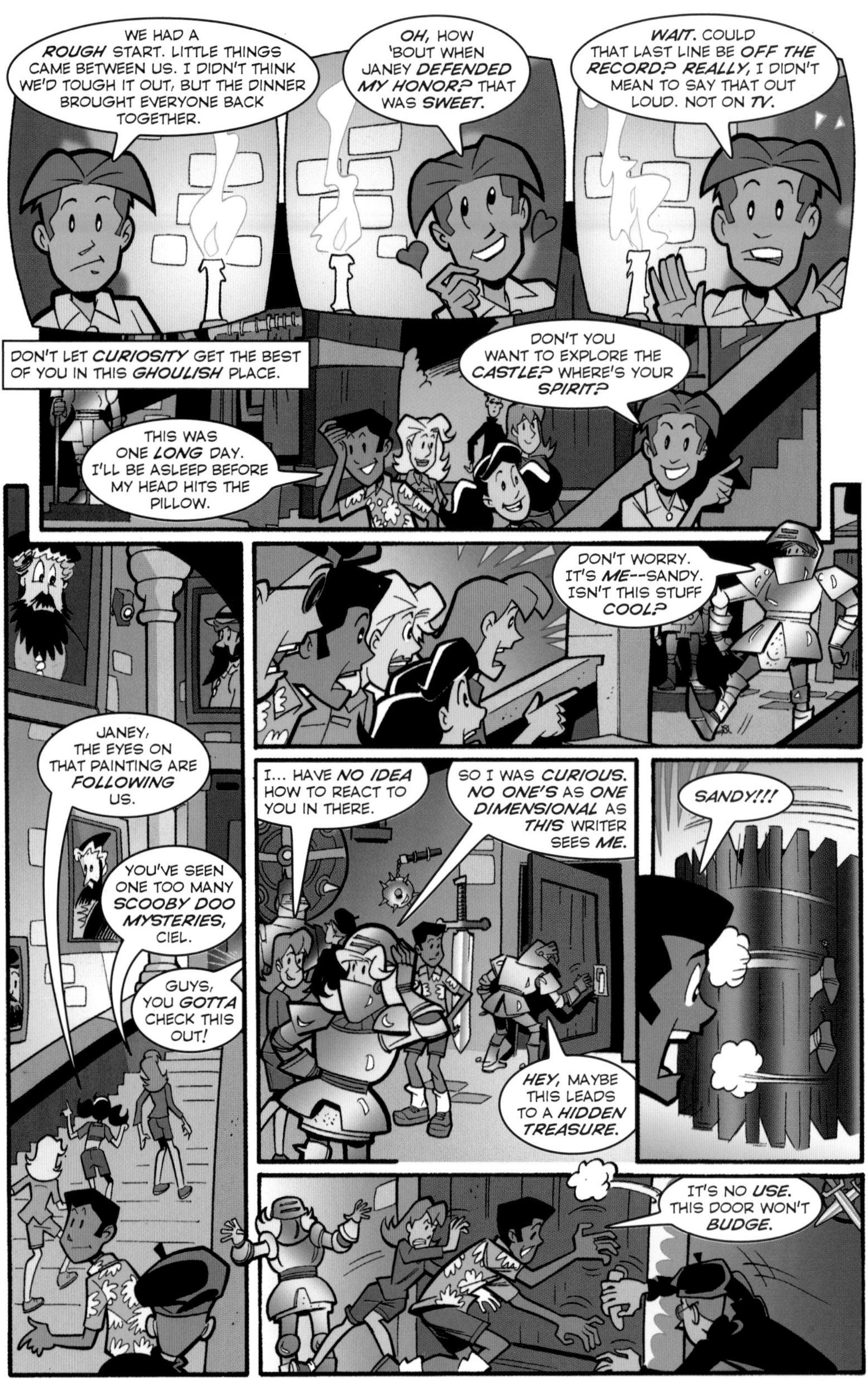
WE HAD A ROUGH START. LITTLE THINGS CAME BETWEEN US. I DIDN'T THINK WE'D TOUGH IT OUT, BUT THE DINNER BROUGHT EVERYONE BACK TOGETHER.
OH, HOW 'BOUT WHEN JANEY DEFENDED MY HONOR? THAT WAS SWEET.
WAIT. COULD THAT LAST LINE BE OFF THE RECORD? REALLY, I DIDN'T MEAN TO SAY THAT OUT LOUD. NOT ON TV.
DON'T LET CURIOSITY GET THE BEST OF YOU IN THIS GHOULISH PLACE.
DON'T YOU WANT TO EXPLORE THE CASTLE? WHERE'S YOUR SPIRIT?
THIS WAS ONE LONG DAY. I'LL BE ASLEEP BEFORE MY HEAD HITS THE PILLOW.
JANEY, THE EYES ON THAT PAINTING ARE FOLLOWING US.
YOU'VE SEEN ONE TOO MANY SCOOBY DOO MYSTERIES, CIEL.
GUYS, YOU GOTTA CHECK THIS OUT!
DON'T WORRY. IT'S ME--SANDY. ISN'T THIS STUFF COOL?
I... HAVE NO IDEA HOW TO REACT TO YOU IN THERE.
SO I WAS CURIOUS. NO ONE'S AS ONE DIMENSIONAL AS THIS WRITER SEES ME.
HEY, MAYBE THIS LEADS TO A HIDDEN TREASURE.
SANDY!!!
IT'S NO USE. THIS DOOR WON'T BUDGE.

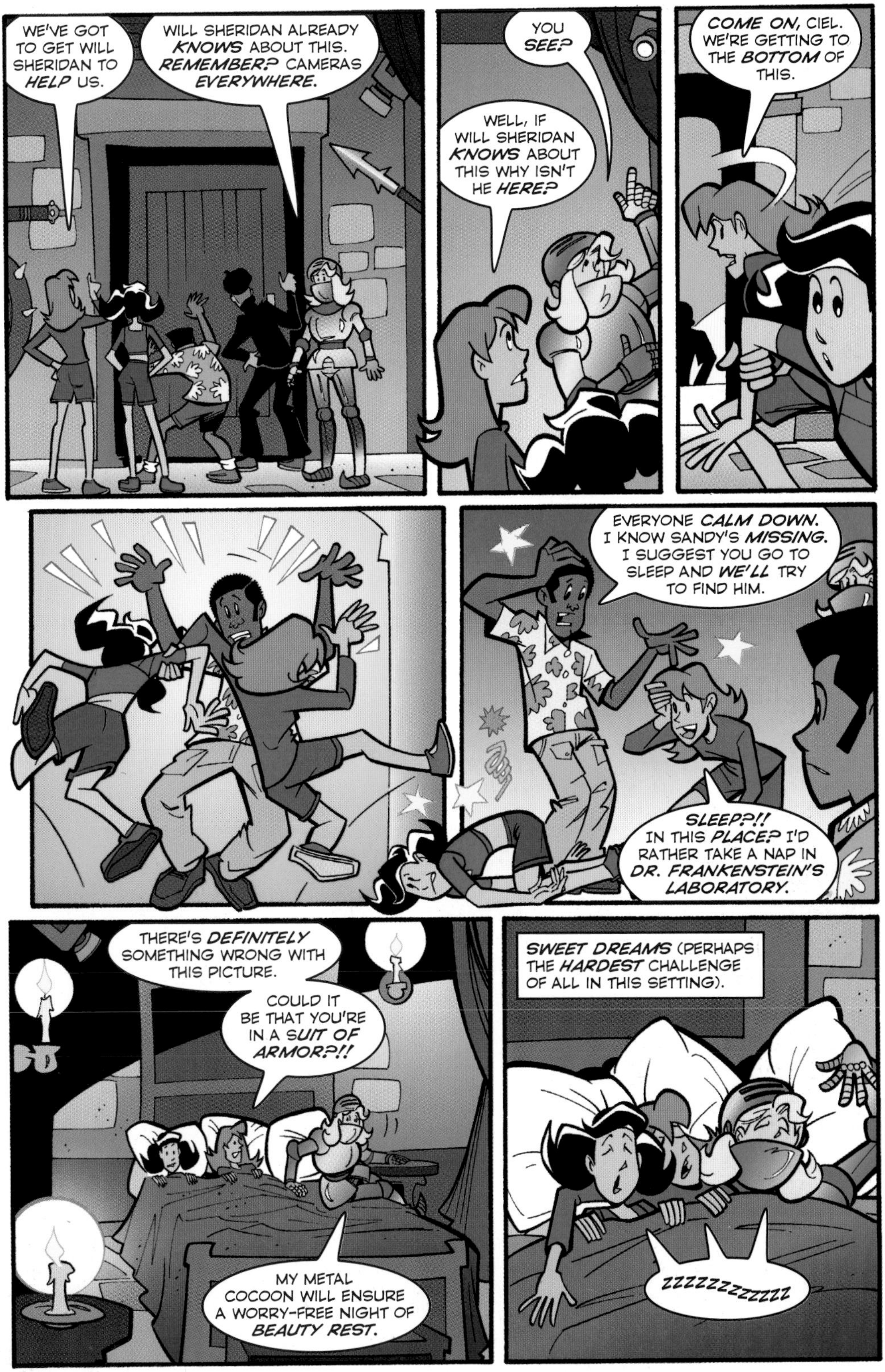

WE'VE GOT TO GET WILL SHERIDAN TO HELP US.
WILL SHERIDAN ALREADY KNOWS ABOUT THIS. REMEMBER? CAMERAS EVERYWHERE.
YOU SEE?
WELL, IF WILL SHERIDAN KNOWS ABOUT THIS WHY ISN'T HE HERE?
COME ON, CIEL. WE'RE GETTING TO THE BOTTOM OF THIS.
EVERYONE CALM DOWN. I KNOW SANDY'S MISSING. I SUGGEST YOU GO TO SLEEP AND WE'LL TRY TO FIND HIM.
SLEEP?!! IN THIS PLACE? I'D RATHER TAKE A NAP IN DR. FRANKENSTEIN'S LABORATORY.
THERE'S DEFINITELY SOMETHING WRONG WITH THIS PICTURE.
COULD IT BE THAT YOU'RE IN A SUIT OF ARMOR?!!
MY METAL COCOON WILL ENSURE A WORRY-FREE NIGHT OF BEAUTY REST.
SWEET DREAMS (PERHAPS THE HARDEST CHALLENGE OF ALL IN THIS SETTING).
ZZZZZZZZZZZZ

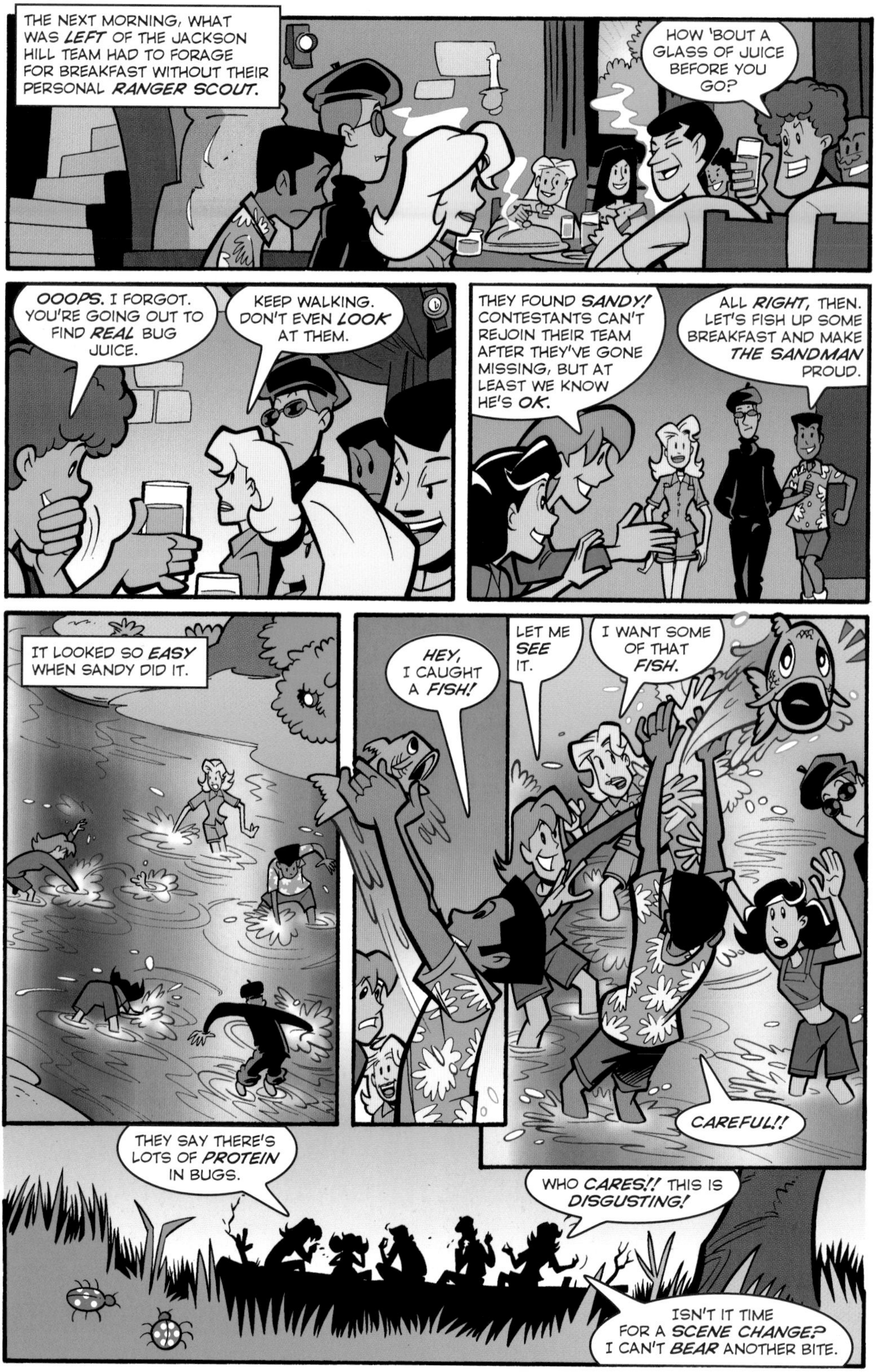
THE NEXT MORNING, WHAT WAS LEFT OF THE JACKSON HILL TEAM HAD TO FORAGE FOR BREAKFAST WITHOUT THEIR PERSONAL RANGER SCOUT.
HOW 'BOUT A GLASS OF JUICE BEFORE YOU GO?
OOOPS. I FORGOT. YOU'RE GOING OUT TO FIND REAL BUG JUICE.
KEEP WALKING. DON'T EVEN LOOK AT THEM.
THEY FOUND SANDY! CONTESTANTS CAN'T REJOIN THEIR TEAM AFTER THEY'VE GONE MISSING, BUT AT LEAST WE KNOW HE'S OK.
ALL RIGHT, THEN. LET'S FISH UP SOME BREAKFAST AND MAKE THE SANDMAN PROUD.
IT LOOKED SO EASY WHEN SANDY DID IT.
HEY, I CAUGHT A FISH!
LET ME SEE IT.
I WANT SOME OF THAT FISH.
CAREFUL!!
THEY SAY THERE'S LOTS OF PROTEIN IN BUGS.
WHO CARES!! THIS IS DISGUSTING!
ISN'T IT TIME FOR A SCENE CHANGE? I CAN'T BEAR ANOTHER BITE.

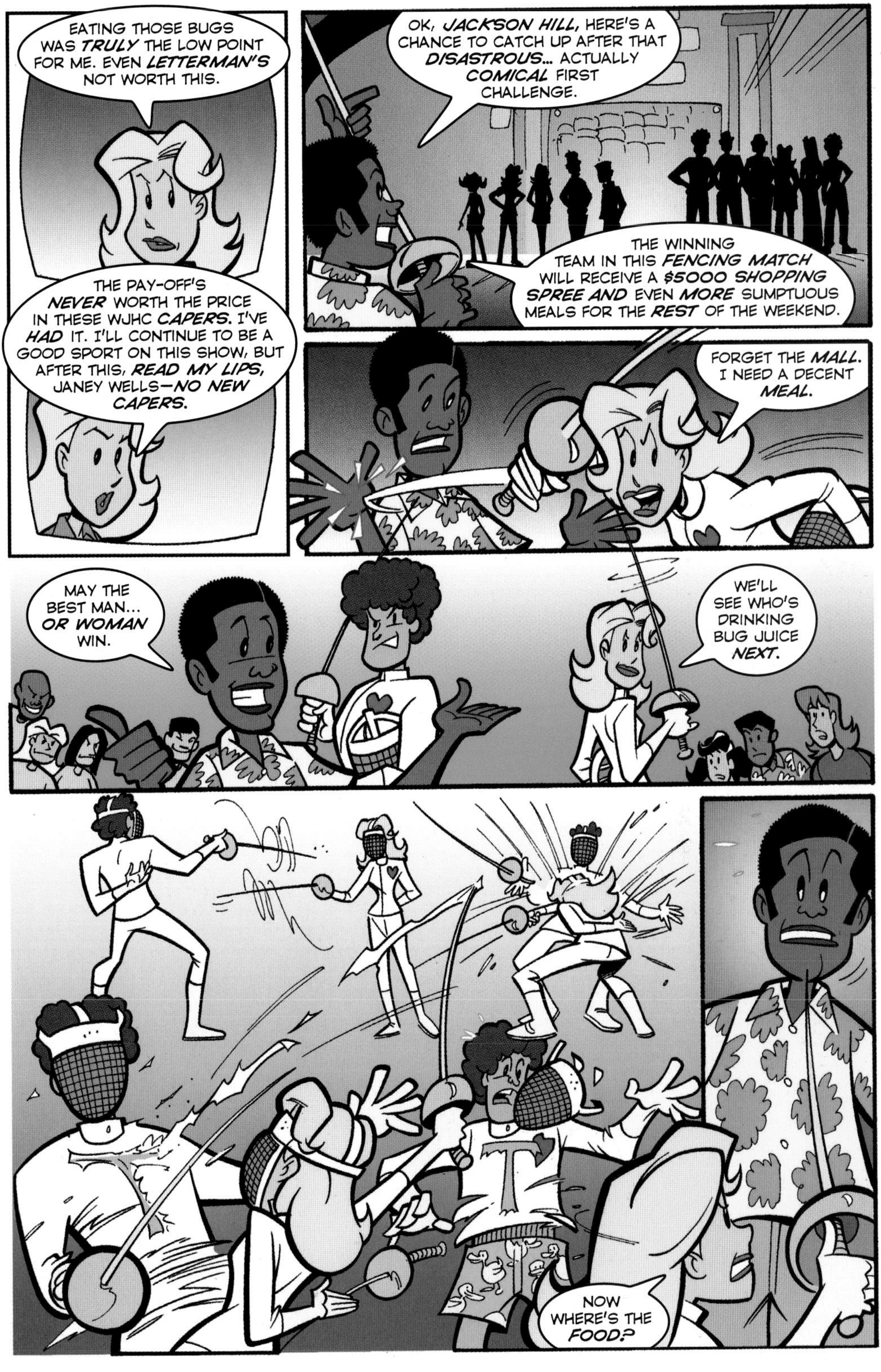
EATING THOSE BUGS WAS TRULY THE LOW POINT FOR ME. EVEN LETTERMAN'S NOT WORTH THIS.
THE PAY-OFF'S NEVER WORTH THE PRICE IN THESE WJHC CAPERS. I'VE HAD IT. I'LL CONTINUE TO BE A GOOD SPORT ON THIS SHOW, BUT AFTER THIS, READ MY LIPS, JANEY WELLS—NO NEW CAPERS.
OK, JACKSON HILL, HERE'S A CHANCE TO CATCH UP AFTER THAT DISASTROUS... ACTUALLY COMICAL FIRST CHALLENGE.
THE WINNING TEAM IN THIS FENCING MATCH WILL RECEIVE A $5000 SHOPPING SPREE AND EVEN MORE SUMPTUOUS MEALS FOR THE REST OF THE WEEKEND.
FORGET THE MALL. I NEED A DECENT MEAL.
MAY THE BEST MAN... OR WOMAN WIN.
WE'LL SEE WHO'S DRINKING BUG JUICE NEXT.
NOW WHERE'S THE FOOD?

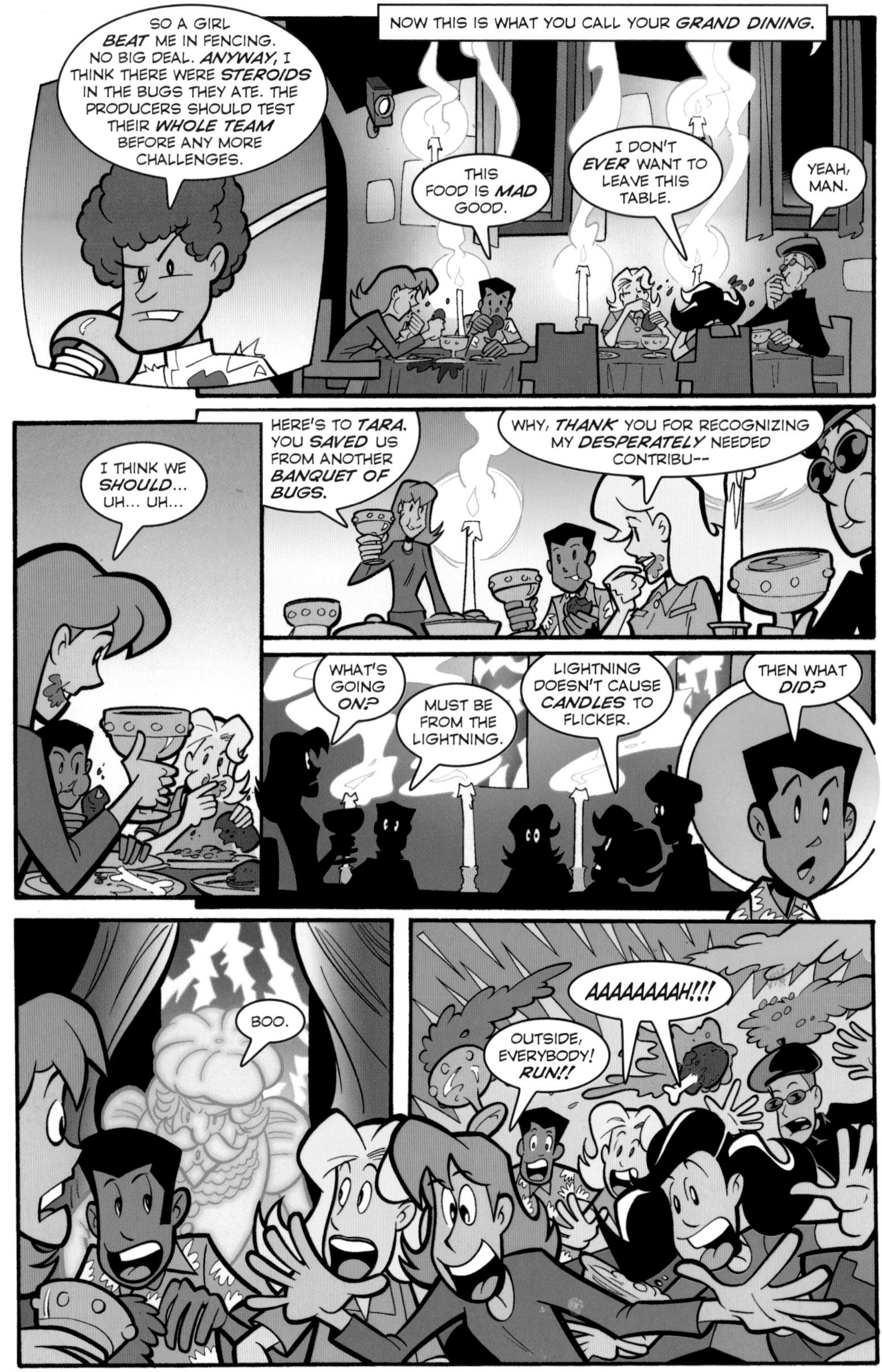

SO A GIRL BEAT ME IN FENCING. NO BIG DEAL. ANYWAY, I THINK THERE WERE STEROIDS IN THE BUGS THEY ATE. THE PRODUCERS SHOULD TEST THEIR WHOLE TEAM BEFORE ANY MORE CHALLENGES.
NOW THIS IS WHAT YOU CALL YOUR GRAND DINING.
THIS FOOD IS MAD GOOD.
I DON'T EVER WANT TO LEAVE THIS TABLE.
YEAH, MAN.
I THINK WE SHOULD... UH... UH...
HERE'S TO TARA. YOU SAVED US FROM ANOTHER BANQUET OF BUGS.
WHY, THANK YOU FOR RECOGNIZING MY DESPERATELY NEEDED CONTRIBU--
WHAT'S GOING ON?
MUST BE FROM THE LIGHTNING.
LIGHTNING DOESN'T CAUSE CANDLES TO FLICKER.
THEN WHAT DID?
BOO.
AAAAAAAAH!!!
OUTSIDE, EVERYBODY! RUN!!

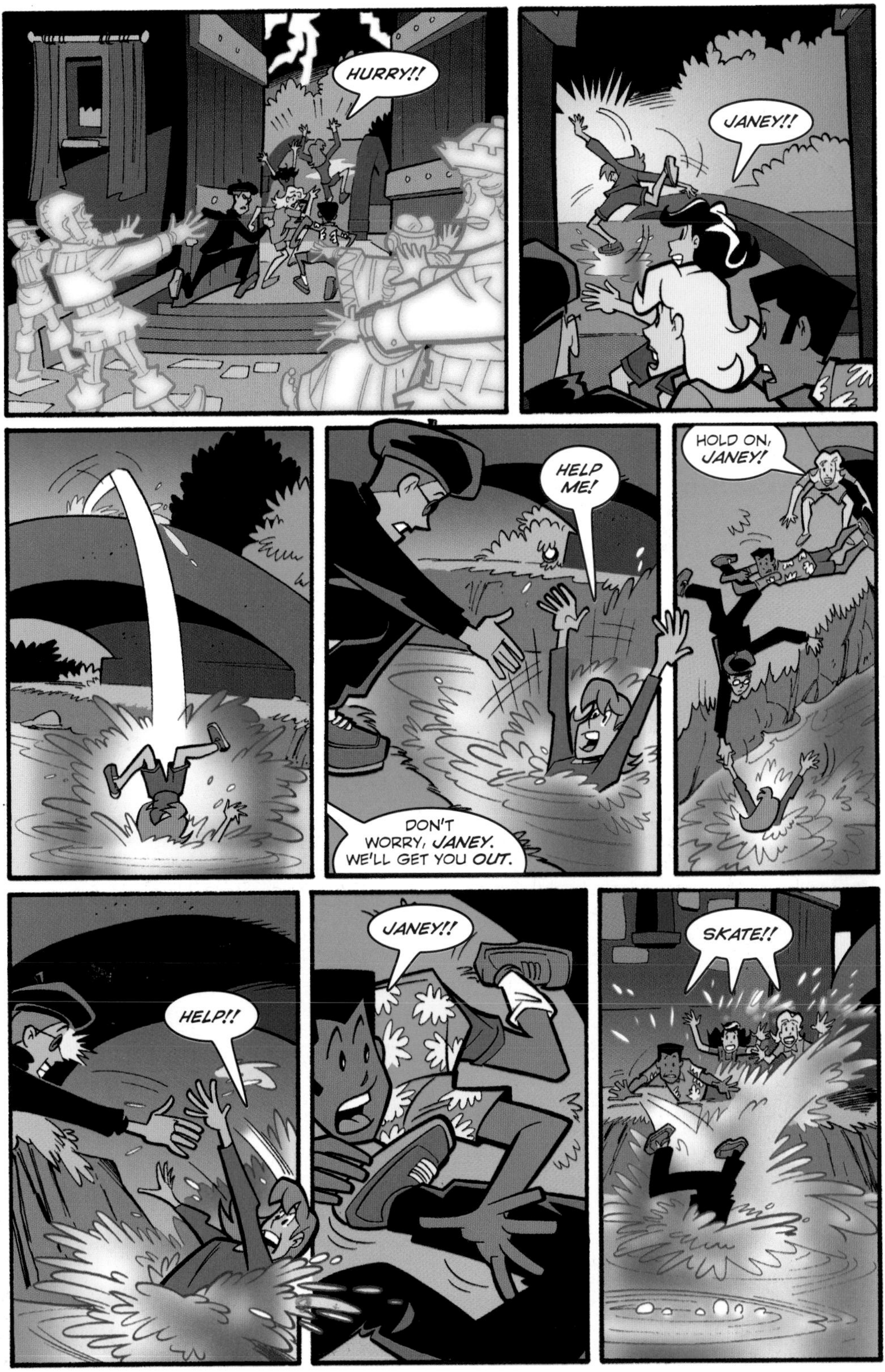
HURRY!!
JANEY!!
HELP ME!
DON'T WORRY, JANEY. WE'LL GET YOU OUT.
HOLD ON, JANEY!
HELP!!
JANEY!!
SKATE!!

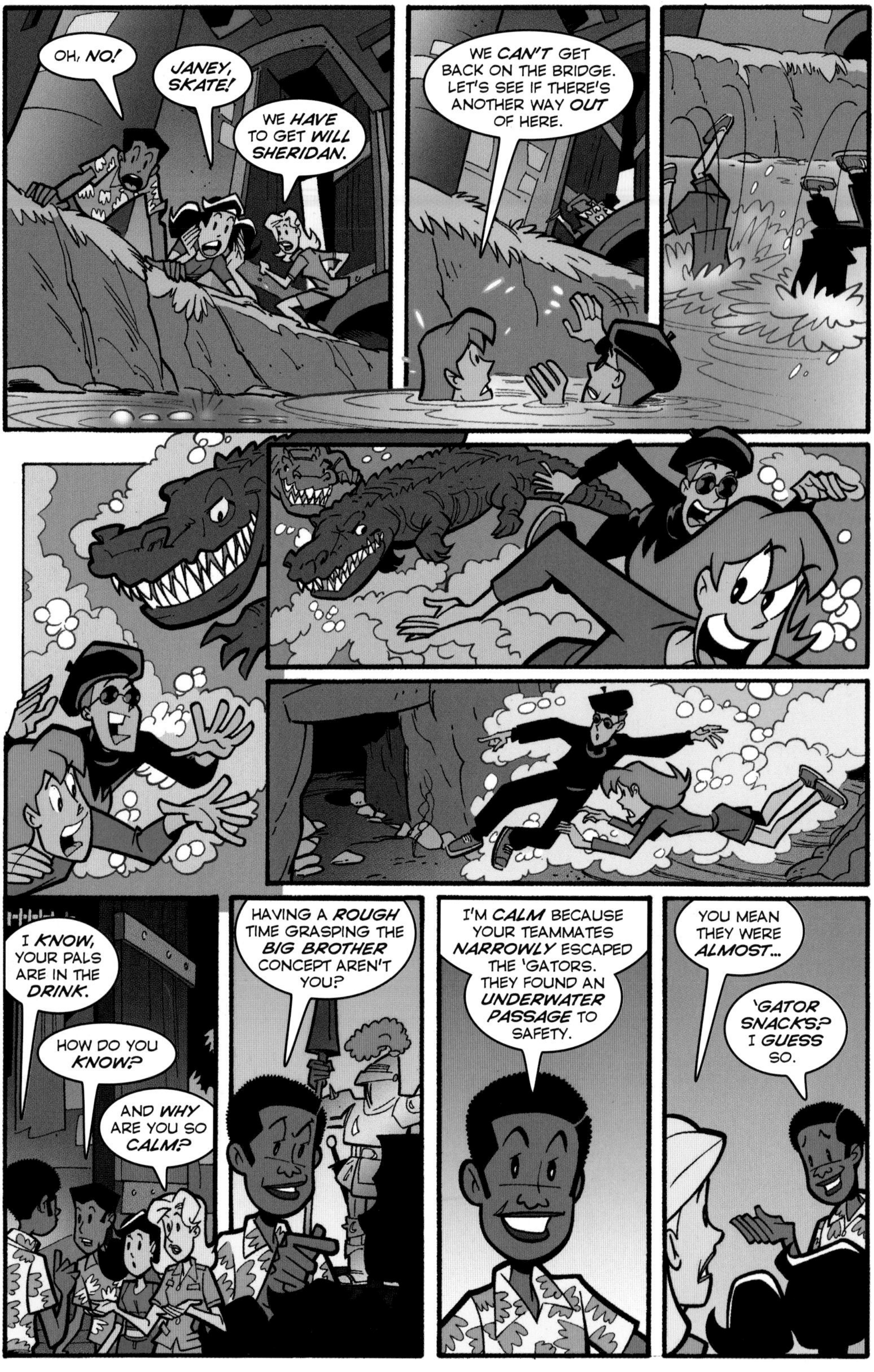
OH, NO!
JANEY, SKATE!
WE HAVE TO GET WILL SHERIDAN.
WE CAN'T GET BACK ON THE BRIDGE. LET'S SEE IF THERE'S ANOTHER WAY OUT OF HERE.
I KNOW, YOUR PALS ARE IN THE DRINK.
HOW DO YOU KNOW?
AND WHY ARE YOU SO CALM?
HAVING A ROUGH TIME GRASPING THE BIG BROTHER CONCEPT AREN'T YOU?
I'M CALM BECAUSE YOUR TEAMMATES NARROWLY ESCAPED THE 'GATORS. THEY FOUND AN UNDERWATER PASSAGE TO SAFETY.
YOU MEAN THEY WERE ALMOST...
'GATOR SNACKS? I GUESS SO.

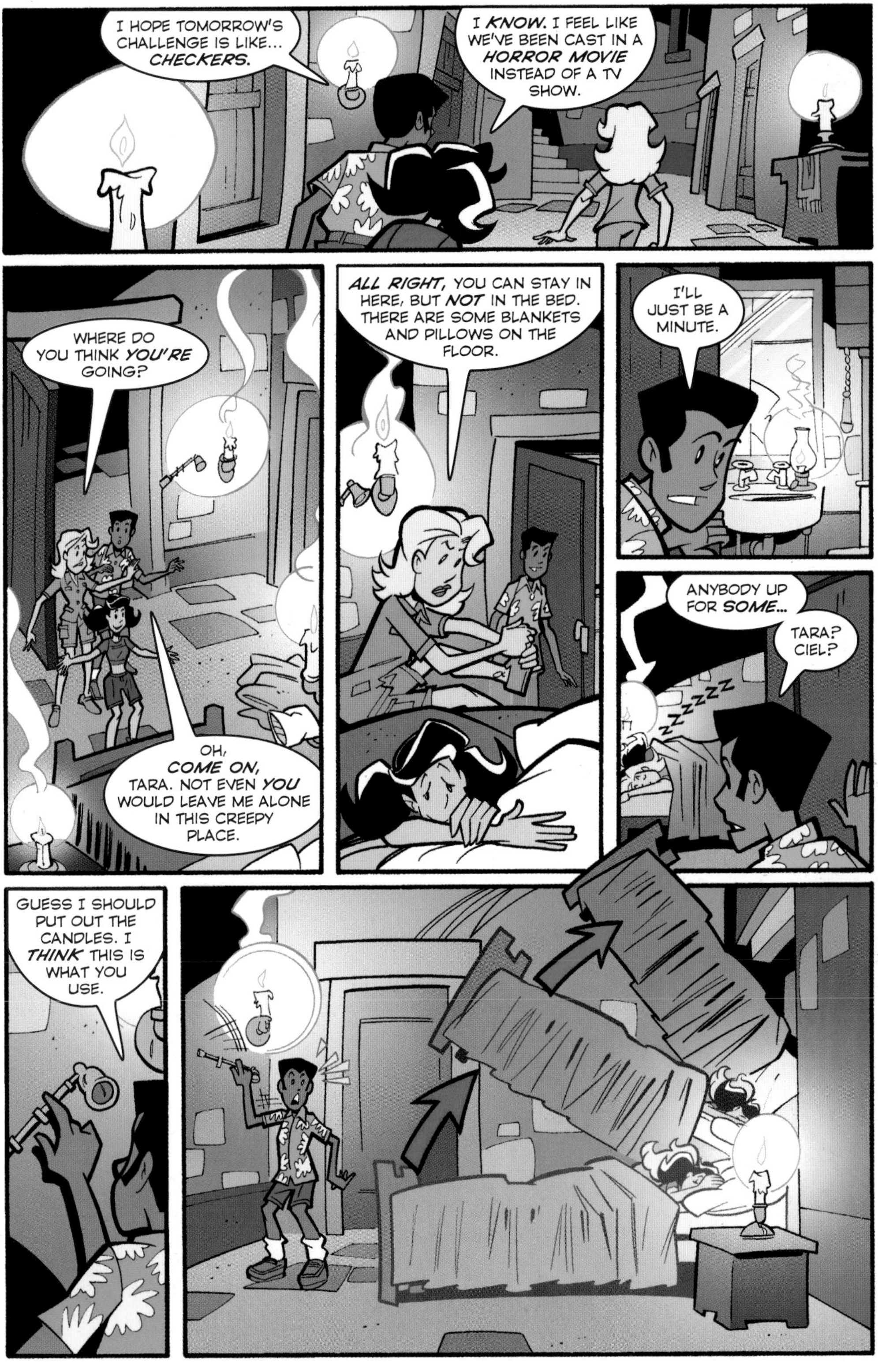
I HOPE TOMORROW'S CHALLENGE IS LIKE... CHECKERS.
I KNOW. I FEEL LIKE WE'VE BEEN CAST IN A HORROR MOVIE INSTEAD OF A TV SHOW.
WHERE DO YOU THINK YOU'RE GOING?
OH, COME ON, TARA. NOT EVEN YOU WOULD LEAVE ME ALONE IN THIS CREEPY PLACE.
ALL RIGHT, YOU CAN STAY IN HERE, BUT NOT IN THE BED. THERE ARE SOME BLANKETS AND PILLOWS ON THE FLOOR.
I'LL JUST BE A MINUTE.
ANYBODY UP FOR SOME...
TARA? CIEL?
ZZZZZZ
GUESS I SHOULD PUT OUT THE CANDLES. I THINK THIS IS WHAT YOU USE.

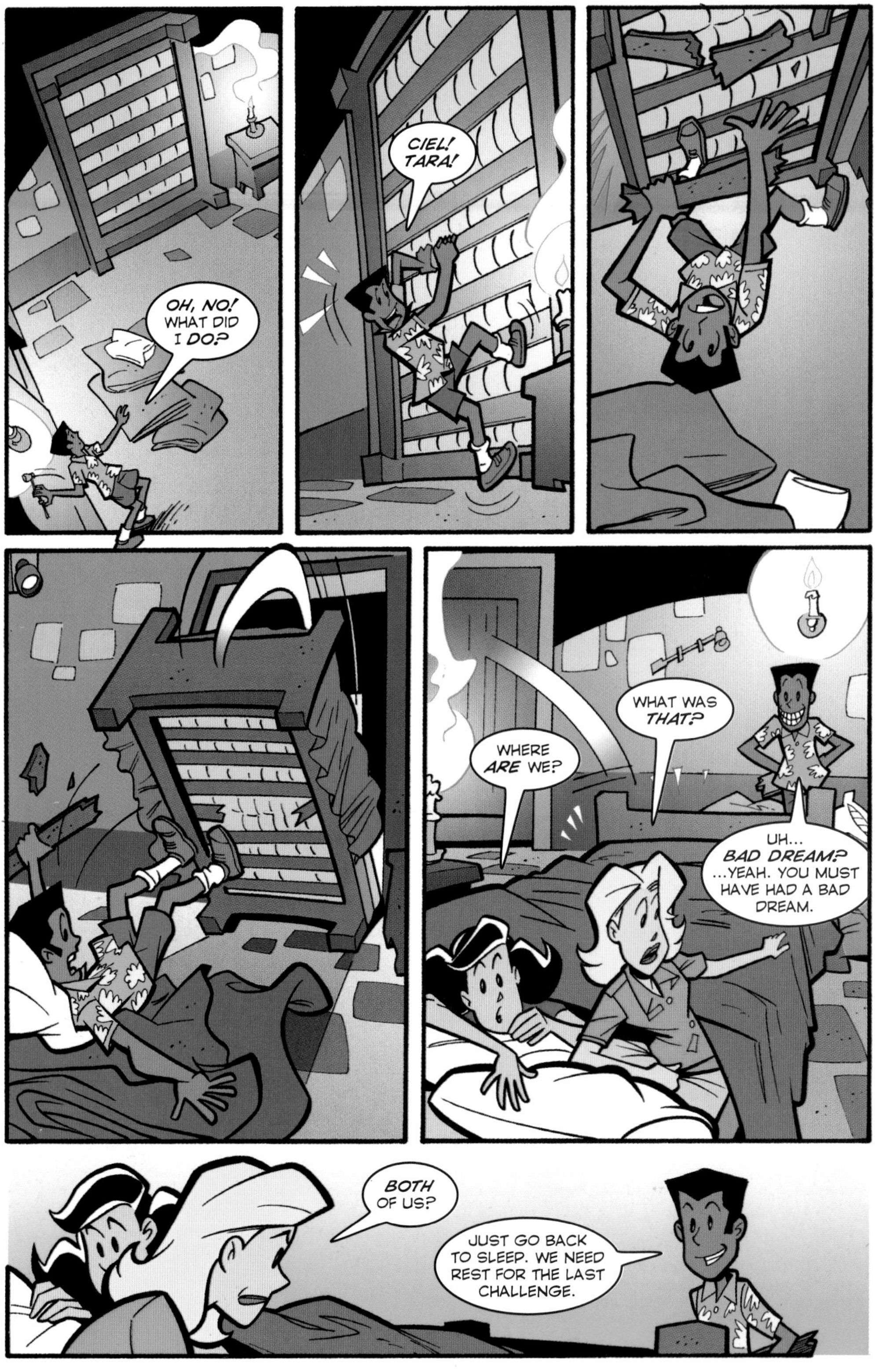
OH, NO! WHAT DID I DO?
CIEL! TARA!
WHAT WAS THAT?
WHERE ARE WE?
UH... BAD DREAM? ...YEAH. YOU MUST HAVE HAD A BAD DREAM.
BOTH OF US?
JUST GO BACK TO SLEEP. WE NEED REST FOR THE LAST CHALLENGE.

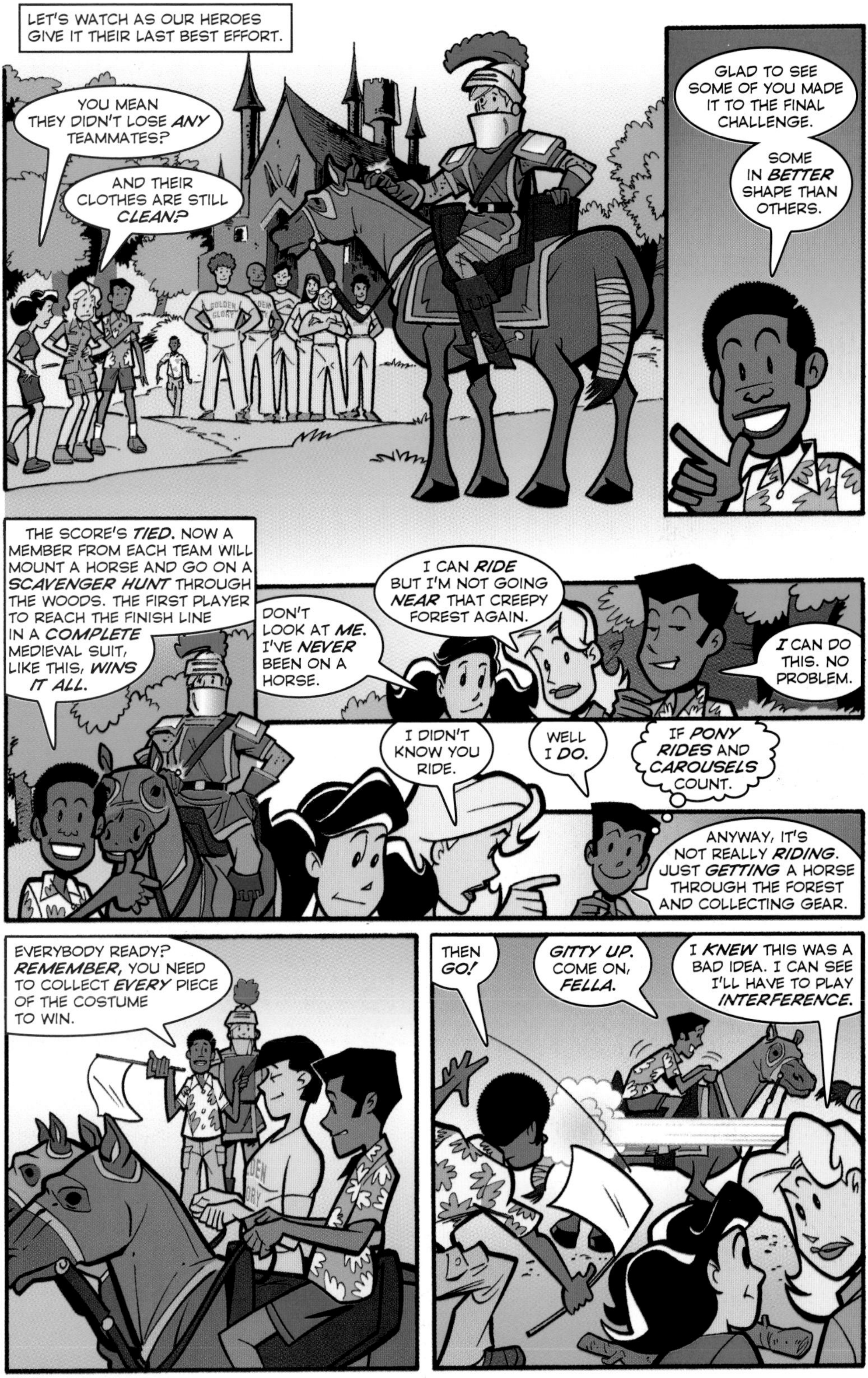
LET'S WATCH AS OUR HEROES GIVE IT THEIR LAST BEST EFFORT.
YOU MEAN THEY DIDN'T LOSE ANY TEAMMATES?
AND THEIR CLOTHES ARE STILL CLEAN?
GOLDEN GLORY
GLAD TO SEE SOME OF YOU MADE IT TO THE FINAL CHALLENGE.
SOME IN BETTER SHAPE THAN OTHERS.
THE SCORE'S TIED. NOW A MEMBER FROM EACH TEAM WILL MOUNT A HORSE AND GO ON A SCAVENGER HUNT THROUGH THE WOODS. THE FIRST PLAYER TO REACH THE FINISH LINE IN A COMPLETE MEDIEVAL SUIT, LIKE THIS, WINS IT ALL.
DON'T LOOK AT ME. I'VE NEVER BEEN ON A HORSE.
I CAN RIDE BUT I'M NOT GOING NEAR THAT CREEPY FOREST AGAIN.
I CAN DO THIS. NO PROBLEM.
I DIDN'T KNOW YOU RIDE.
WELL I DO.
IF PONY RIDES AND CAROUSELS COUNT.
ANYWAY, IT'S NOT REALLY RIDING. JUST GETTING A HORSE THROUGH THE FOREST AND COLLECTING GEAR.
EVERYBODY READY? REMEMBER, YOU NEED TO COLLECT EVERY PIECE OF THE COSTUME TO WIN.
THEN GO!
GITTY UP. COME ON, FELLA.
I KNEW THIS WAS A BAD IDEA. I CAN SEE I'LL HAVE TO PLAY INTERFERENCE.

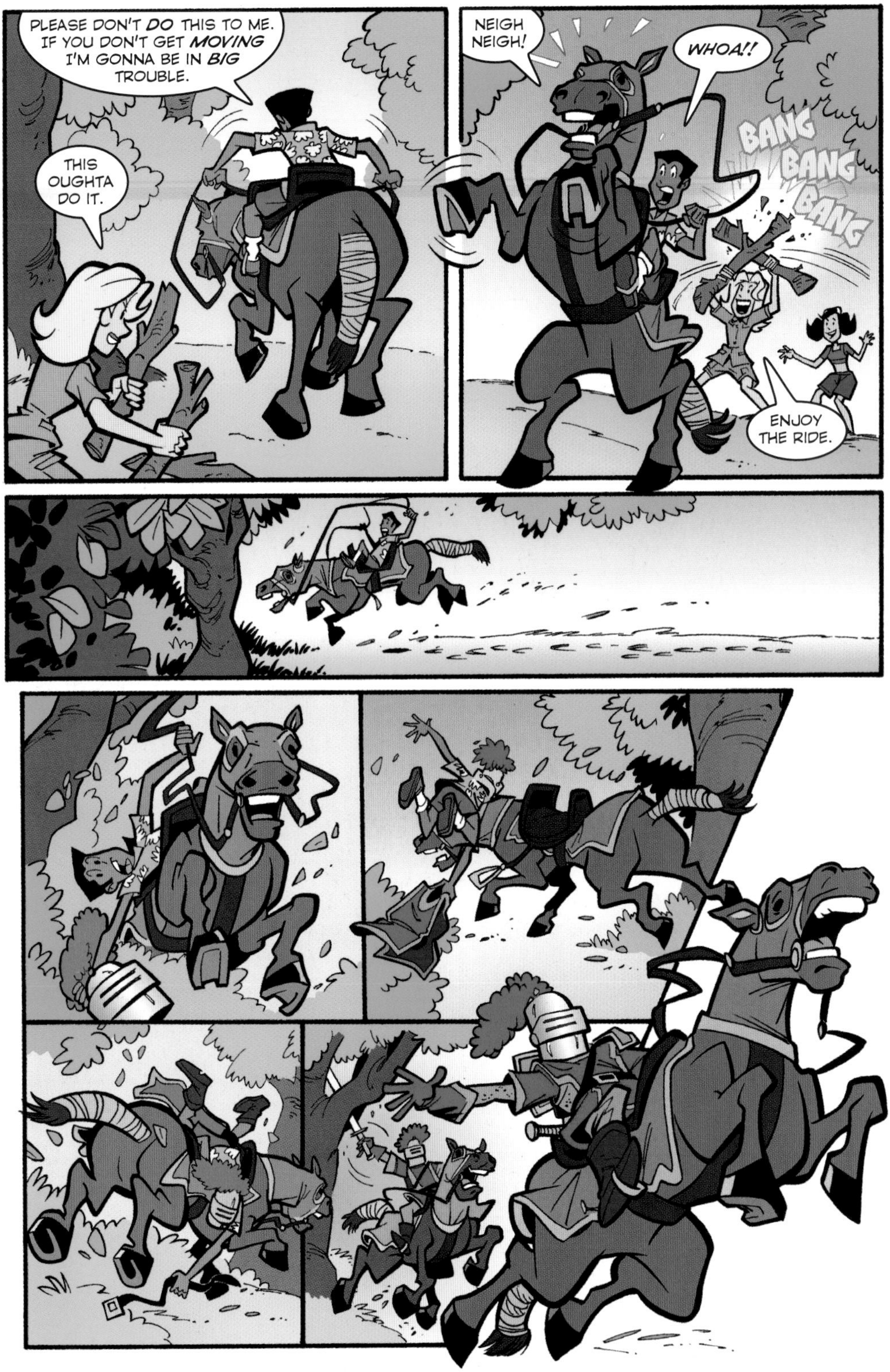
PLEASE DON'T DO THIS TO ME. IF YOU DON'T GET MOVING I'M GONNA BE IN BIG TROUBLE.
THIS OUGHTA DO IT.
NEIGH NEIGH!
WHOA!!
BANG
BANG
BANG
ENJOY THE RIDE.

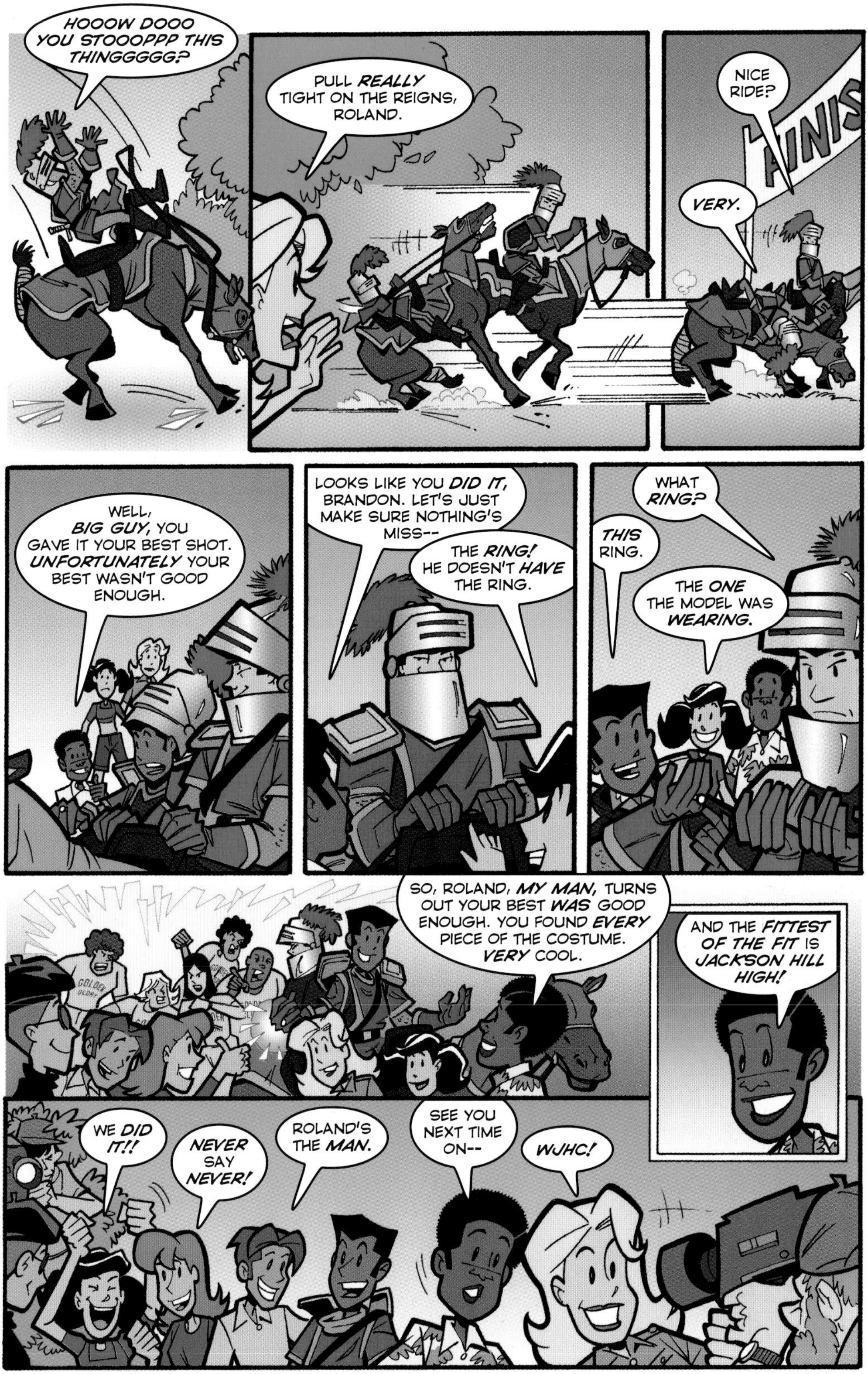
HOOOW DOOO YOU STOOOPPP THIS THINGGGGG?
PULL REALLY TIGHT ON THE REIGNS, ROLAND.
NICE RIDE?
VERY.
WELL, BIG GUY, YOU GAVE IT YOUR BEST SHOT. UNFORTUNATELY YOUR BEST WASN'T GOOD ENOUGH.
LOOKS LIKE YOU DID IT, BRANDON. LET'S JUST MAKE SURE NOTHING'S MISS--
THE RING! HE DOESN'T HAVE THE RING.
WHAT RING?
THIS RING.
THE ONE THE MODEL WAS WEARING.
SO, ROLAND, MY MAN, TURNS OUT YOUR BEST WAS GOOD ENOUGH. YOU FOUND EVERY PIECE OF THE COSTUME. VERY COOL.
AND THE FITTEST OF THE FIT IS JACKSON HILL HIGH!
WE DID IT!!
NEVER SAY NEVER!
ROLAND'S THE MAN.
SEE YOU NEXT TIME ON--
WJHC!

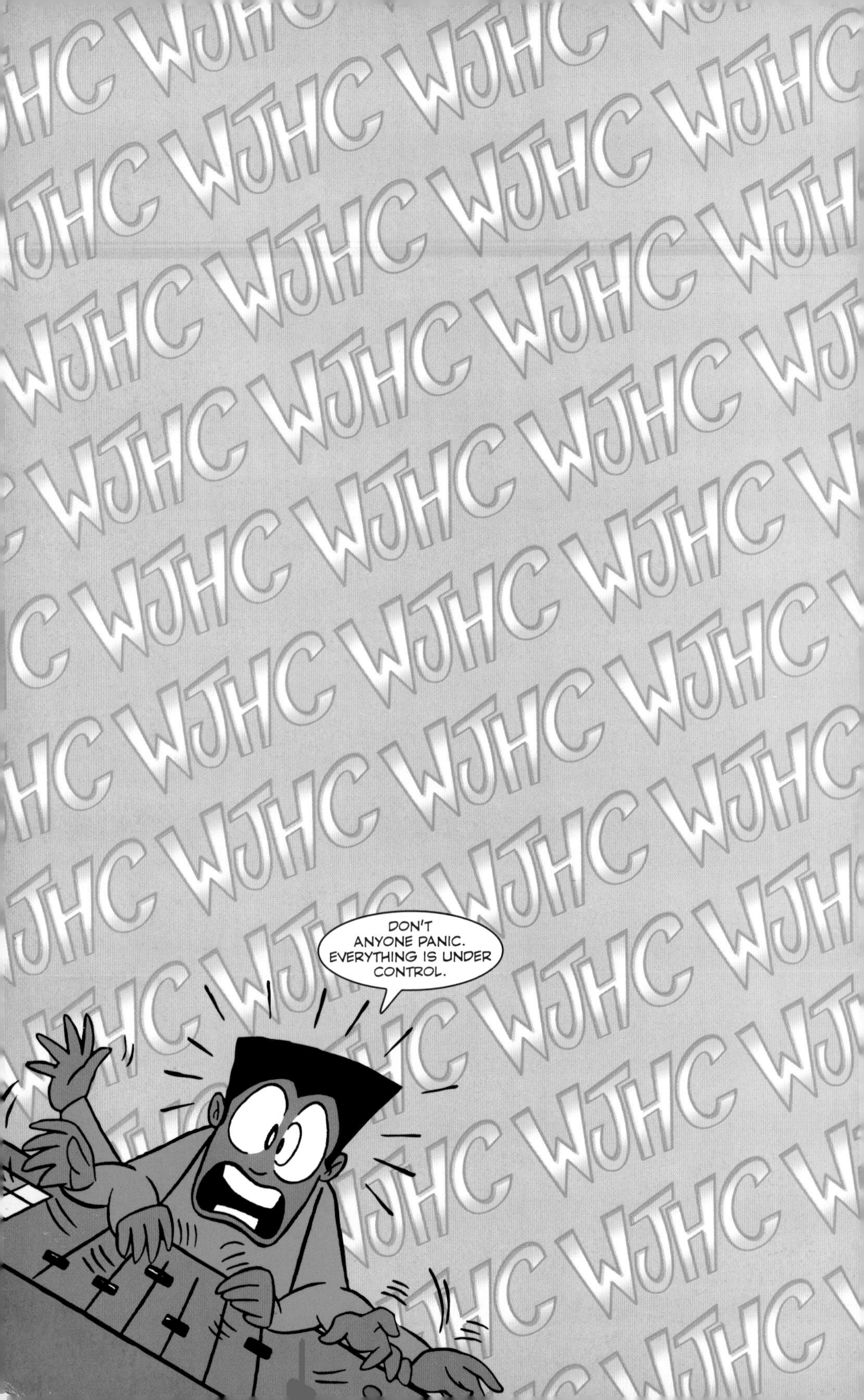
WJHC
DON'T ANYONE PANIC. EVERYTHING IS UNDER CONTROL.

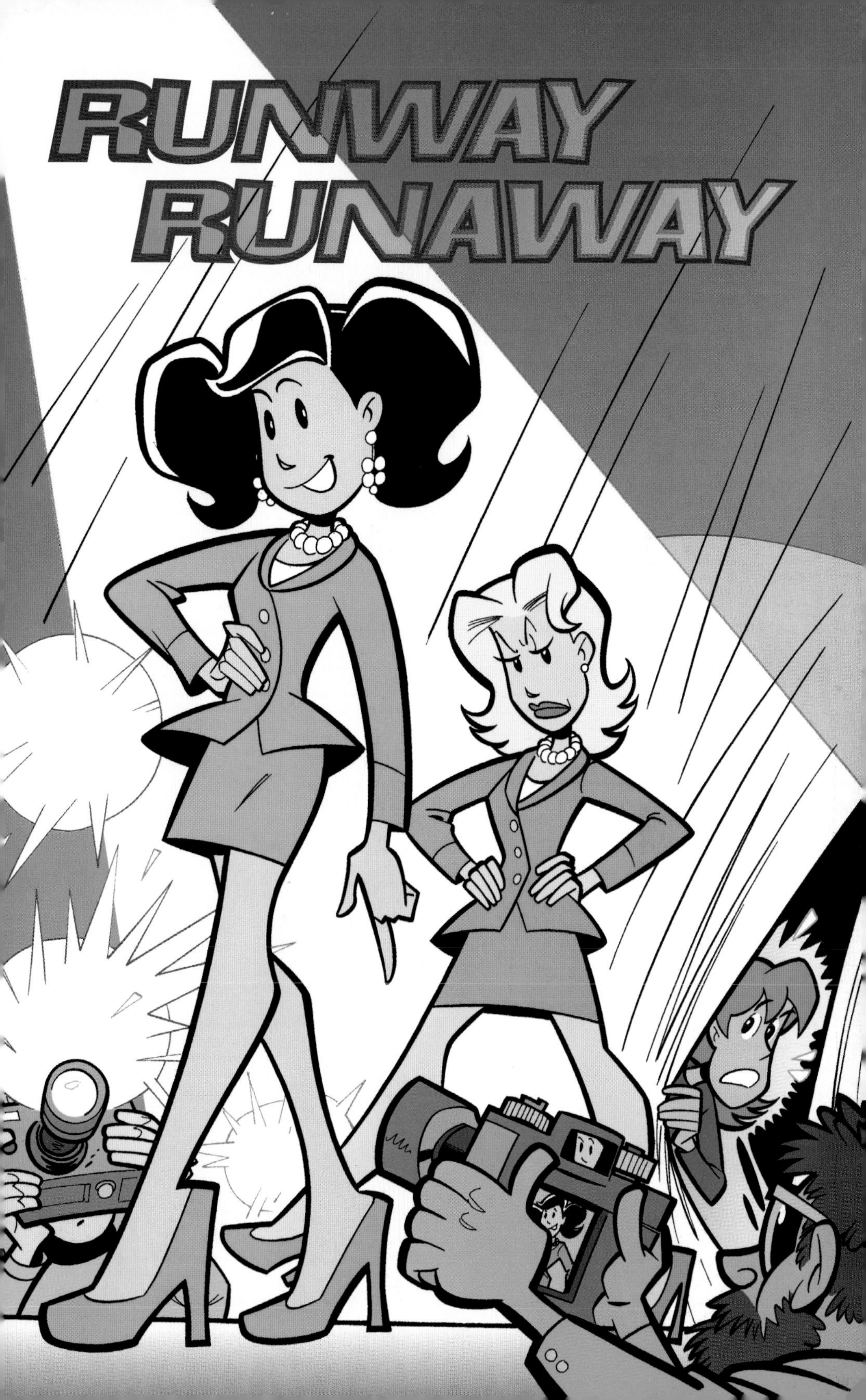
RUNWAY
RUNAWAY

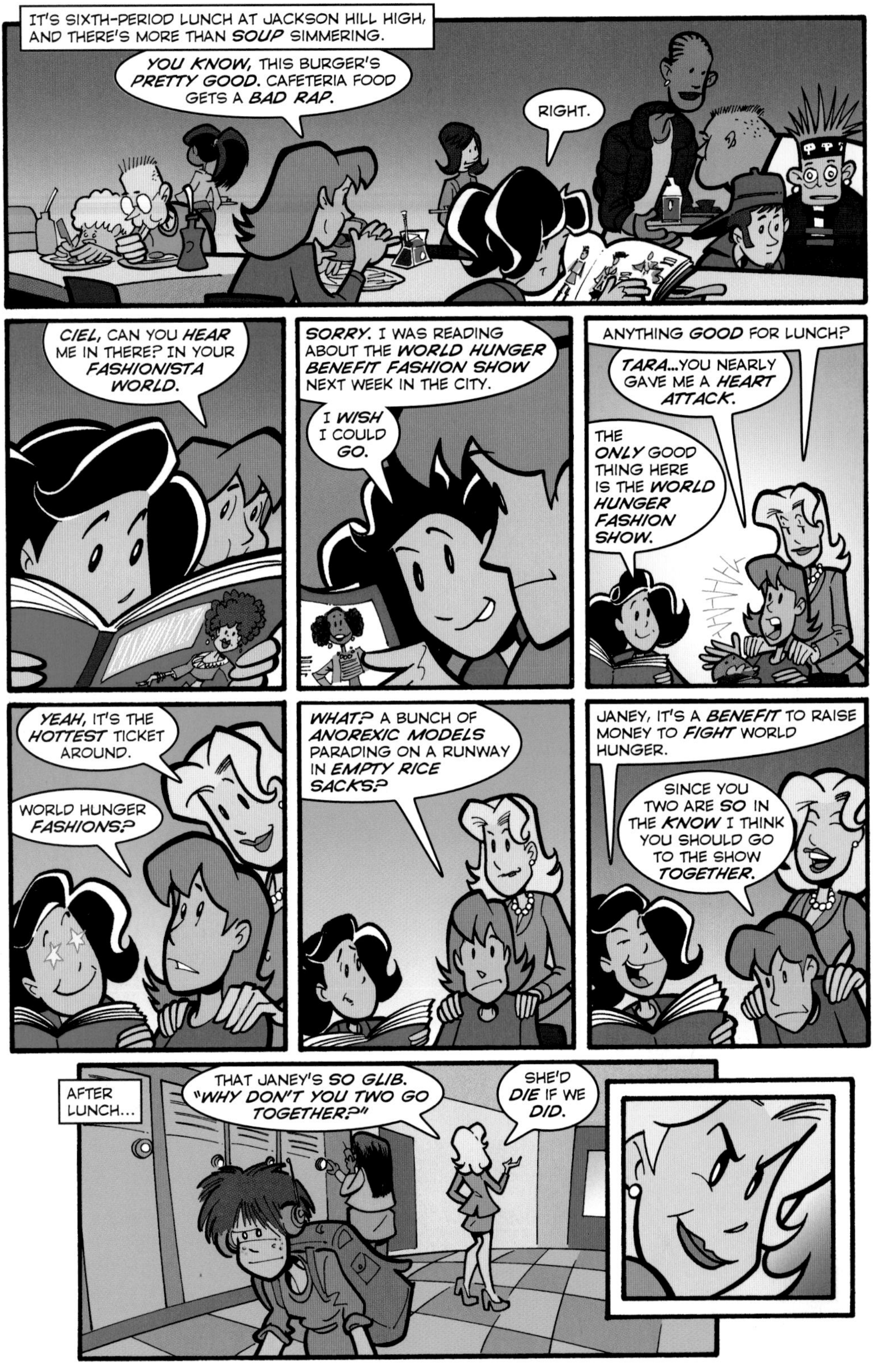
IT'S SIXTH-PERIOD LUNCH AT JACKSON HILL HIGH, AND THERE'S MORE THAN SOUP SIMMERING.
YOU KNOW, THIS BURGER'S PRETTY GOOD. CAFETERIA FOOD GETS A BAD RAP.
RIGHT.
CIEL, CAN YOU HEAR ME IN THERE? IN YOUR FASHIONISTA WORLD.
SORRY. I WAS READING ABOUT THE WORLD HUNGER BENEFIT FASHION SHOW NEXT WEEK IN THE CITY.
I WISH I COULD GO.
ANYTHING GOOD FOR LUNCH?
TARA...YOU NEARLY GAVE ME A HEART ATTACK.
THE ONLY GOOD THING HERE IS THE WORLD HUNGER FASHION SHOW.
YEAH, IT'S THE HOTTEST TICKET AROUND.
WORLD HUNGER FASHIONS?
WHAT? A BUNCH OF ANOREXIC MODELS PARADING ON A RUNWAY IN EMPTY RICE SACKS?
JANEY, IT'S A BENEFIT TO RAISE MONEY TO FIGHT WORLD HUNGER.
SINCE YOU TWO ARE SO IN THE KNOW I THINK YOU SHOULD GO TO THE SHOW TOGETHER.
AFTER LUNCH...
THAT JANEY'S SO GLIB. "WHY DON'T YOU TWO GO TOGETHER?"
SHE'D DIE IF WE DID.

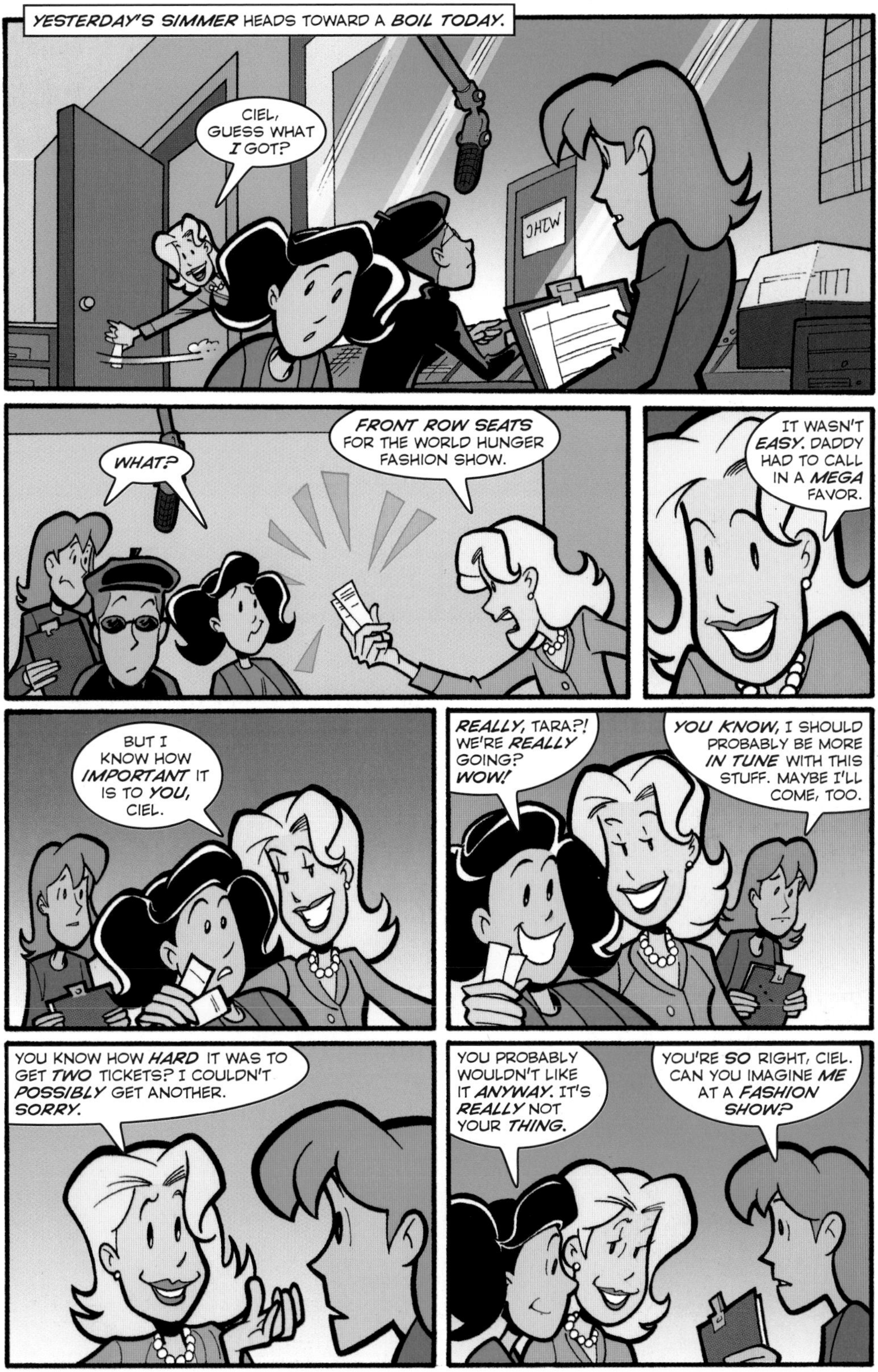
YESTERDAY'S SIMMER HEADS TOWARD A BOIL TODAY.
CIEL, GUESS WHAT I GOT?
WHAT?
FRONT ROW SEATS FOR THE WORLD HUNGER FASHION SHOW.
IT WASN'T EASY. DADDY HAD TO CALL IN A MEGA FAVOR.
BUT I KNOW HOW IMPORTANT IT IS TO YOU, CIEL.
REALLY, TARA?! WE'RE REALLY GOING? WOW!
YOU KNOW, I SHOULD PROBABLY BE MORE IN TUNE WITH THIS STUFF. MAYBE I'LL COME, TOO.
YOU KNOW HOW HARD IT WAS TO GET TWO TICKETS? I COULDN'T POSSIBLY GET ANOTHER. SORRY.
YOU PROBABLY WOULDN'T LIKE IT ANYWAY. IT'S REALLY NOT YOUR THING.
YOU'RE SO RIGHT, CIEL. CAN YOU IMAGINE ME AT A FASHION SHOW?

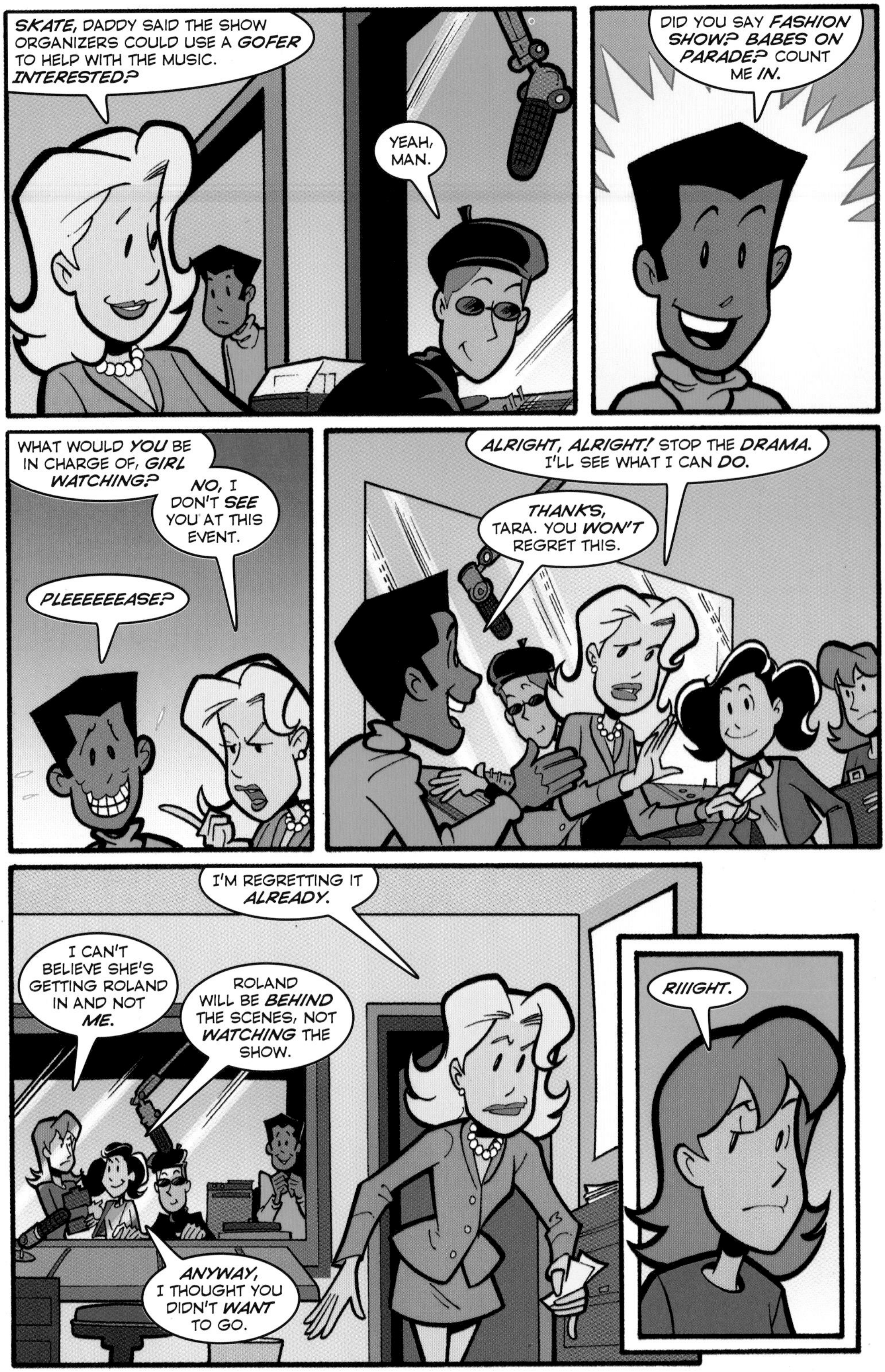
SKATE, DADDY SAID THE SHOW ORGANIZERS COULD USE A GOFER TO HELP WITH THE MUSIC. INTERESTED?
YEAH, MAN.
DID YOU SAY FASHION SHOW? BABES ON PARADE? COUNT ME IN.
WHAT WOULD YOU BE IN CHARGE OF, GIRL WATCHING?
NO, I DON'T SEE YOU AT THIS EVENT.
PLEEEEEEASE?
ALRIGHT, ALRIGHT! STOP THE DRAMA. I'LL SEE WHAT I CAN DO.
THANKS, TARA. YOU WON'T REGRET THIS.
I'M REGRETTING IT ALREADY.
I CAN'T BELIEVE SHE'S GETTING ROLAND IN AND NOT ME.
ROLAND WILL BE BEHIND THE SCENES, NOT WATCHING THE SHOW.
ANYWAY, I THOUGHT YOU DIDN'T WANT TO GO.
RIIIGHT.

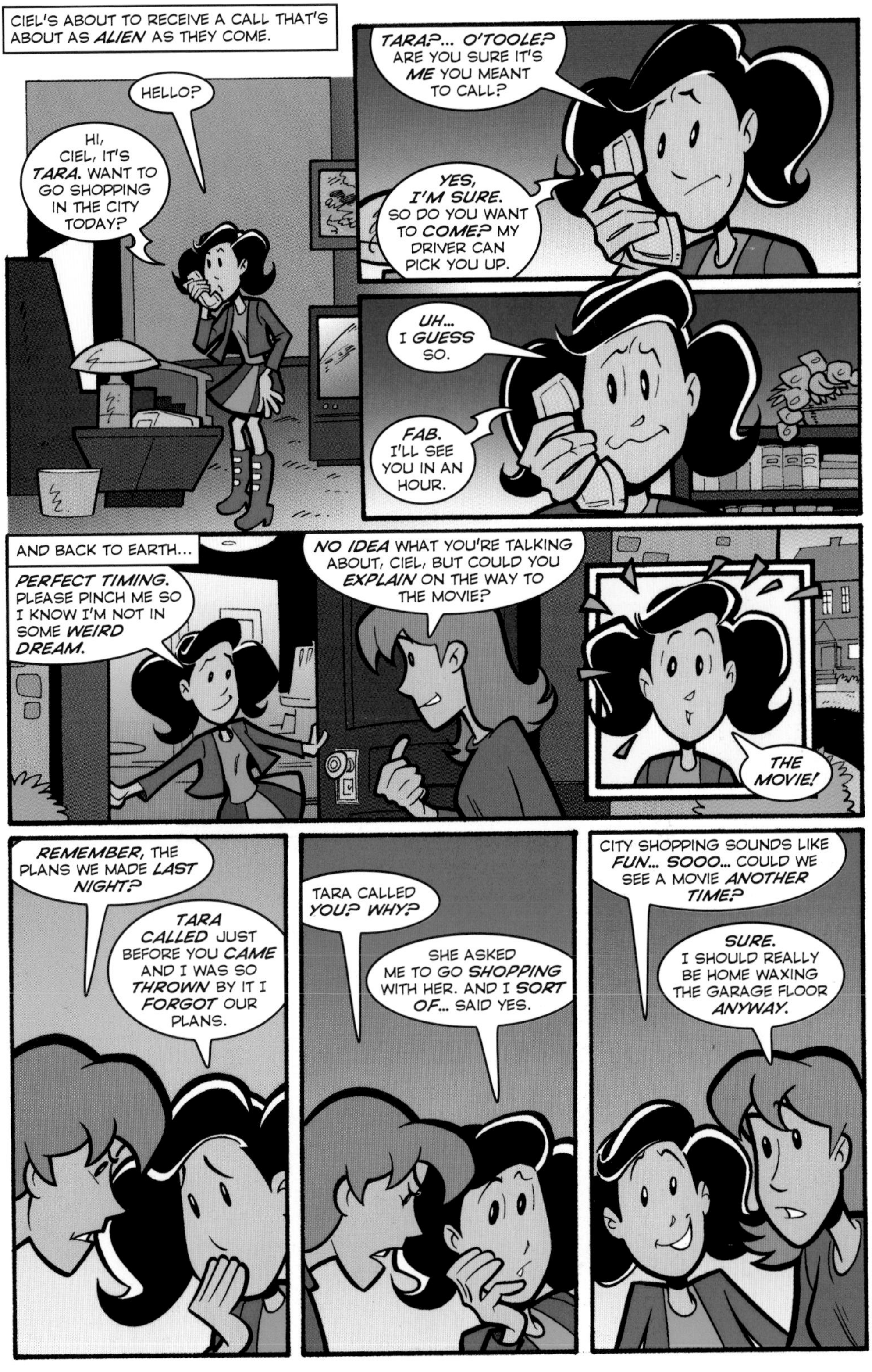
CIEL'S ABOUT TO RECEIVE A CALL THAT'S ABOUT AS ALIEN AS THEY COME.
HELLO?
HI, CIEL, IT'S TARA. WANT TO GO SHOPPING IN THE CITY TODAY?
TARA?... O'TOOLE? ARE YOU SURE IT'S ME YOU MEANT TO CALL?
YES, I'M SURE. SO DO YOU WANT TO COME? MY DRIVER CAN PICK YOU UP.
UH... I GUESS SO.
FAB. I'LL SEE YOU IN AN HOUR.
AND BACK TO EARTH...
PERFECT TIMING. PLEASE PINCH ME SO I KNOW I'M NOT IN SOME WEIRD DREAM.
NO IDEA WHAT YOU'RE TALKING ABOUT, CIEL, BUT COULD YOU EXPLAIN ON THE WAY TO THE MOVIE?
THE MOVIE!
REMEMBER, THE PLANS WE MADE LAST NIGHT?
TARA CALLED JUST BEFORE YOU CAME AND I WAS SO THROWN BY IT I FORGOT OUR PLANS.
TARA CALLED YOU? WHY?
SHE ASKED ME TO GO SHOPPING WITH HER. AND I SORT OF... SAID YES.
CITY SHOPPING SOUNDS LIKE FUN... SOOO... COULD WE SEE A MOVIE ANOTHER TIME?
SURE. I SHOULD REALLY BE HOME WAXING THE GARAGE FLOOR ANYWAY.

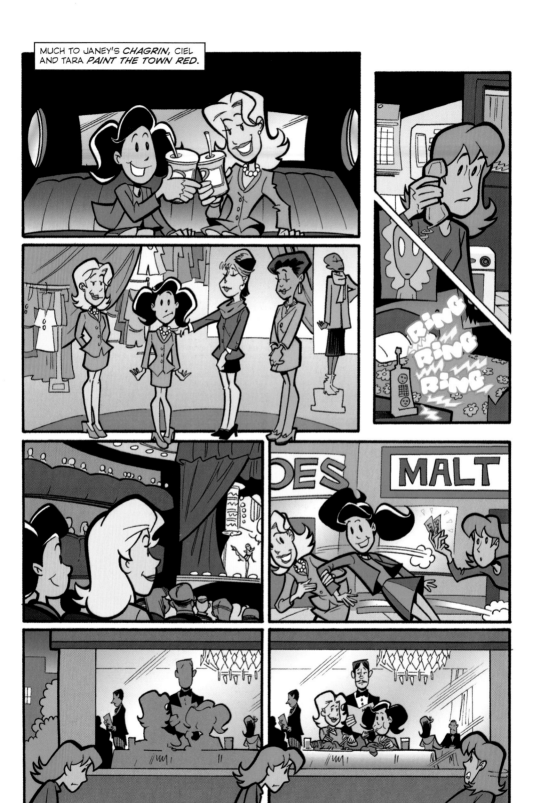

MUCH TO JANEY'S *CHAGRIN*, CIEL AND TARA *PAINT THE TOWN RED*.

RING RING RING

DES MALT

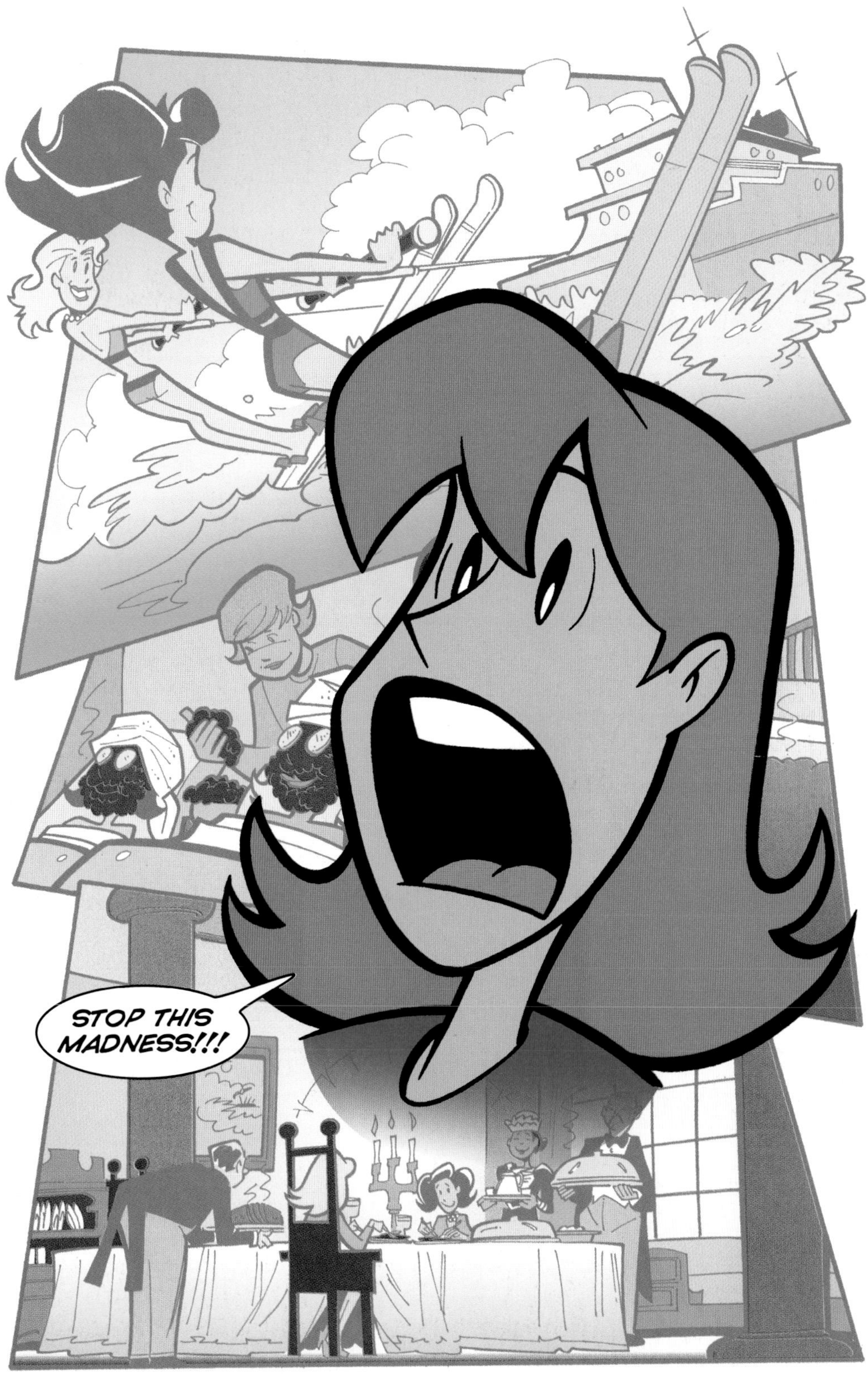
STOP THIS MADNESS!!!

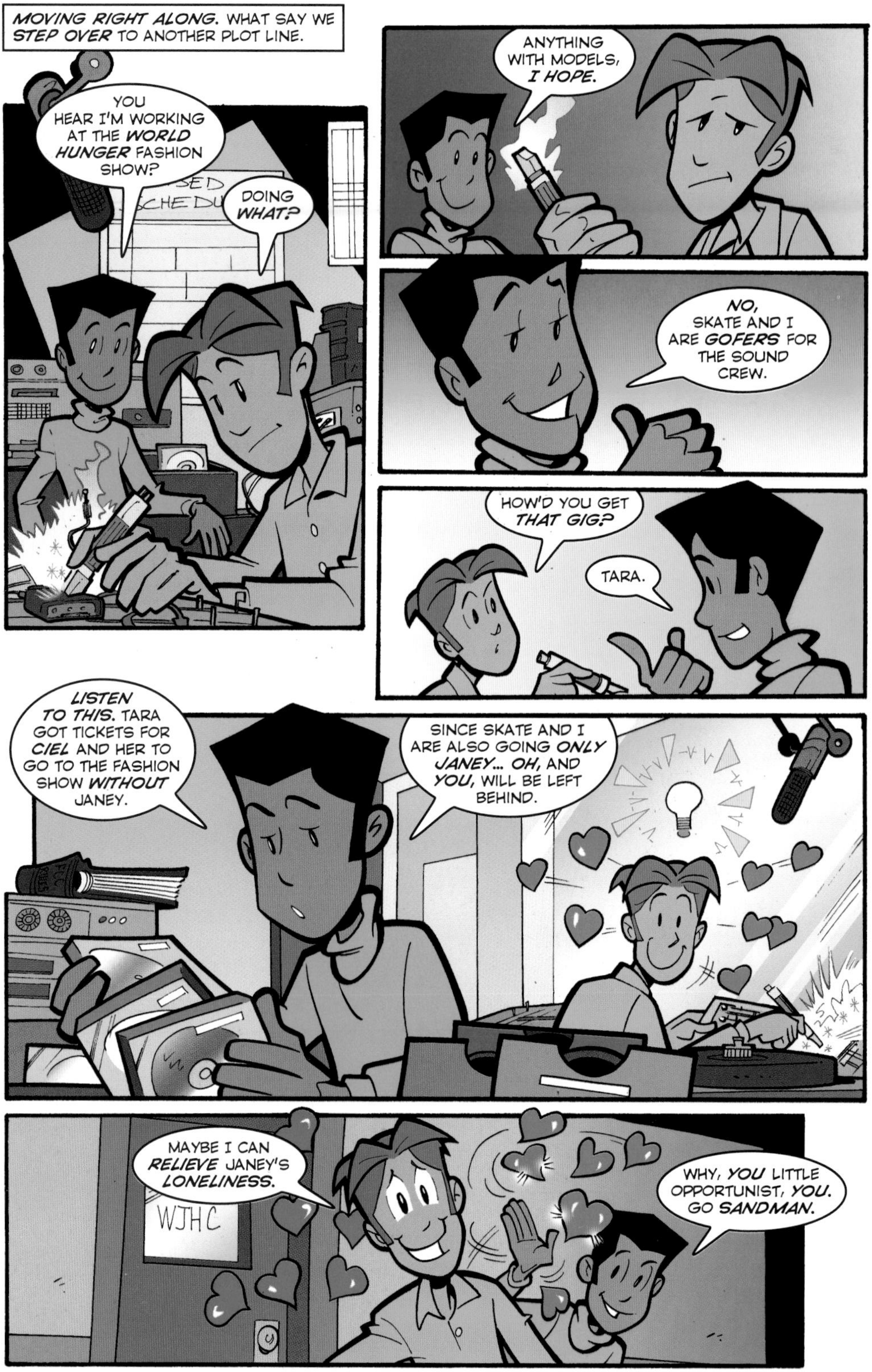
MOVING RIGHT ALONG. WHAT SAY WE STEP OVER TO ANOTHER PLOT LINE.
YOU HEAR I'M WORKING AT THE WORLD HUNGER FASHION SHOW?
DOING WHAT?
ANYTHING WITH MODELS, I HOPE.
NO, SKATE AND I ARE GOFERS FOR THE SOUND CREW.
HOW'D YOU GET THAT GIG?
TARA.
LISTEN TO THIS. TARA GOT TICKETS FOR CIEL AND HER TO GO TO THE FASHION SHOW WITHOUT JANEY.
SINCE SKATE AND I ARE ALSO GOING ONLY JANEY... OH, AND YOU, WILL BE LEFT BEHIND.
MAYBE I CAN RELIEVE JANEY'S LONELINESS.
WJHC
WHY, YOU LITTLE OPPORTUNIST, YOU. GO SANDMAN.

TODAY'S THE DAY. ROLAND AND SKATE GET BEHIND THE SCENES EARLY.

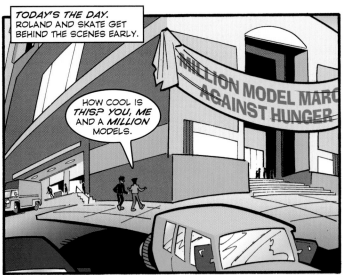

HOW COOL IS *THIS?* YOU, *ME* AND A *MILLION* MODELS.

MILLION MODEL MARCH AGAINST HUNGER

JOHN O'TOOLE SENT YOU TWO OVER HERE, *HUH?*

HANG *TIGHT* AND I'LL LET YOU KNOW WHAT I NEED. OH, *ONE RULE...*

...*DON'T* GO NEAR THE *MODELS.*

BACK AT SCHOOL...

SORRY I HAVEN'T BEEN *AROUND* MUCH. TARA'S BEEN *WHIPPING* ME AROUND TOWN.

MAYBE WE HAD HER *WRONG.* SHE'S BEEN *PRETTY* COOL.

AND NOW THIS *FASHION SHOW.* I *STILL* CAN'T BELIEVE I'M GOING.

ME *EITHER.*

I HAVE TO MEET TARA.

LIGHTEN UP, JANEY. I'M JUST FRIENDS WITH YOU *AND* TARA NOW.

SURE, CIEL.

57

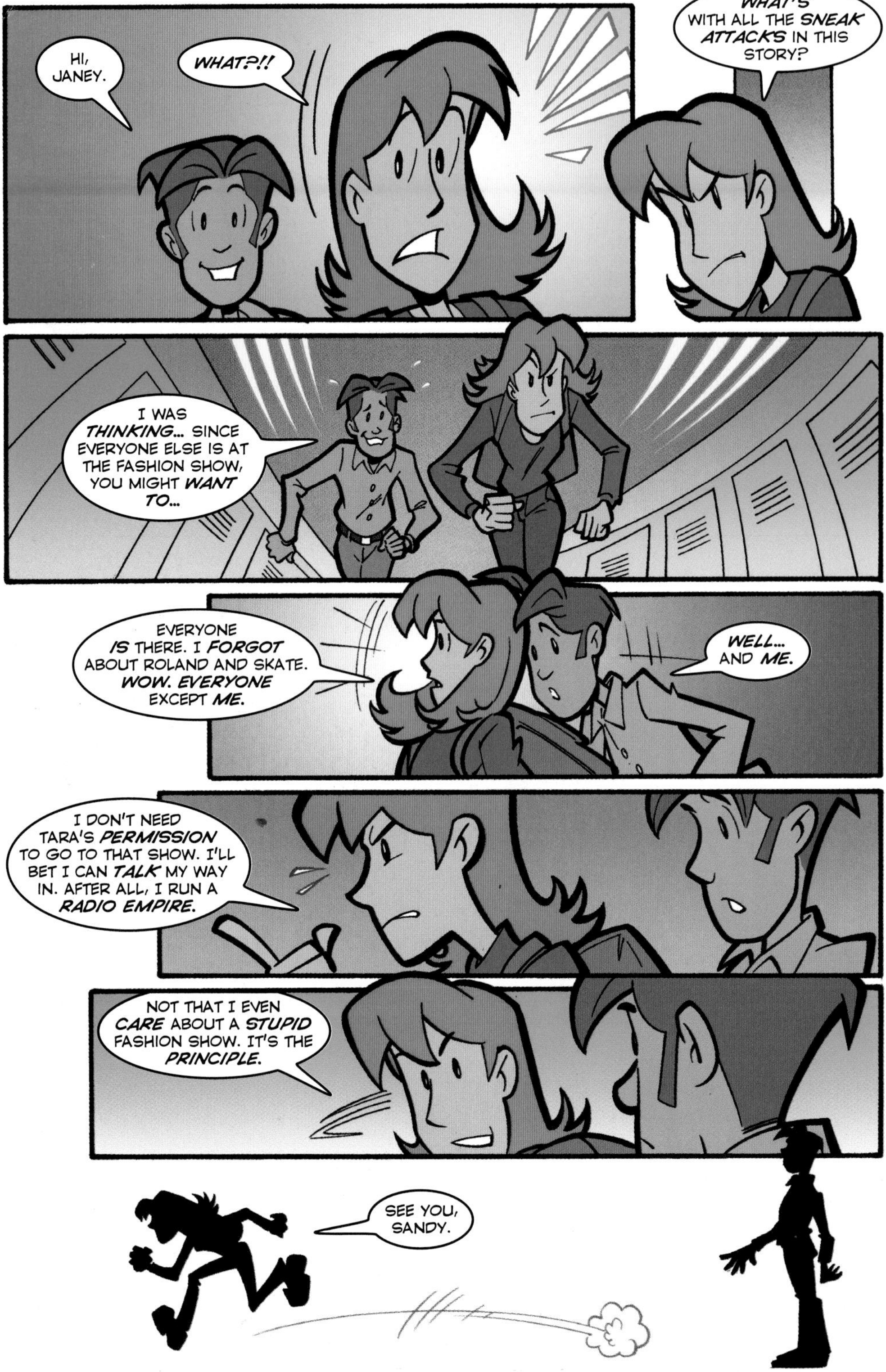
HI, JANEY.
WHAT?!!
WHAT'S WITH ALL THE SNEAK ATTACKS IN THIS STORY?
I WAS THINKING... SINCE EVERYONE ELSE IS AT THE FASHION SHOW, YOU MIGHT WANT TO...
EVERYONE IS THERE. I FORGOT ABOUT ROLAND AND SKATE. WOW. EVERYONE EXCEPT ME.
WELL... AND ME.
I DON'T NEED TARA'S PERMISSION TO GO TO THAT SHOW. I'LL BET I CAN TALK MY WAY IN. AFTER ALL, I RUN A RADIO EMPIRE.
NOT THAT I EVEN CARE ABOUT A STUPID FASHION SHOW. IT'S THE PRINCIPLE.
SEE YOU, SANDY.

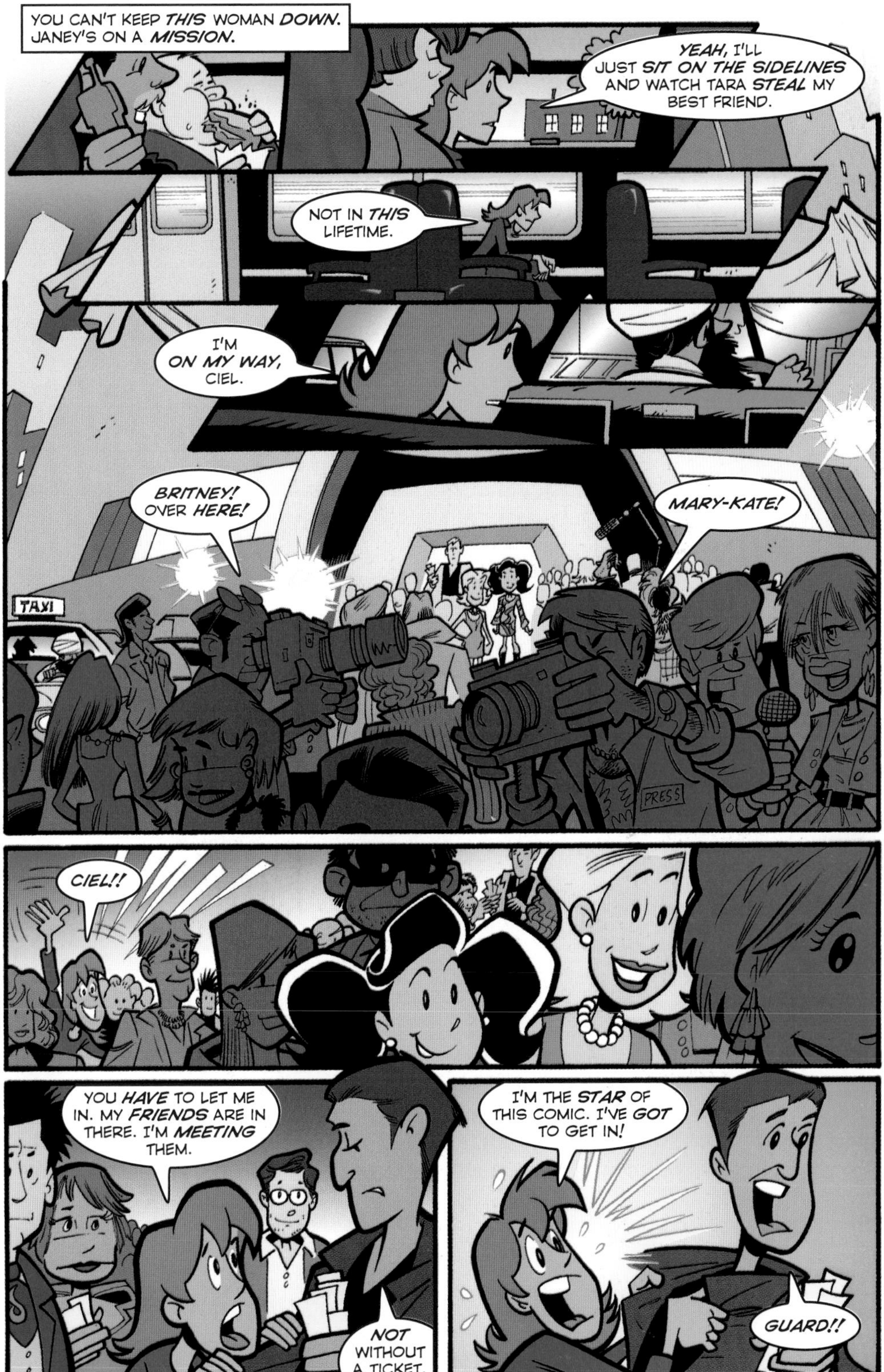
YOU CAN'T KEEP THIS WOMAN DOWN. JANEY'S ON A MISSION.
YEAH, I'LL JUST SIT ON THE SIDELINES AND WATCH TARA STEAL MY BEST FRIEND.
NOT IN THIS LIFETIME.
I'M ON MY WAY, CIEL.
BRITNEY! OVER HERE!
MARY-KATE!
TAXI
PRESS
CIEL!!
YOU HAVE TO LET ME IN. MY FRIENDS ARE IN THERE. I'M MEETING THEM.
NOT WITHOUT A TICKET.
I'M THE STAR OF THIS COMIC. I'VE GOT TO GET IN!
GUARD!!

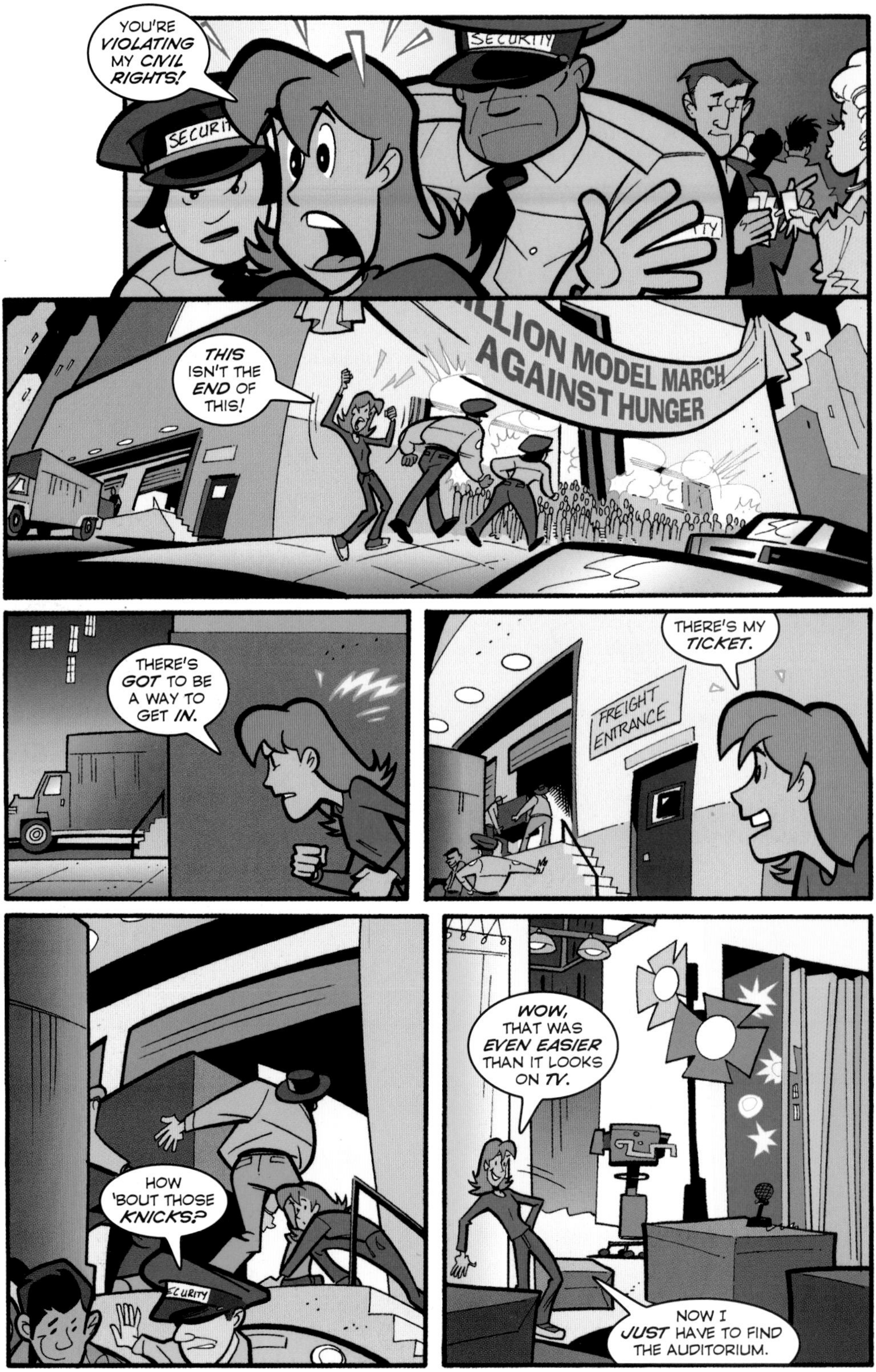
YOU'RE VIOLATING MY CIVIL RIGHTS!
SECURITY
SECURITY
LLION MODEL MARCH AGAINST HUNGER
THIS ISN'T THE END OF THIS!
THERE'S GOT TO BE A WAY TO GET IN.
THERE'S MY TICKET.
FREIGHT ENTRANCE
HOW 'BOUT THOSE KNICKS?
SECURITY
WOW, THAT WAS EVEN EASIER THAN IT LOOKS ON TV.
NOW I JUST HAVE TO FIND THE AUDITORIUM.

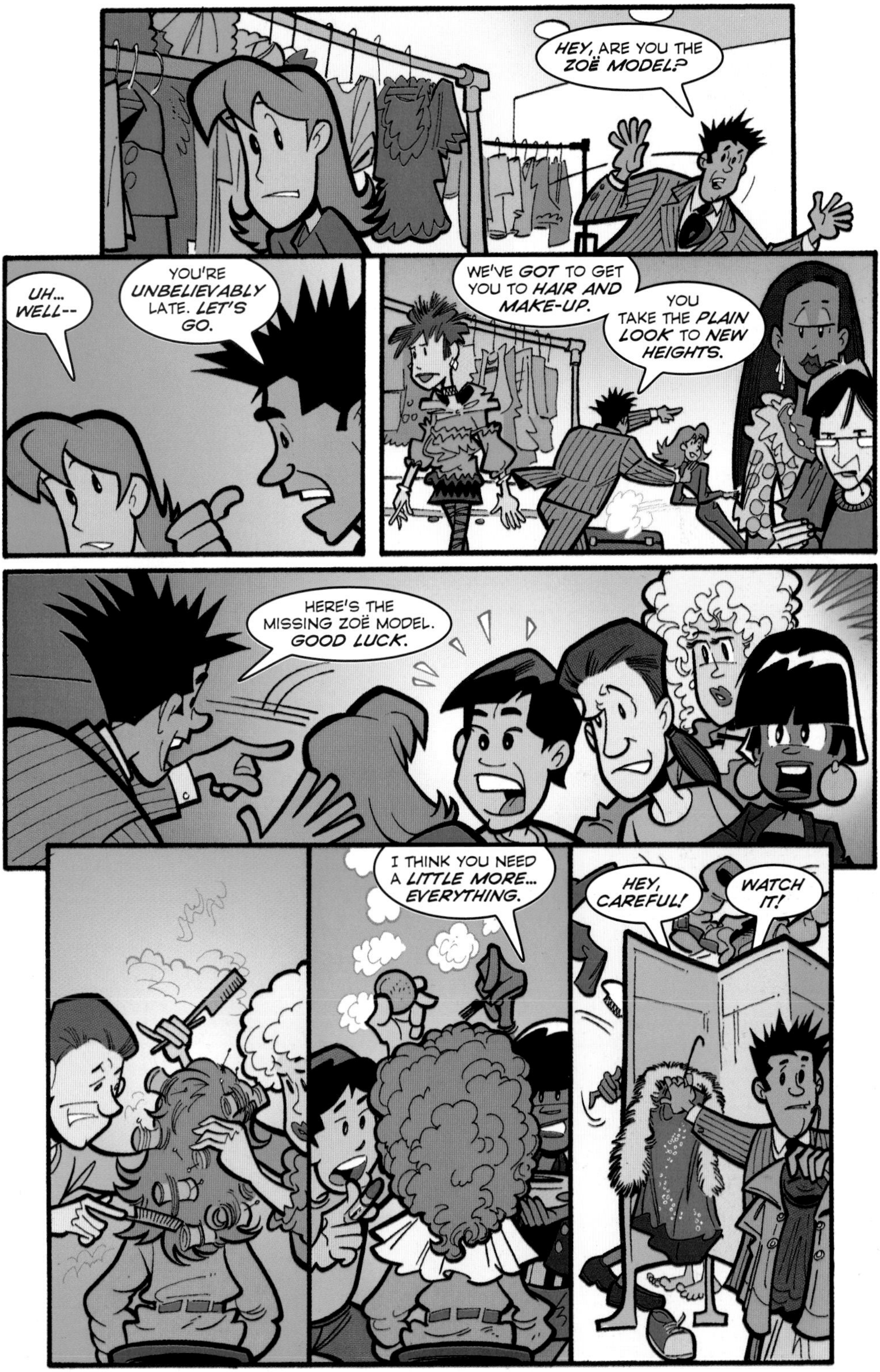
HEY, ARE YOU THE ZOË MODEL?
UH... WELL--
YOU'RE UNBELIEVABLY LATE. LET'S GO.
WE'VE GOT TO GET YOU TO HAIR AND MAKE-UP.
YOU TAKE THE PLAIN LOOK TO NEW HEIGHTS.
HERE'S THE MISSING ZOË MODEL. GOOD LUCK.
I THINK YOU NEED A LITTLE MORE... EVERYTHING.
HEY, CAREFUL!
WATCH IT!

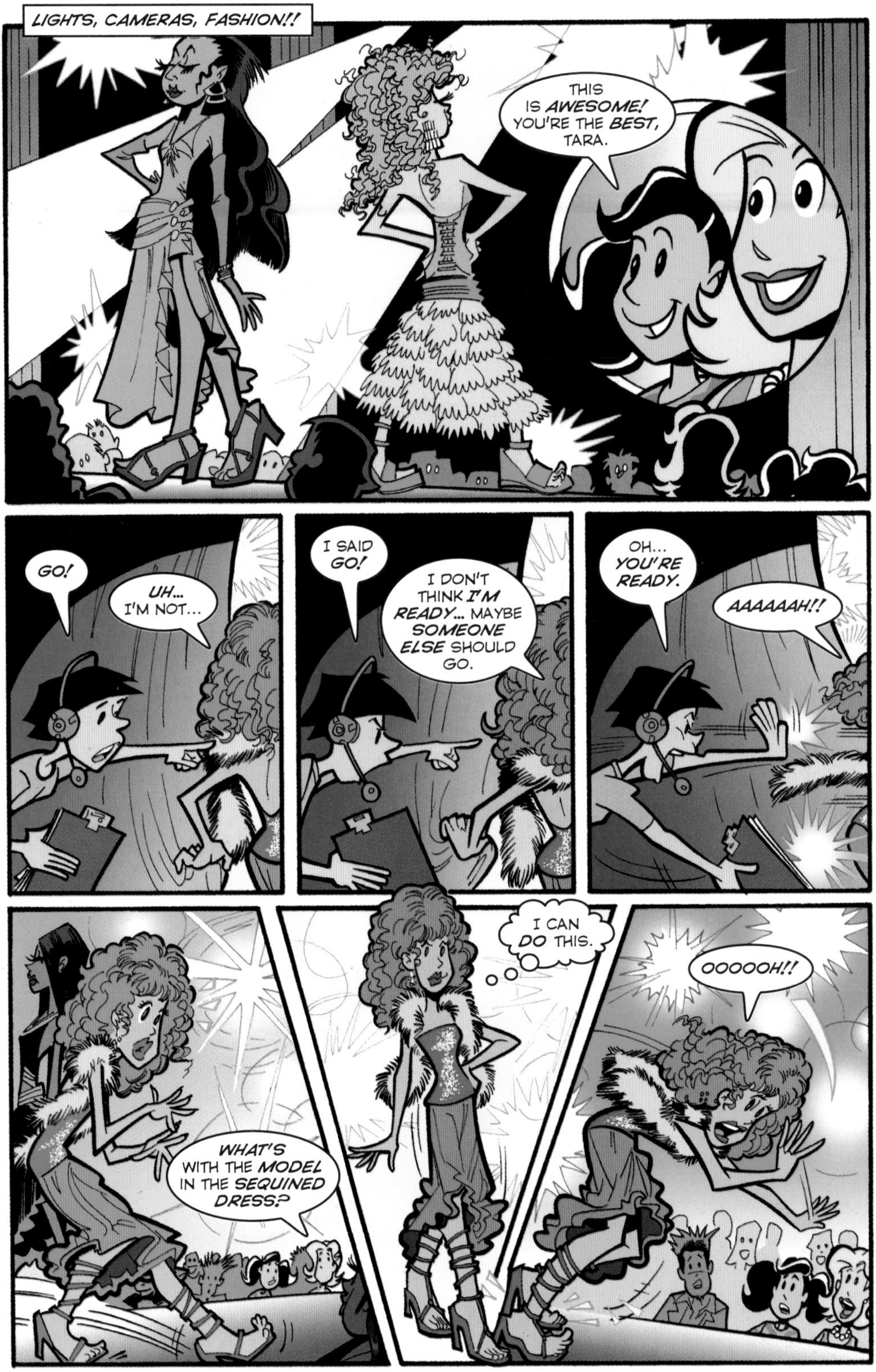
LIGHTS, CAMERAS, FASHION!!
THIS IS AWESOME! YOU'RE THE BEST, TARA.
GO!
UH... I'M NOT...
I SAID GO!
I DON'T THINK I'M READY... MAYBE SOMEONE ELSE SHOULD GO.
OH... YOU'RE READY.
AAAAAAH!!
WHAT'S WITH THE MODEL IN THE SEQUINED DRESS?
I CAN DO THIS.
OOOOOH!!

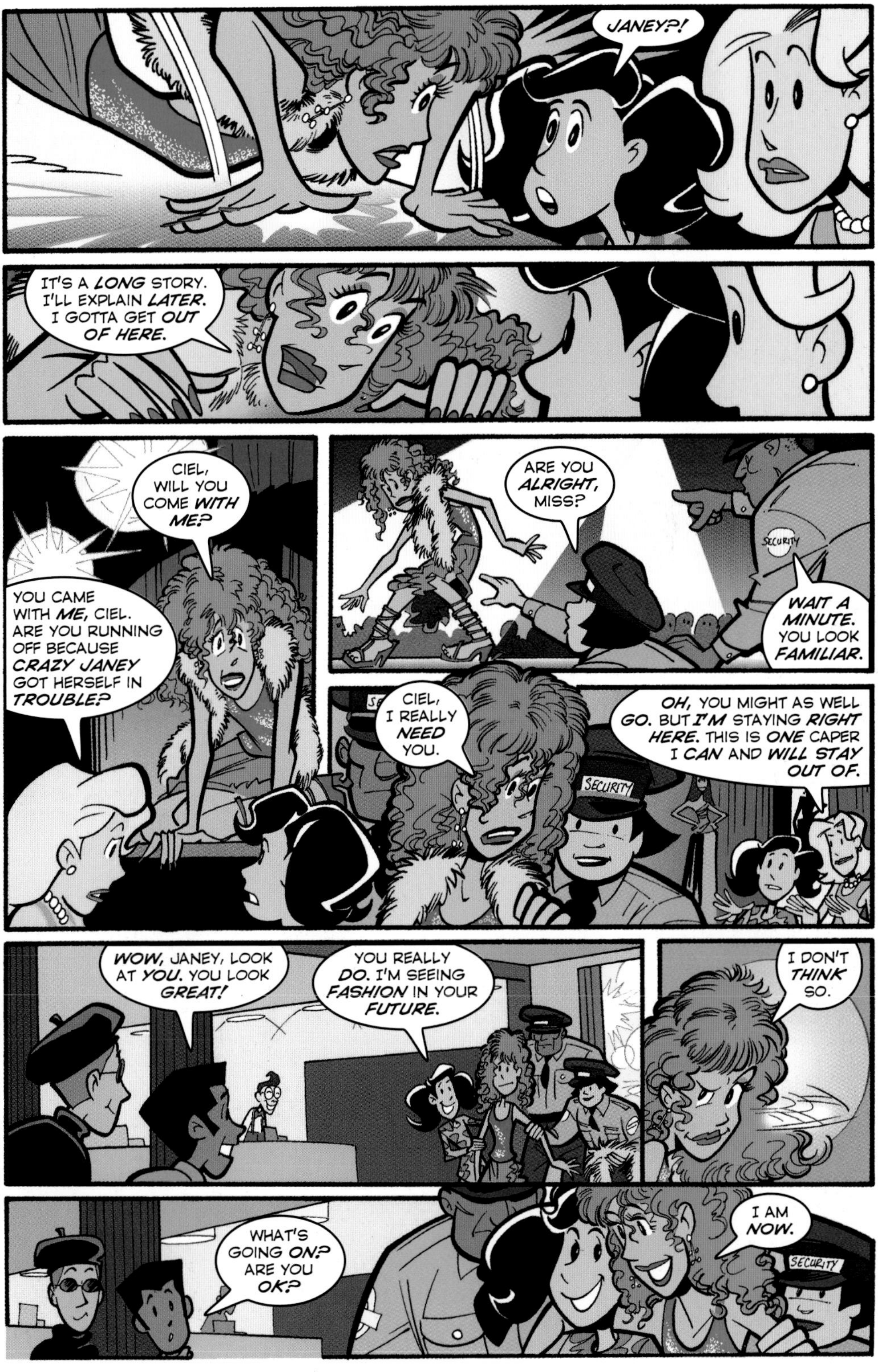
JANEY?!
IT'S A LONG STORY. I'LL EXPLAIN LATER. I GOTTA GET OUT OF HERE.
CIEL, WILL YOU COME WITH ME?
YOU CAME WITH ME, CIEL. ARE YOU RUNNING OFF BECAUSE CRAZY JANEY GOT HERSELF IN TROUBLE?
ARE YOU ALRIGHT, MISS?
SECURITY
WAIT A MINUTE. YOU LOOK FAMILIAR.
CIEL, I REALLY NEED YOU.
OH, YOU MIGHT AS WELL GO. BUT I'M STAYING RIGHT HERE. THIS IS ONE CAPER I CAN AND WILL STAY OUT OF.
SECURITY
WOW, JANEY, LOOK AT YOU. YOU LOOK GREAT!
YOU REALLY DO. I'M SEEING FASHION IN YOUR FUTURE.
I DON'T THINK SO.
WHAT'S GOING ON? ARE YOU OK?
I AM NOW.
SECURITY

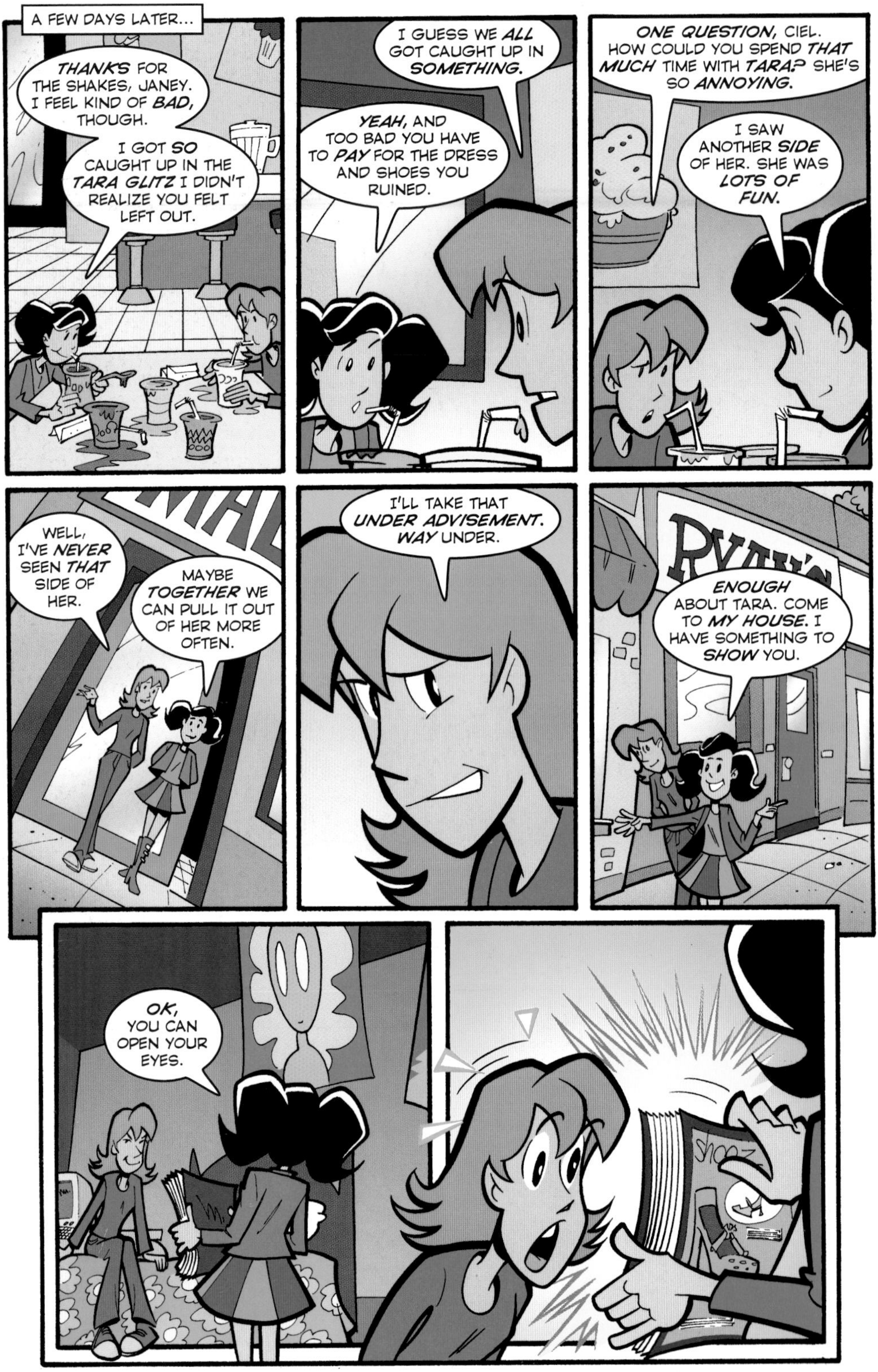
A FEW DAYS LATER...
THANKS FOR THE SHAKES, JANEY. I FEEL KIND OF BAD, THOUGH.
I GOT SO CAUGHT UP IN THE TARA GLITZ I DIDN'T REALIZE YOU FELT LEFT OUT.
I GUESS WE ALL GOT CAUGHT UP IN SOMETHING.
YEAH, AND TOO BAD YOU HAVE TO PAY FOR THE DRESS AND SHOES YOU RUINED.
ONE QUESTION, CIEL. HOW COULD YOU SPEND THAT MUCH TIME WITH TARA? SHE'S SO ANNOYING.
I SAW ANOTHER SIDE OF HER. SHE WAS LOTS OF FUN.
WELL, I'VE NEVER SEEN THAT SIDE OF HER.
MAYBE TOGETHER WE CAN PULL IT OUT OF HER MORE OFTEN.
I'LL TAKE THAT UNDER ADVISEMENT. WAY UNDER.
ENOUGH ABOUT TARA. COME TO MY HOUSE. I HAVE SOMETHING TO SHOW YOU.
OK, YOU CAN OPEN YOUR EYES.

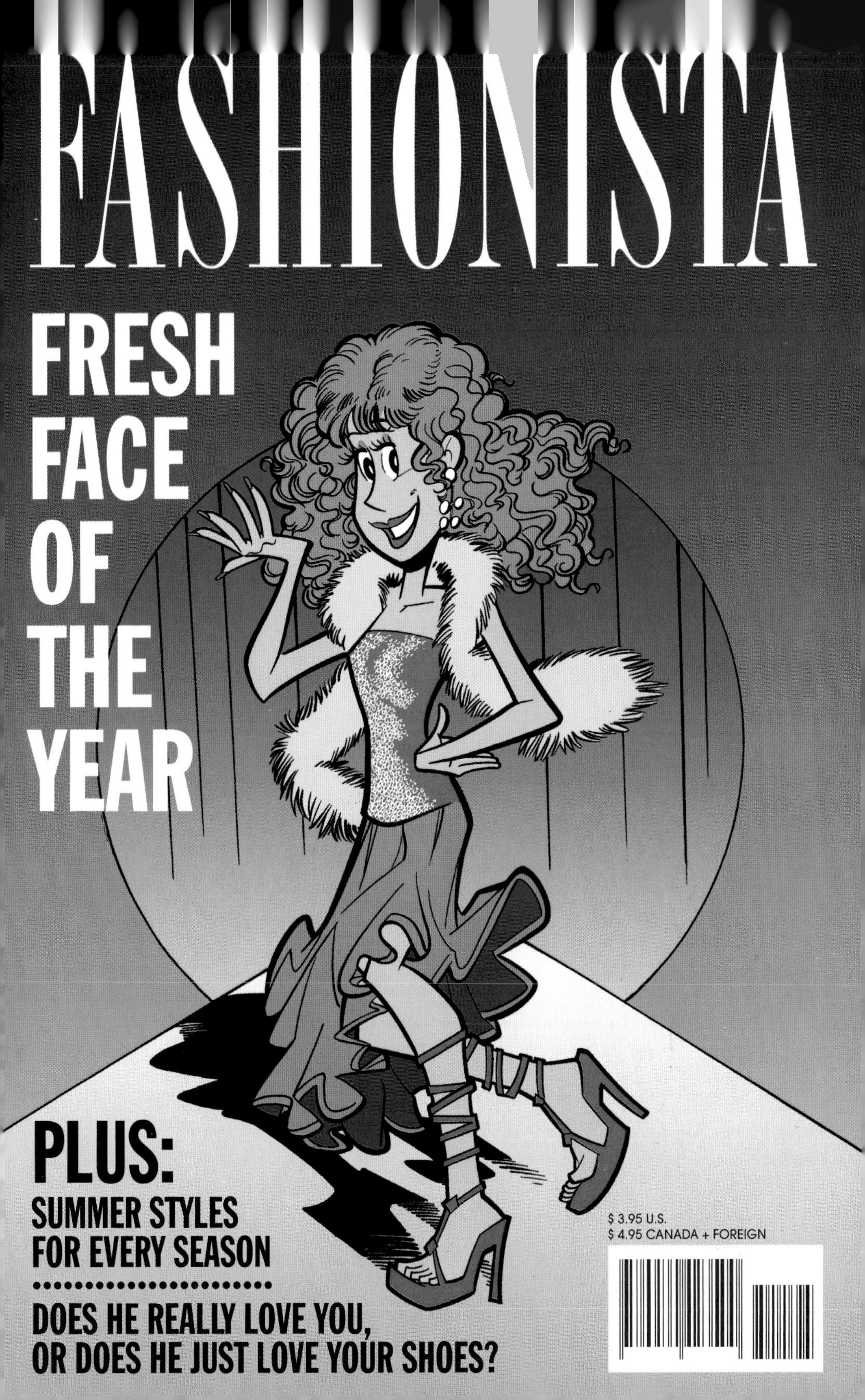
FASHIONISTA
FRESH FACE OF THE YEAR
PLUS:
SUMMER STYLES FOR EVERY SEASON
DOES HE REALLY LOVE YOU, OR DOES HE JUST LOVE YOUR SHOES?
$ 3.95 U.S.
$ 4.95 CANADA + FOREIGN

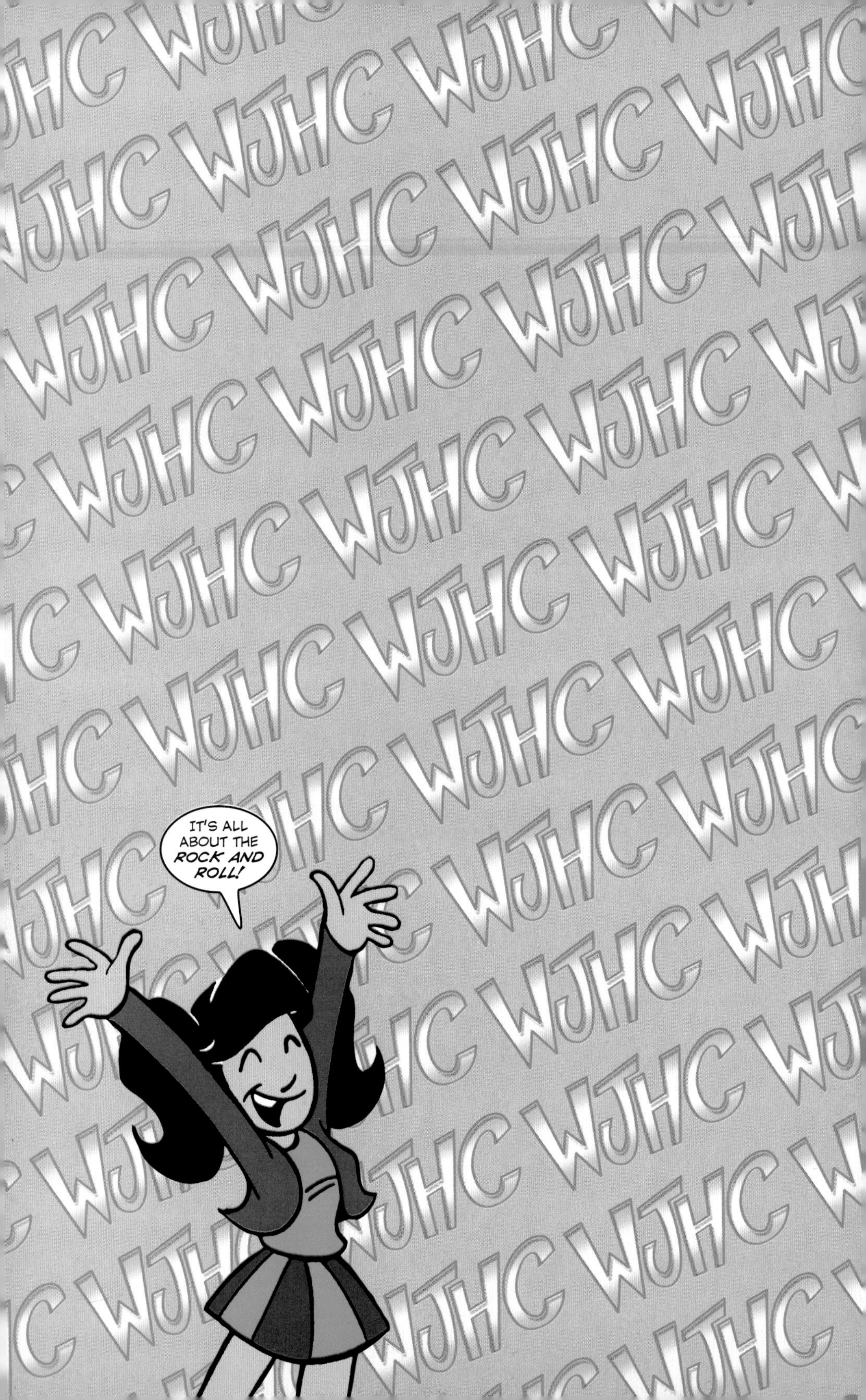
IT'S ALL ABOUT THE *ROCK AND ROLL!*

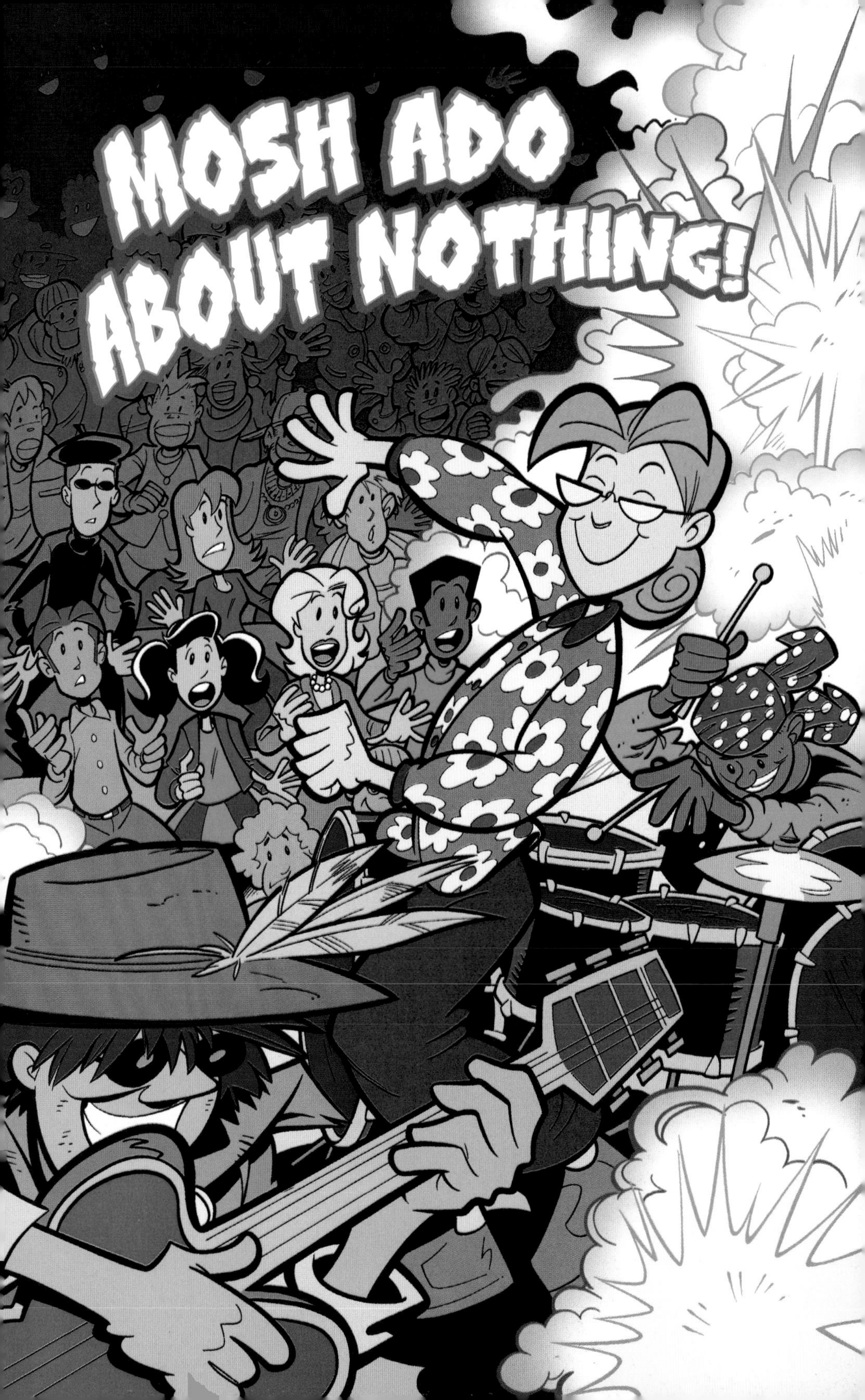
MOSH ADO ABOUT NOTHING!

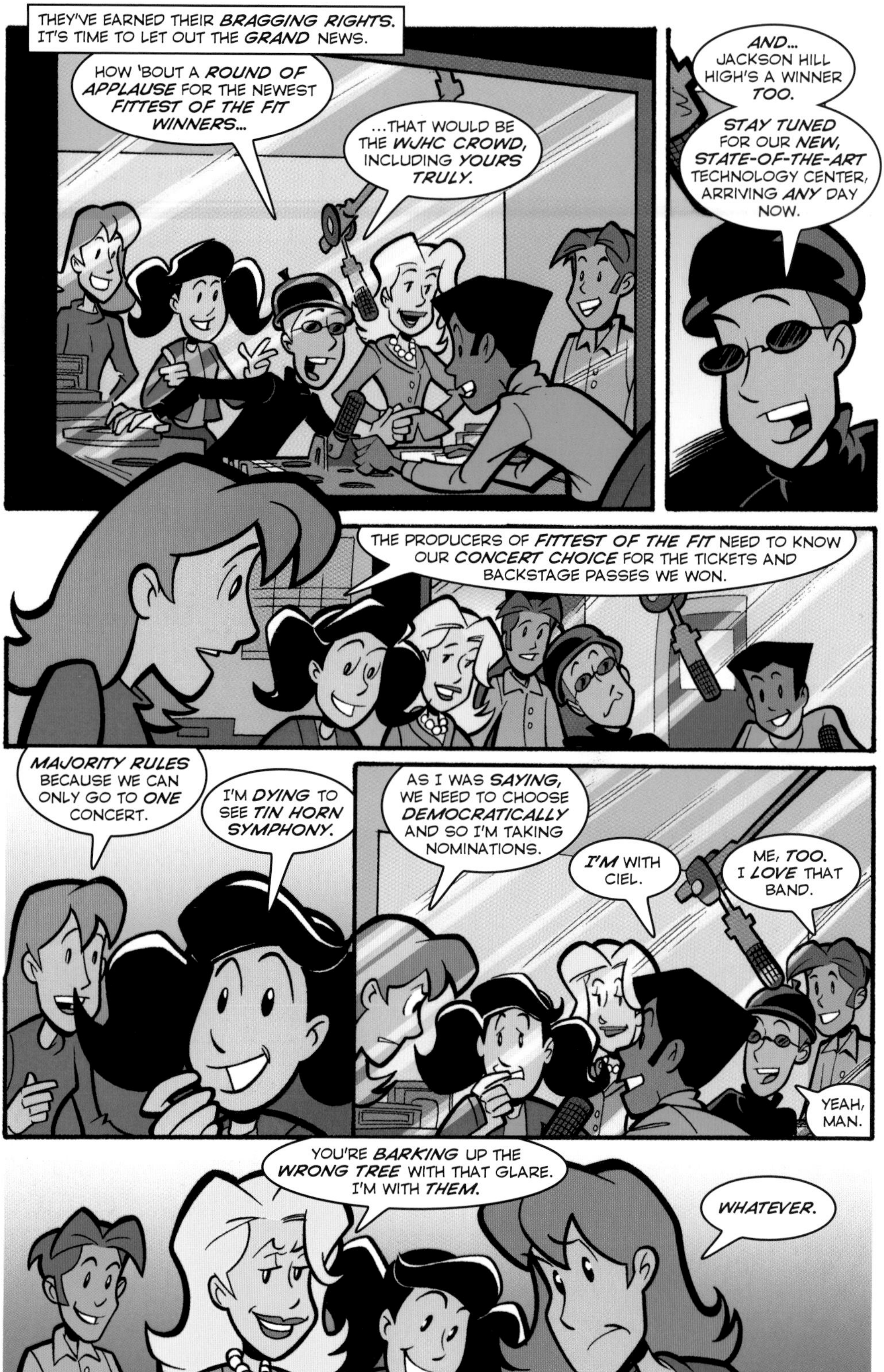
THEY'VE EARNED THEIR BRAGGING RIGHTS. IT'S TIME TO LET OUT THE GRAND NEWS.
HOW 'BOUT A ROUND OF APPLAUSE FOR THE NEWEST FITTEST OF THE FIT WINNERS...
...THAT WOULD BE THE WJHC CROWD, INCLUDING YOURS TRULY.
AND... JACKSON HILL HIGH'S A WINNER TOO.
STAY TUNED FOR OUR NEW, STATE-OF-THE-ART TECHNOLOGY CENTER, ARRIVING ANY DAY NOW.
THE PRODUCERS OF FITTEST OF THE FIT NEED TO KNOW OUR CONCERT CHOICE FOR THE TICKETS AND BACKSTAGE PASSES WE WON.
MAJORITY RULES BECAUSE WE CAN ONLY GO TO ONE CONCERT.
I'M DYING TO SEE TIN HORN SYMPHONY.
AS I WAS SAYING, WE NEED TO CHOOSE DEMOCRATICALLY AND SO I'M TAKING NOMINATIONS.
I'M WITH CIEL.
ME, TOO. I LOVE THAT BAND.
YEAH, MAN.
YOU'RE BARKING UP THE WRONG TREE WITH THAT GLARE. I'M WITH THEM.
WHATEVER.

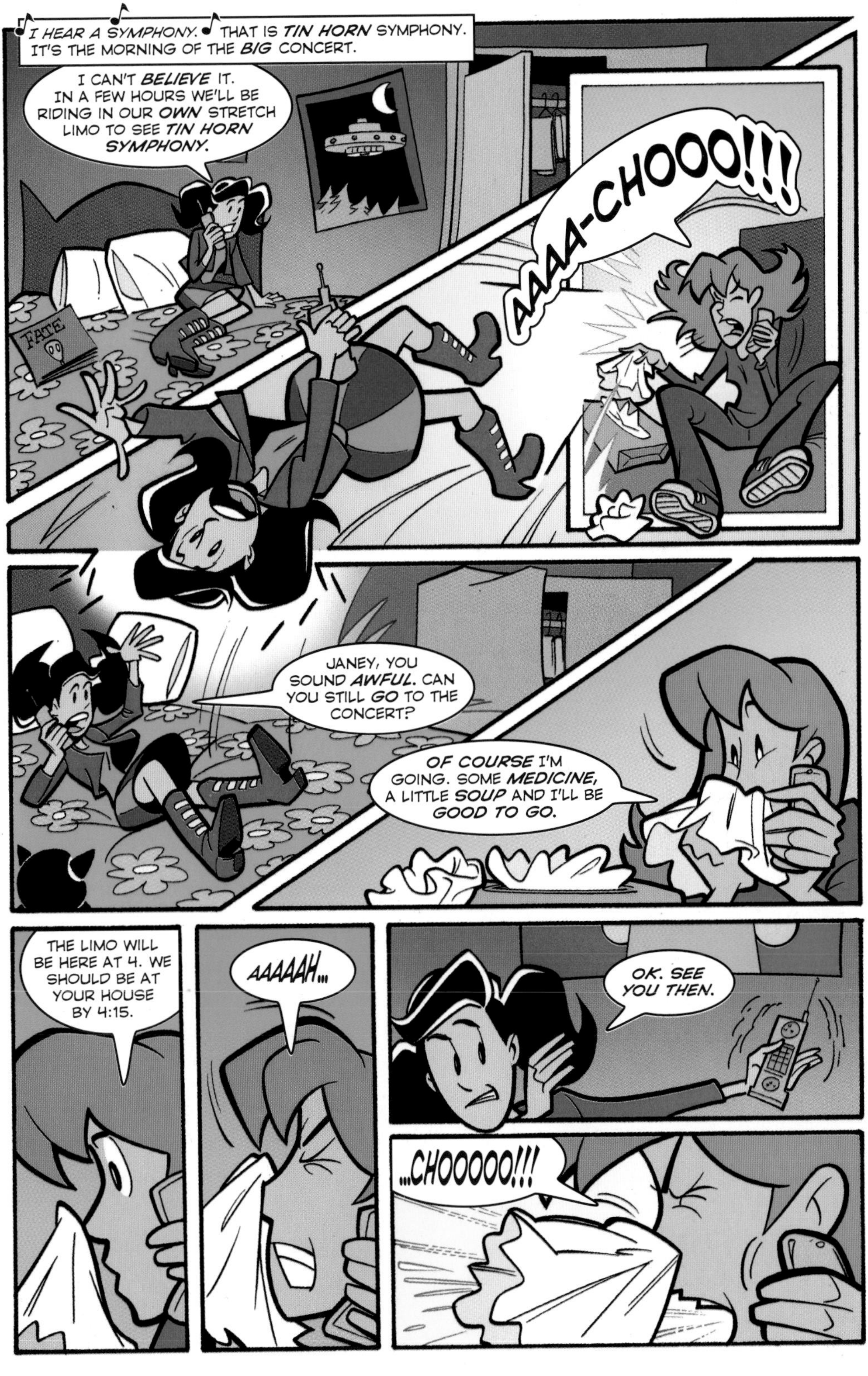
I HEAR A SYMPHONY. THAT IS TIN HORN SYMPHONY. IT'S THE MORNING OF THE BIG CONCERT.
I CAN'T BELIEVE IT. IN A FEW HOURS WE'LL BE RIDING IN OUR OWN STRETCH LIMO TO SEE TIN HORN SYMPHONY.
FATE
AAAA-CHOOO!!!
JANEY, YOU SOUND AWFUL. CAN YOU STILL GO TO THE CONCERT?
OF COURSE I'M GOING. SOME MEDICINE, A LITTLE SOUP AND I'LL BE GOOD TO GO.
THE LIMO WILL BE HERE AT 4. WE SHOULD BE AT YOUR HOUSE BY 4:15.
AAAAAH...
OK. SEE YOU THEN.
...CHOOOOO!!!

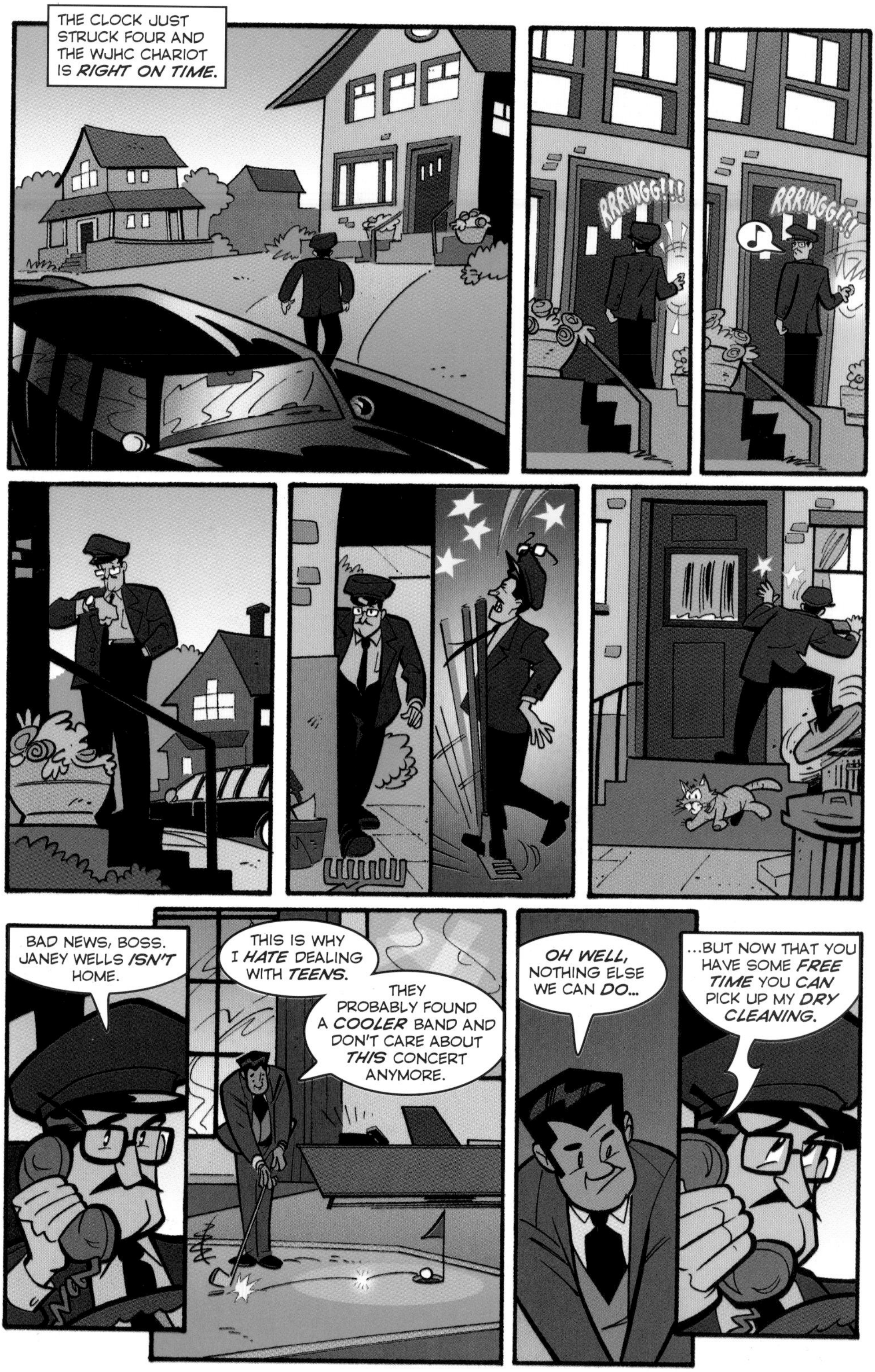
THE CLOCK JUST STRUCK FOUR AND THE WJHC CHARIOT IS RIGHT ON TIME.
RRRINGG!!!
RRRINGG!!!
BAD NEWS, BOSS. JANEY WELLS ISN'T HOME.
THIS IS WHY I HATE DEALING WITH TEENS.
THEY PROBABLY FOUND A COOLER BAND AND DON'T CARE ABOUT THIS CONCERT ANYMORE.
OH WELL, NOTHING ELSE WE CAN DO...
...BUT NOW THAT YOU HAVE SOME FREE TIME YOU CAN PICK UP MY DRY CLEANING.

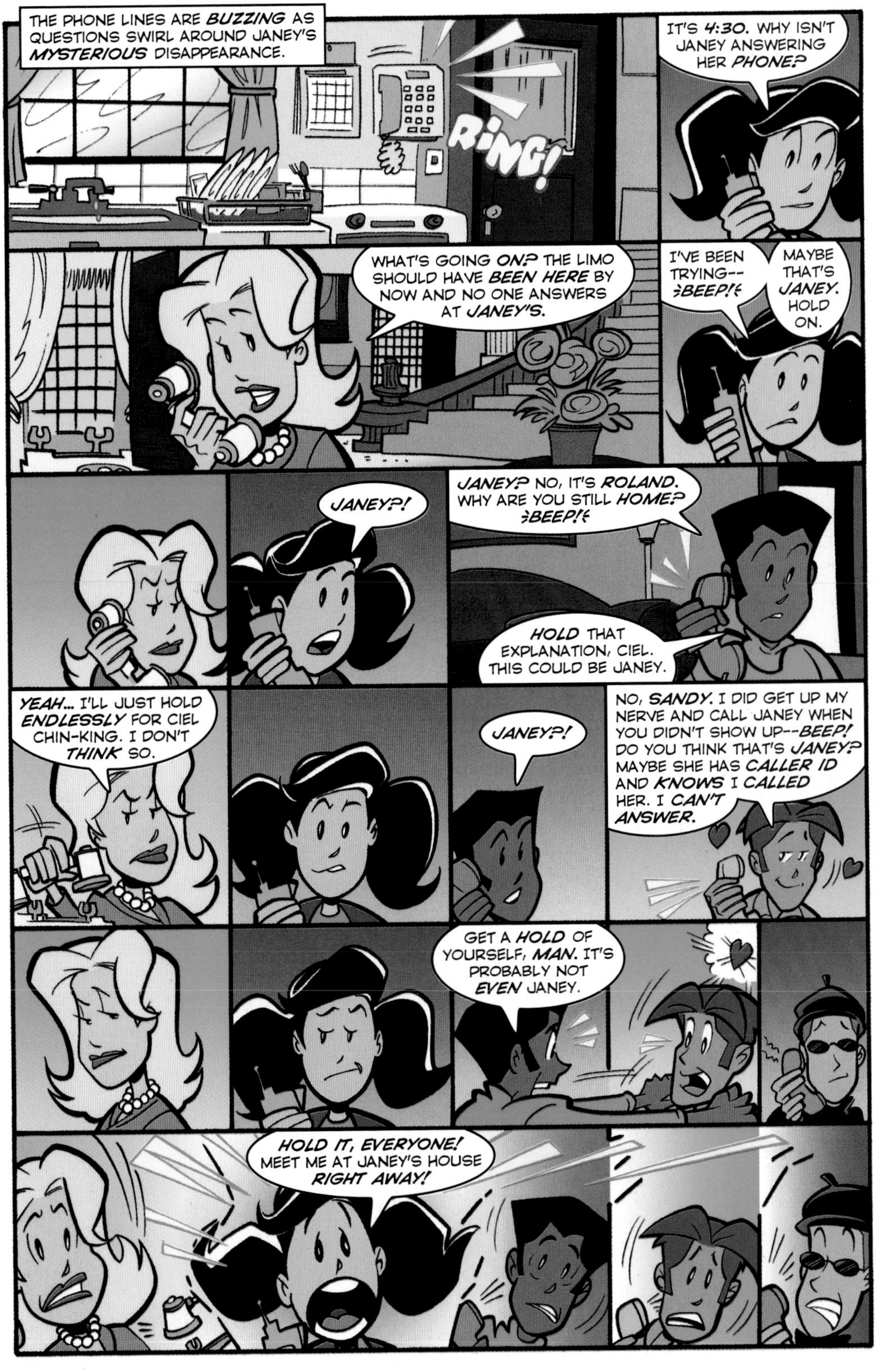
THE PHONE LINES ARE BUZZING AS QUESTIONS SWIRL AROUND JANEY'S MYSTERIOUS DISAPPEARANCE.
RING!
IT'S 4:30. WHY ISN'T JANEY ANSWERING HER PHONE?
WHAT'S GOING ON? THE LIMO SHOULD HAVE BEEN HERE BY NOW AND NO ONE ANSWERS AT JANEY'S.
I'VE BEEN TRYING-- BEEP!
MAYBE THAT'S JANEY. HOLD ON.
JANEY?!
JANEY? NO, IT'S ROLAND. WHY ARE YOU STILL HOME? BEEP!
HOLD THAT EXPLANATION, CIEL. THIS COULD BE JANEY.
YEAH... I'LL JUST HOLD ENDLESSLY FOR CIEL CHIN-KING. I DON'T THINK SO.
JANEY?!
NO, SANDY. I DID GET UP MY NERVE AND CALL JANEY WHEN YOU DIDN'T SHOW UP--BEEP! DO YOU THINK THAT'S JANEY? MAYBE SHE HAS CALLER ID AND KNOWS I CALLED HER. I CAN'T ANSWER.
GET A HOLD OF YOURSELF, MAN. IT'S PROBABLY NOT EVEN JANEY.
HOLD IT, EVERYONE! MEET ME AT JANEY'S HOUSE RIGHT AWAY!

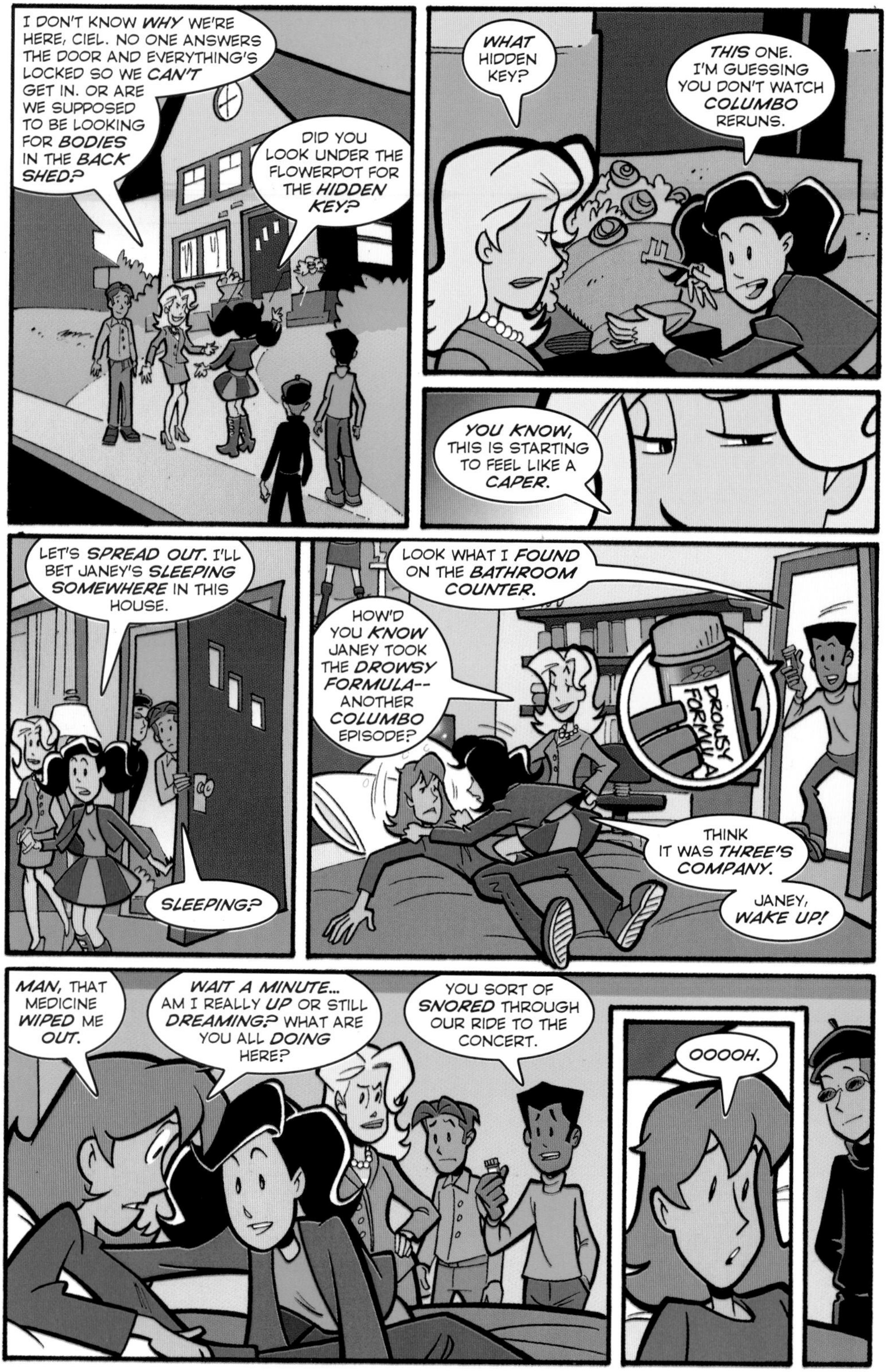
I DON'T KNOW WHY WE'RE HERE, CIEL. NO ONE ANSWERS THE DOOR AND EVERYTHING'S LOCKED SO WE CAN'T GET IN. OR ARE WE SUPPOSED TO BE LOOKING FOR BODIES IN THE BACK SHED?
DID YOU LOOK UNDER THE FLOWERPOT FOR THE HIDDEN KEY?
WHAT HIDDEN KEY?
THIS ONE. I'M GUESSING YOU DON'T WATCH COLUMBO RERUNS.
YOU KNOW, THIS IS STARTING TO FEEL LIKE A CAPER.
LET'S SPREAD OUT. I'LL BET JANEY'S SLEEPING SOMEWHERE IN THIS HOUSE.
SLEEPING?
LOOK WHAT I FOUND ON THE BATHROOM COUNTER.
HOW'D YOU KNOW JANEY TOOK THE DROWSY FORMULA-- ANOTHER COLUMBO EPISODE?
DROWSY FORMULA
THINK IT WAS THREE'S COMPANY.
JANEY, WAKE UP!
MAN, THAT MEDICINE WIPED ME OUT.
WAIT A MINUTE... AM I REALLY UP OR STILL DREAMING? WHAT ARE YOU ALL DOING HERE?
YOU SORT OF SNORED THROUGH OUR RIDE TO THE CONCERT.
OOOOH.

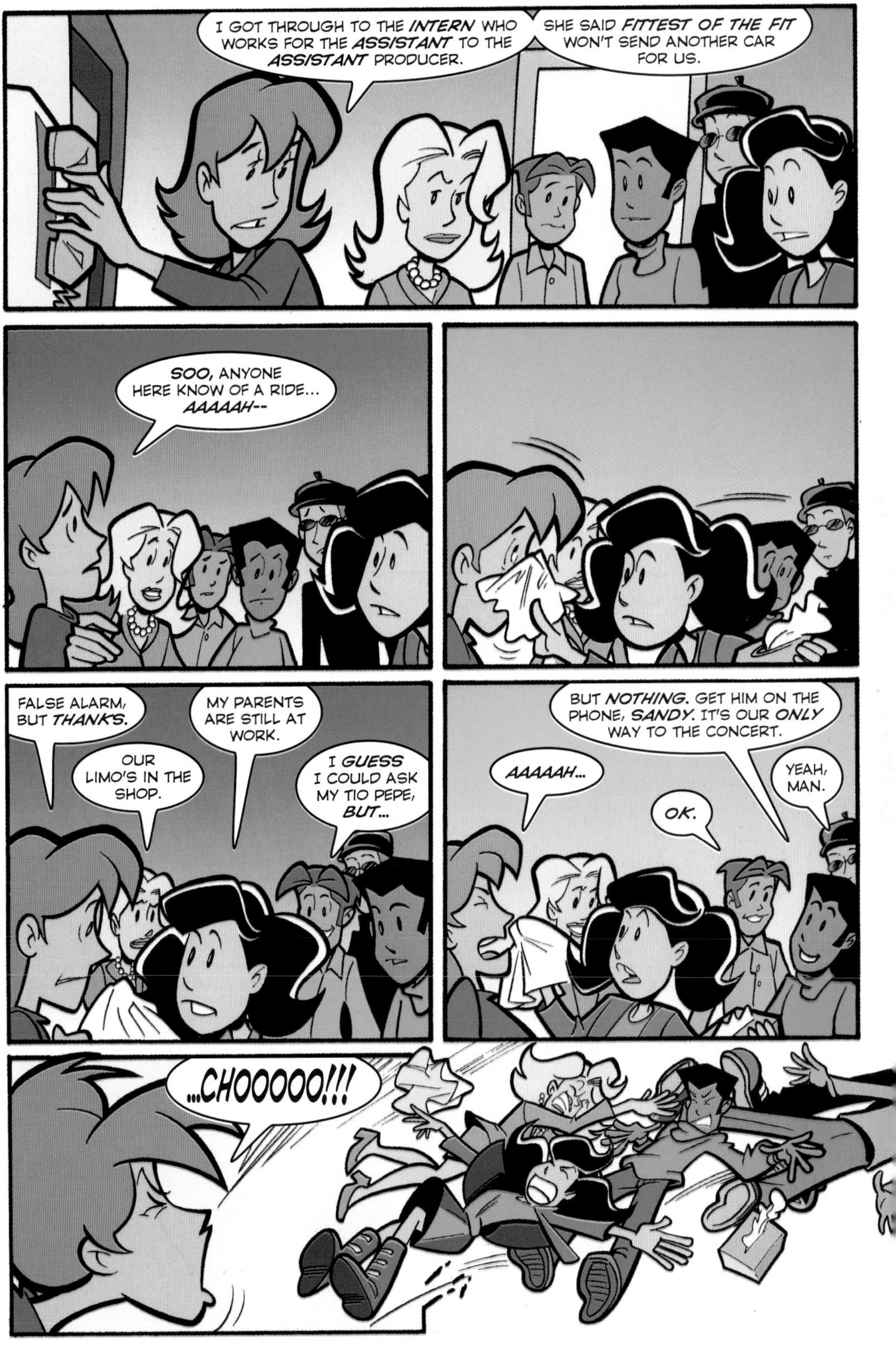
I GOT THROUGH TO THE INTERN WHO WORKS FOR THE ASSISTANT TO THE ASSISTANT PRODUCER.
SHE SAID FITTEST OF THE FIT WON'T SEND ANOTHER CAR FOR US.
SOO, ANYONE HERE KNOW OF A RIDE... AAAAAH--
FALSE ALARM, BUT THANKS.
OUR LIMO'S IN THE SHOP.
MY PARENTS ARE STILL AT WORK.
I GUESS I COULD ASK MY TIO PEPE, BUT...
BUT NOTHING. GET HIM ON THE PHONE, SANDY. IT'S OUR ONLY WAY TO THE CONCERT.
AAAAAH...
OK.
YEAH, MAN.
...CHOOOOO!!!

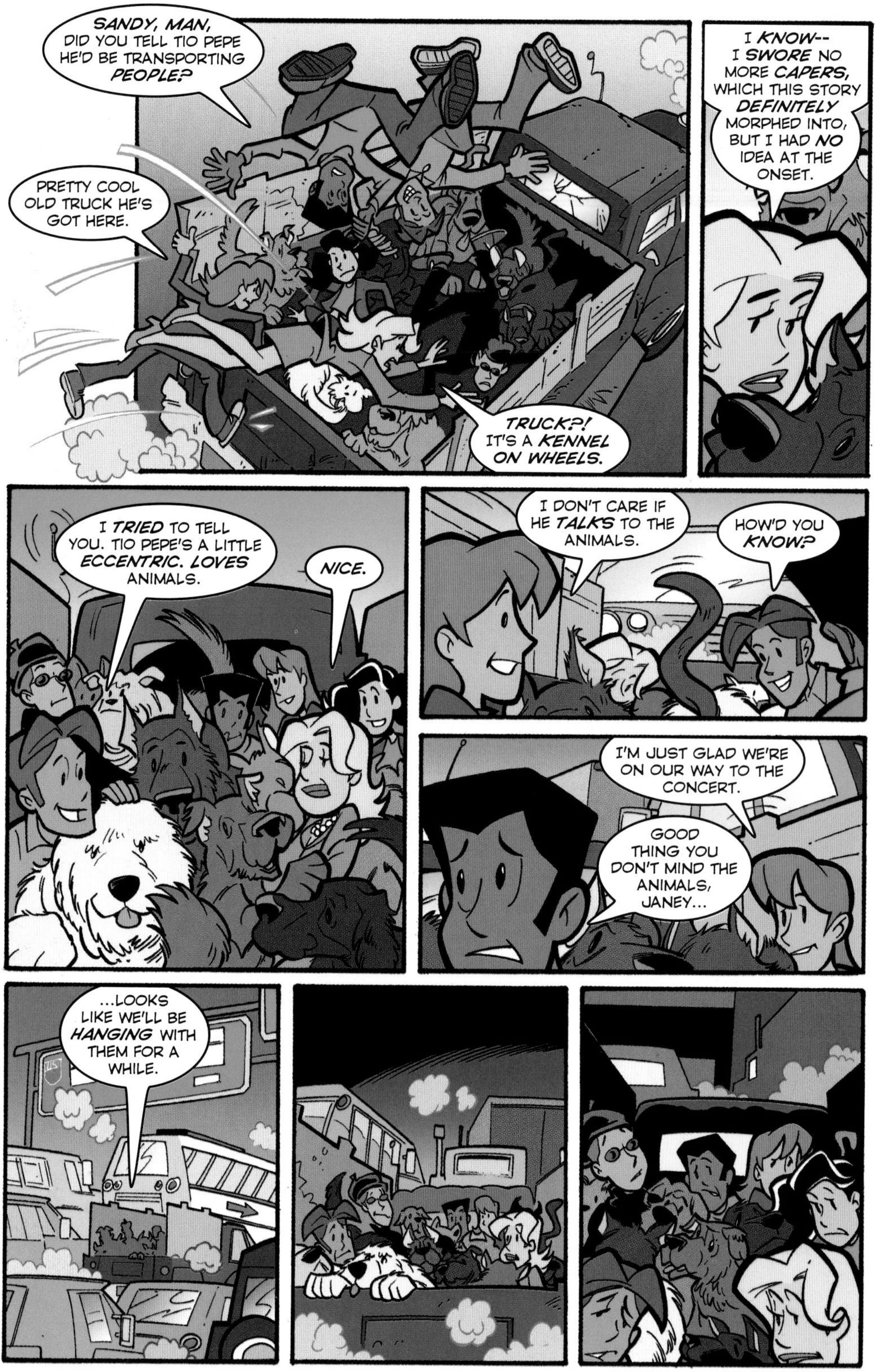
SANDY, MAN, DID YOU TELL TIO PEPE HE'D BE TRANSPORTING PEOPLE?
PRETTY COOL OLD TRUCK HE'S GOT HERE.
TRUCK?! IT'S A KENNEL ON WHEELS.
I KNOW-- I SWORE NO MORE CAPERS, WHICH THIS STORY DEFINITELY MORPHED INTO, BUT I HAD NO IDEA AT THE ONSET.
I TRIED TO TELL YOU. TIO PEPE'S A LITTLE ECCENTRIC. LOVES ANIMALS.
NICE.
I DON'T CARE IF HE TALKS TO THE ANIMALS.
HOW'D YOU KNOW?
I'M JUST GLAD WE'RE ON OUR WAY TO THE CONCERT.
GOOD THING YOU DON'T MIND THE ANIMALS, JANEY...
...LOOKS LIKE WE'LL BE HANGING WITH THEM FOR A WHILE.

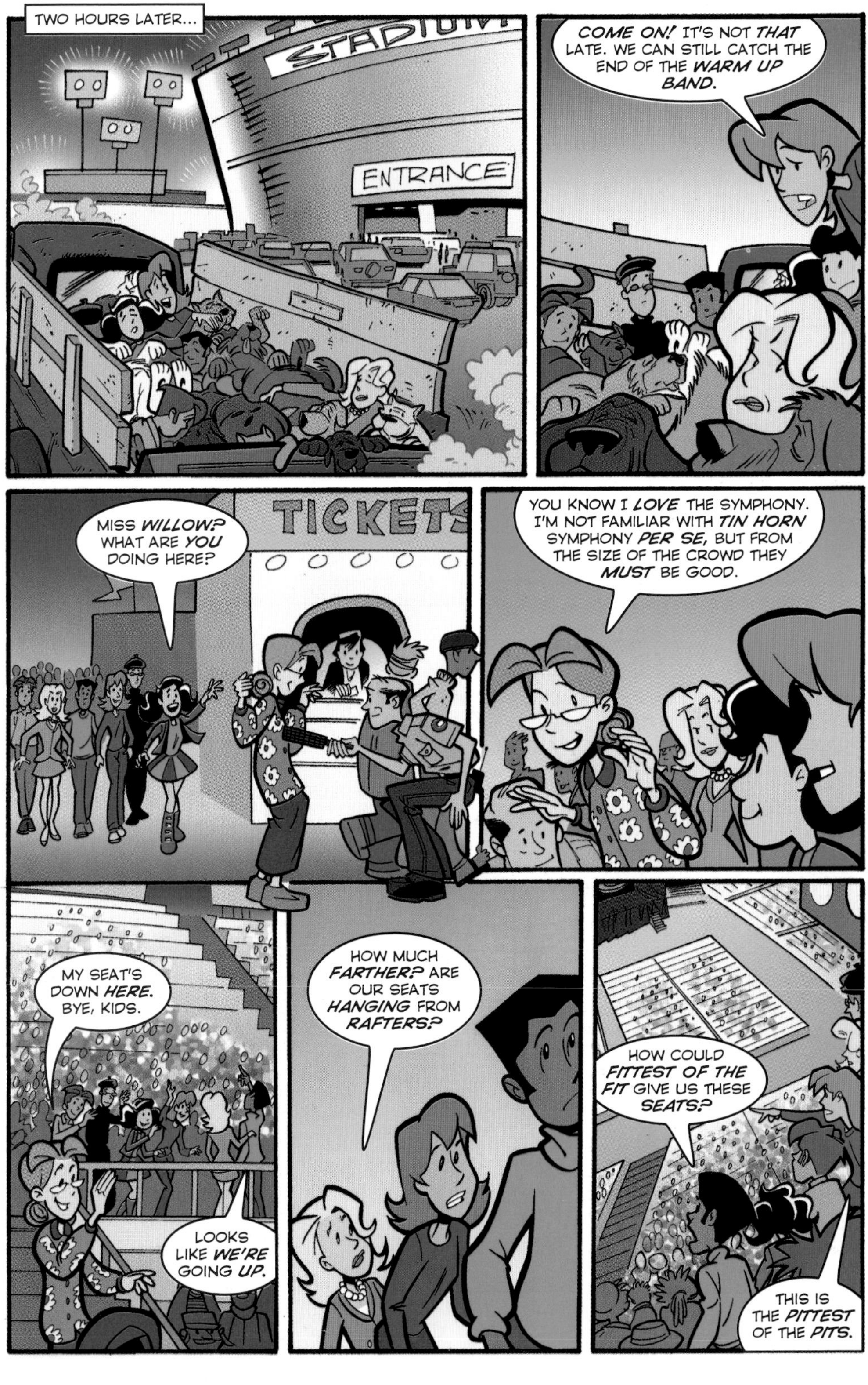
TWO HOURS LATER...
STADIUM
ENTRANCE
COME ON! IT'S NOT THAT LATE. WE CAN STILL CATCH THE END OF THE WARM UP BAND.
TICKETS
MISS WILLOW? WHAT ARE YOU DOING HERE?
YOU KNOW I LOVE THE SYMPHONY. I'M NOT FAMILIAR WITH TIN HORN SYMPHONY PER SE, BUT FROM THE SIZE OF THE CROWD THEY MUST BE GOOD.
MY SEAT'S DOWN HERE. BYE, KIDS.
LOOKS LIKE WE'RE GOING UP.
HOW MUCH FARTHER? ARE OUR SEATS HANGING FROM RAFTERS?
HOW COULD FITTEST OF THE FIT GIVE US THESE SEATS?
THIS IS THE PITTEST OF THE PITS.

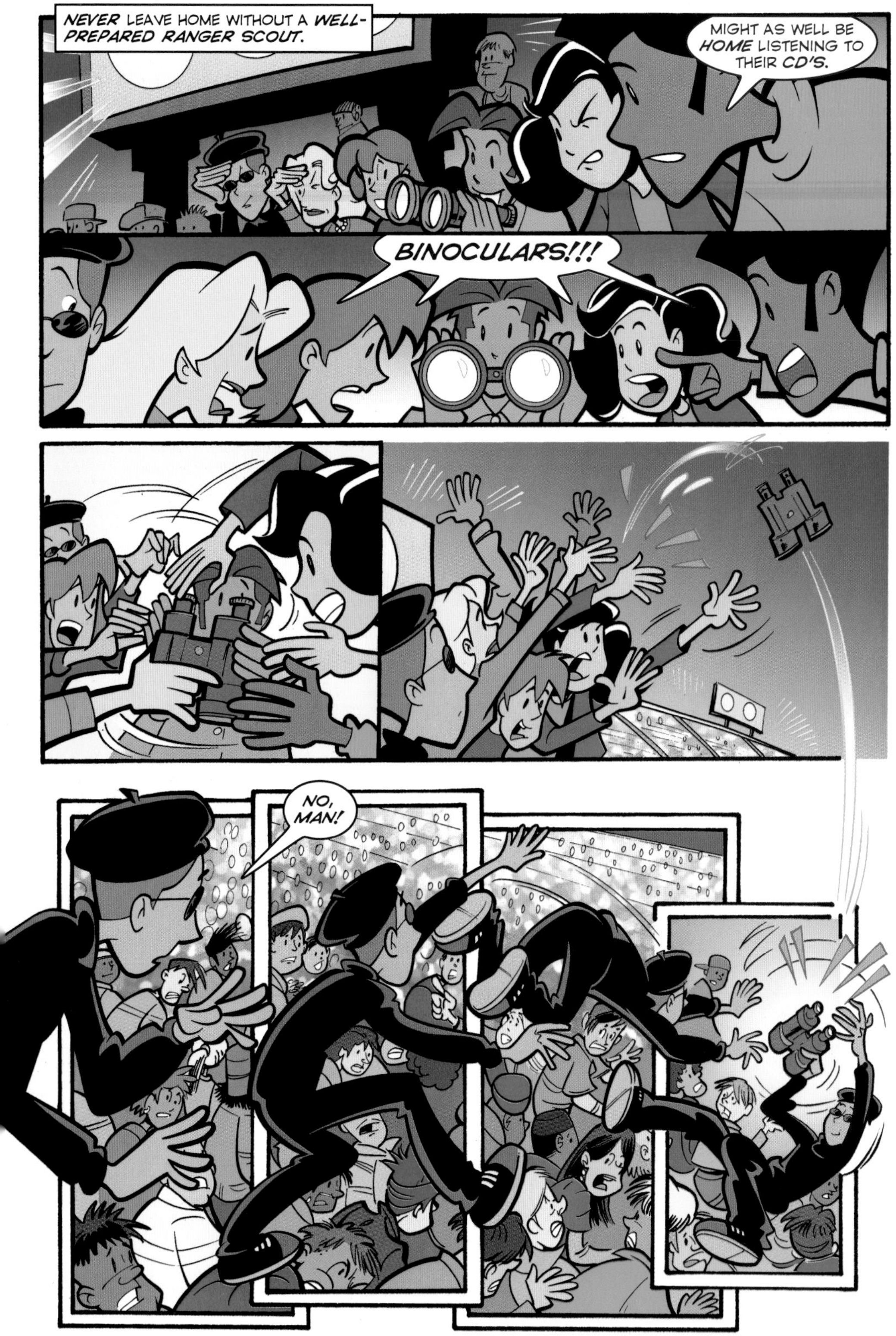
NEVER LEAVE HOME WITHOUT A WELL-PREPARED RANGER SCOUT.
MIGHT AS WELL BE HOME LISTENING TO THEIR CD'S.
BINOCULARS!!!
NO, MAN!

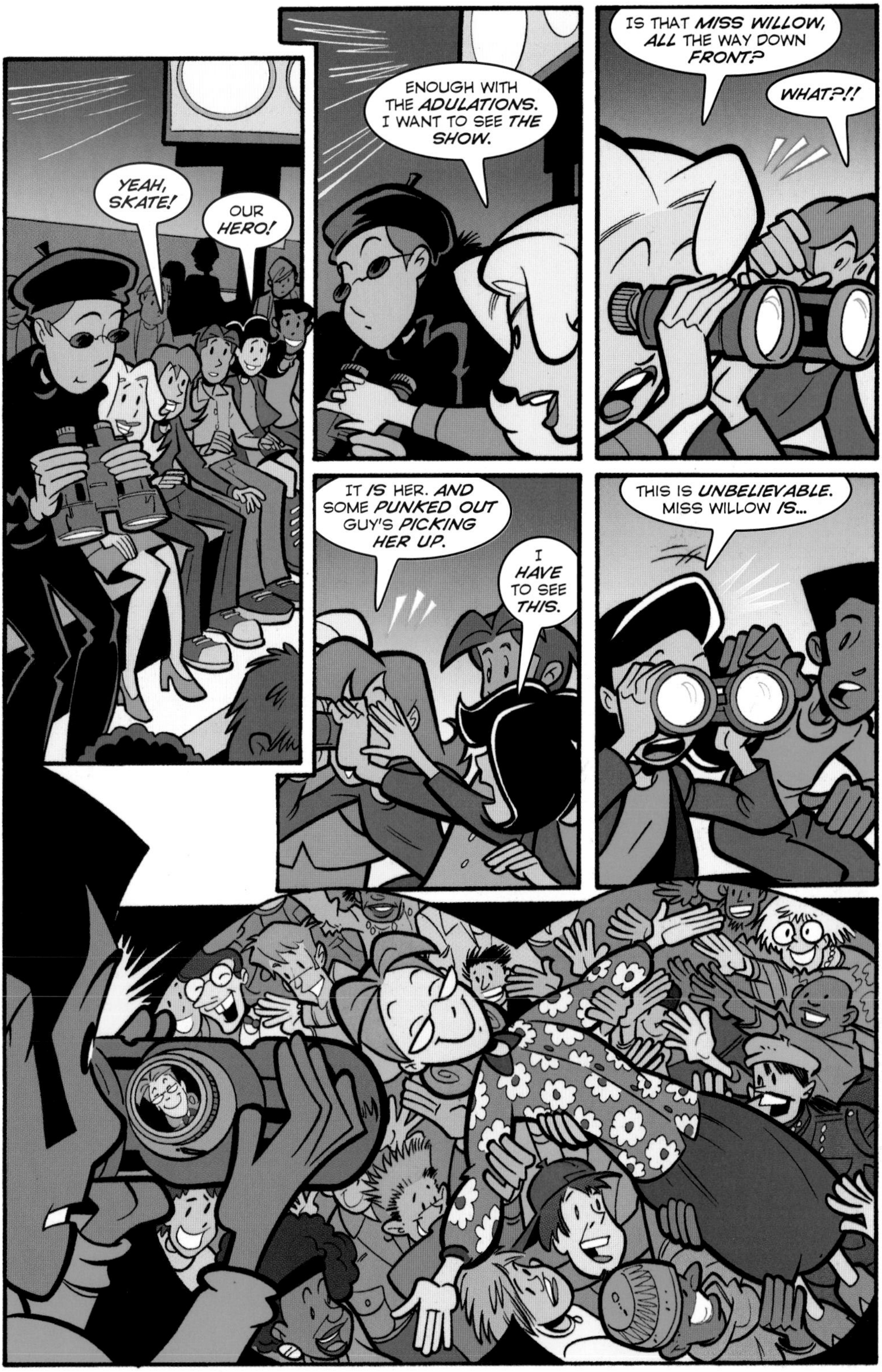
YEAH, SKATE!
OUR HERO!
ENOUGH WITH THE ADULATIONS. I WANT TO SEE THE SHOW.
IS THAT MISS WILLOW, ALL THE WAY DOWN FRONT?
WHAT?!!
IT IS HER. AND SOME PUNKED OUT GUY'S PICKING HER UP.
I HAVE TO SEE THIS.
THIS IS UNBELIEVABLE. MISS WILLOW IS...

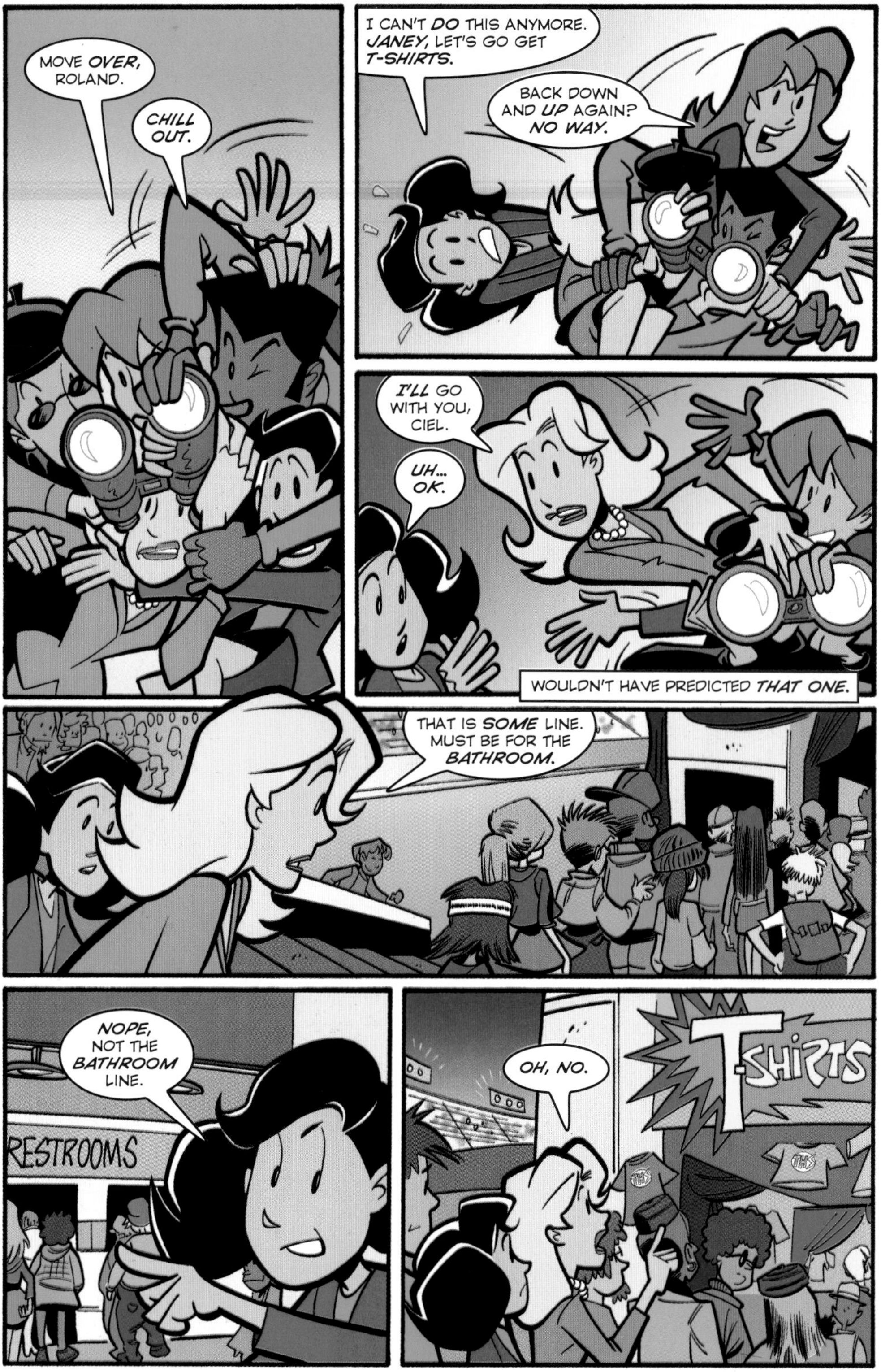
MOVE OVER, ROLAND.
CHILL OUT.
I CAN'T DO THIS ANYMORE. JANEY, LET'S GO GET T-SHIRTS.
BACK DOWN AND UP AGAIN? NO WAY.
I'LL GO WITH YOU, CIEL.
UH... OK.
WOULDN'T HAVE PREDICTED THAT ONE.
THAT IS SOME LINE. MUST BE FOR THE BATHROOM.
NOPE, NOT THE BATHROOM LINE.
RESTROOMS
OH, NO.
T-SHIRTS

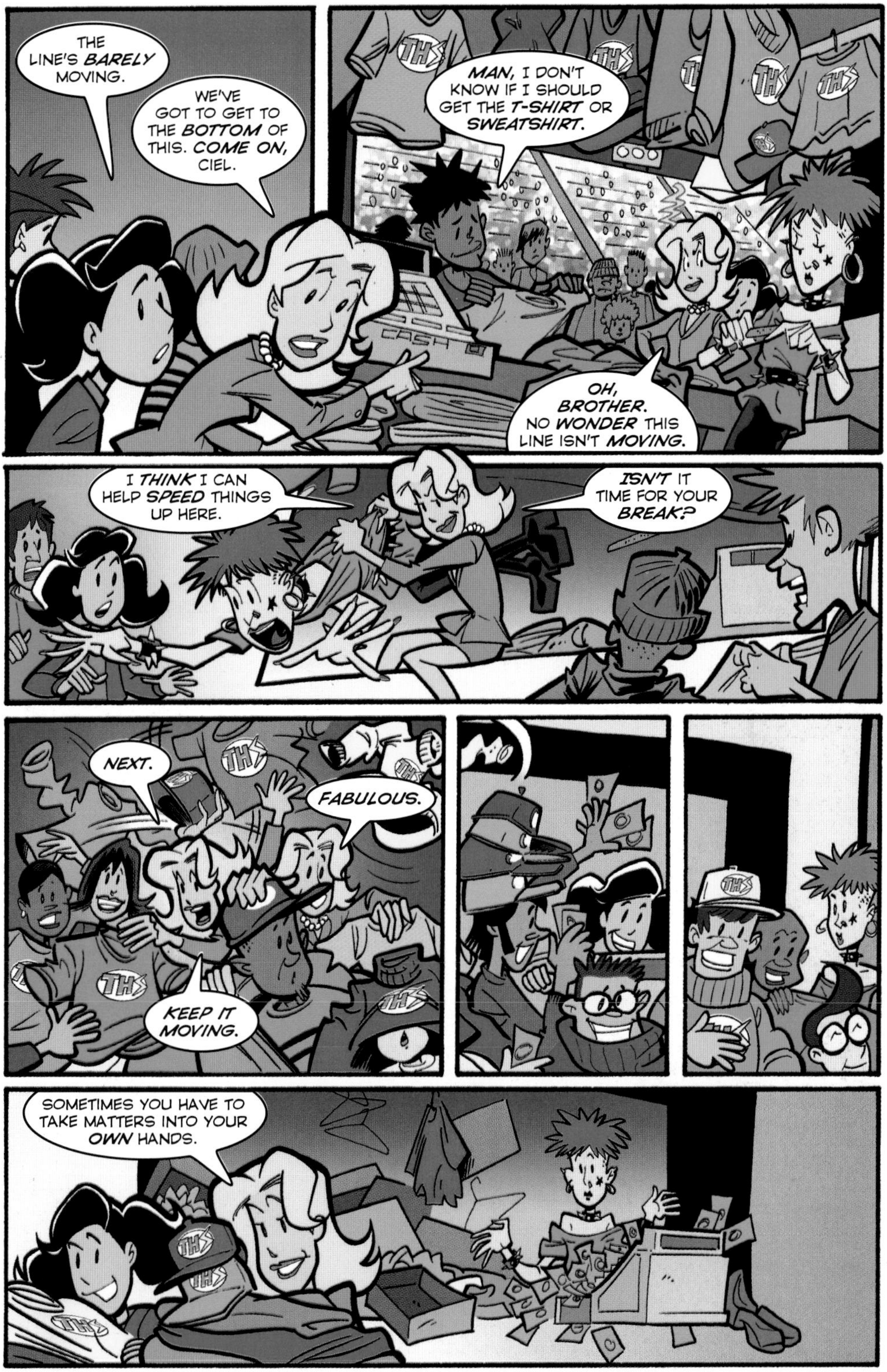
THE LINE'S BARELY MOVING.
WE'VE GOT TO GET TO THE BOTTOM OF THIS. COME ON, CIEL.
MAN, I DON'T KNOW IF I SHOULD GET THE T-SHIRT OR SWEATSHIRT.
CASH
OH, BROTHER. NO WONDER THIS LINE ISN'T MOVING.
I THINK I CAN HELP SPEED THINGS UP HERE.
ISN'T IT TIME FOR YOUR BREAK?
NEXT.
FABULOUS.
KEEP IT MOVING.
SOMETIMES YOU HAVE TO TAKE MATTERS INTO YOUR OWN HANDS.

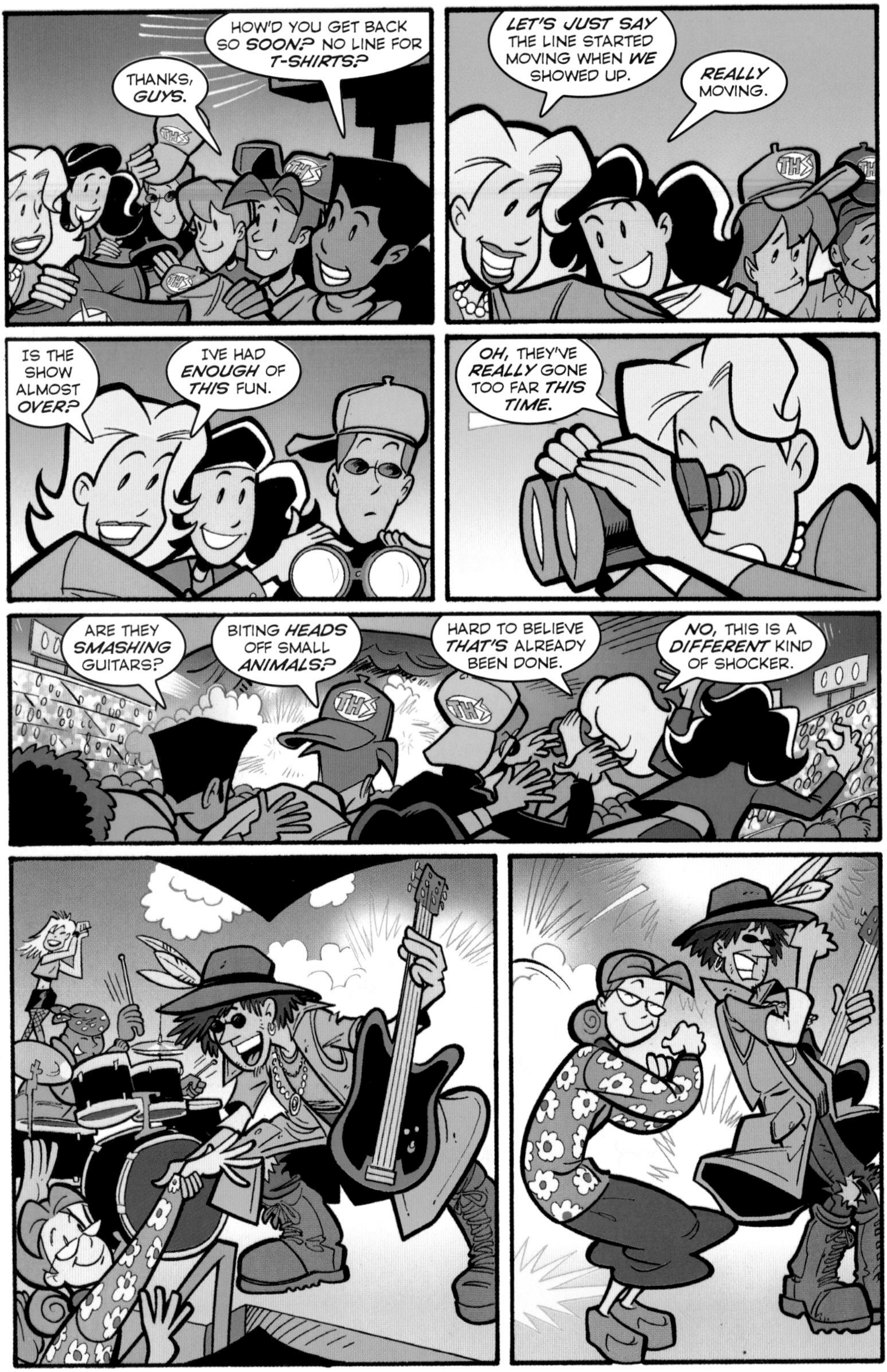
THANKS, GUYS.
HOW'D YOU GET BACK SO SOON? NO LINE FOR T-SHIRTS?
LET'S JUST SAY THE LINE STARTED MOVING WHEN WE SHOWED UP.
REALLY MOVING.
IS THE SHOW ALMOST OVER?
I'VE HAD ENOUGH OF THIS FUN.
OH, THEY'VE REALLY GONE TOO FAR THIS TIME.
ARE THEY SMASHING GUITARS?
BITING HEADS OFF SMALL ANIMALS?
HARD TO BELIEVE THAT'S ALREADY BEEN DONE.
NO, THIS IS A DIFFERENT KIND OF SHOCKER.

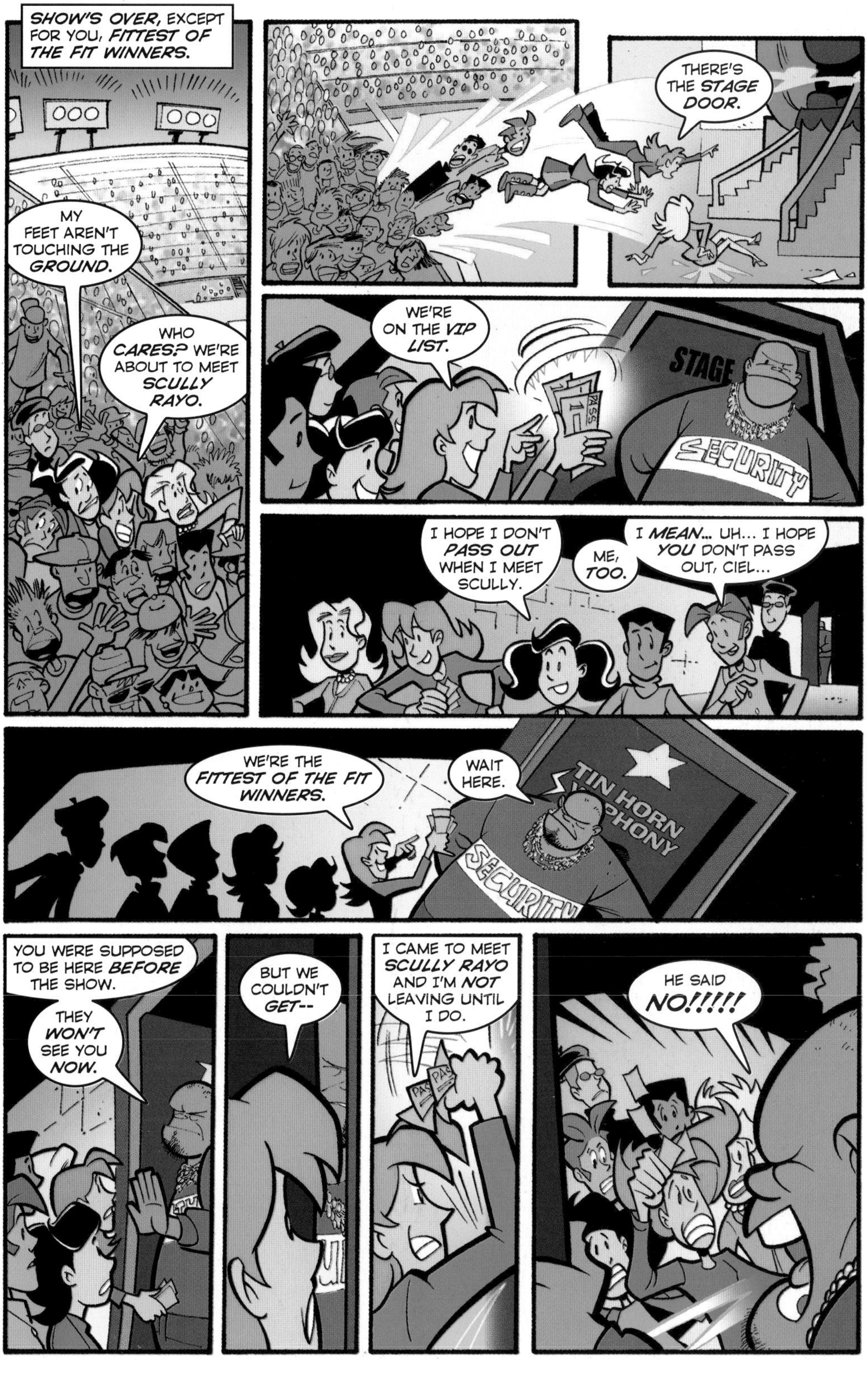
SHOW'S OVER, EXCEPT FOR YOU, FITTEST OF THE FIT WINNERS.
MY FEET AREN'T TOUCHING THE GROUND.
WHO CARES? WE'RE ABOUT TO MEET SCULLY RAYO.
THERE'S THE STAGE DOOR.
WE'RE ON THE VIP LIST.
STAGE
SECURITY
I HOPE I DON'T PASS OUT WHEN I MEET SCULLY.
ME, TOO.
I MEAN... UH... I HOPE YOU DON'T PASS OUT, CIEL...
WE'RE THE FITTEST OF THE FIT WINNERS.
WAIT HERE.
SECURITY
YOU WERE SUPPOSED TO BE HERE BEFORE THE SHOW.
THEY WON'T SEE YOU NOW.
BUT WE COULDN'T GET--
I CAME TO MEET SCULLY RAYO AND I'M NOT LEAVING UNTIL I DO.
HE SAID NO!!!!!!

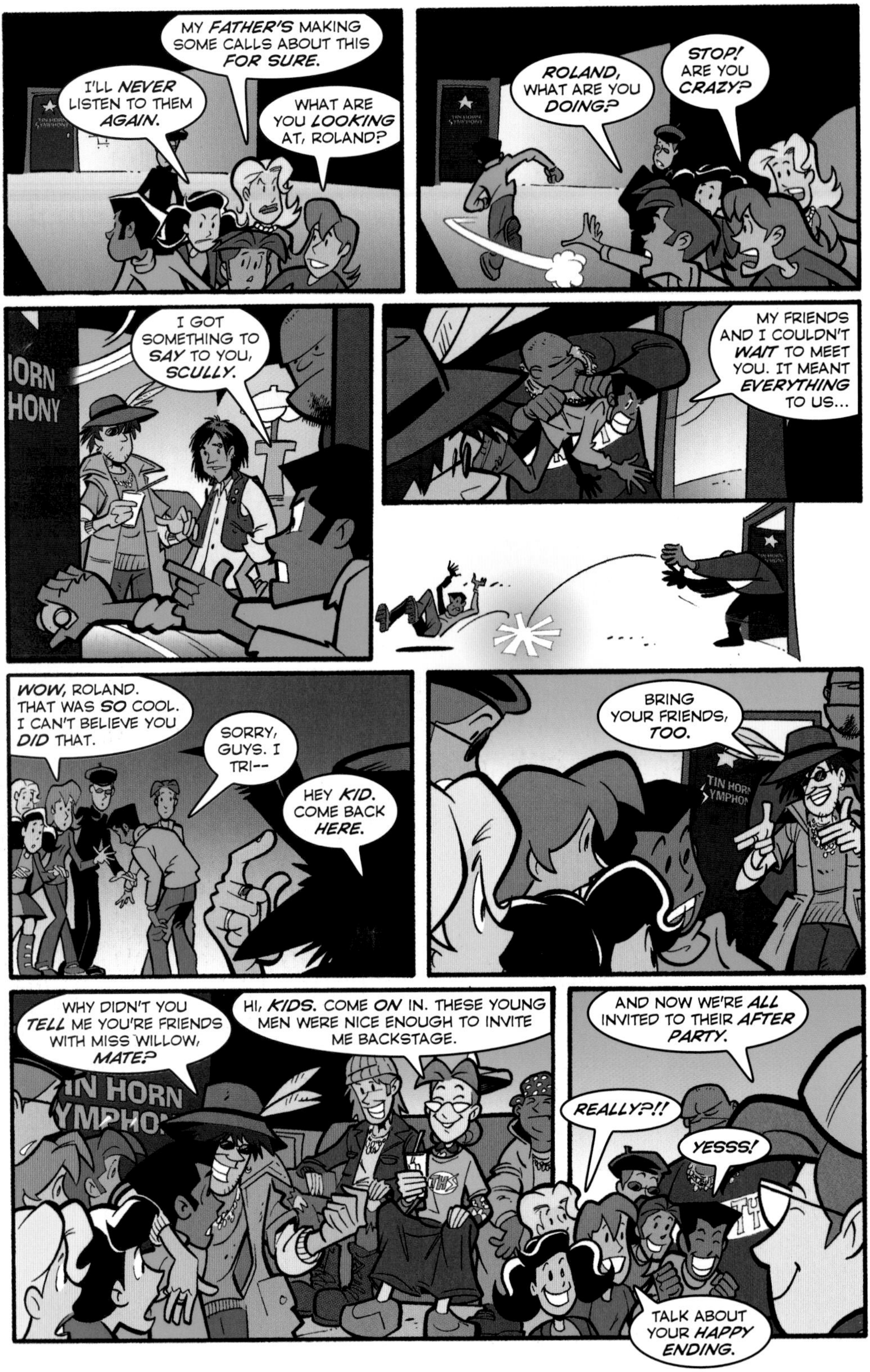
I'LL NEVER LISTEN TO THEM AGAIN.
MY FATHER'S MAKING SOME CALLS ABOUT THIS FOR SURE.
WHAT ARE YOU LOOKING AT, ROLAND?
ROLAND, WHAT ARE YOU DOING?
STOP! ARE YOU CRAZY?
I GOT SOMETHING TO SAY TO YOU, SCULLY.
MY FRIENDS AND I COULDN'T WAIT TO MEET YOU. IT MEANT EVERYTHING TO US...
WOW, ROLAND. THAT WAS SO COOL. I CAN'T BELIEVE YOU DID THAT.
SORRY, GUYS. I TRI--
HEY KID. COME BACK HERE.
BRING YOUR FRIENDS, TOO.
TIN HORN SYMPHON
WHY DIDN'T YOU TELL ME YOU'RE FRIENDS WITH MISS WILLOW, MATE?
HI, KIDS. COME ON IN. THESE YOUNG MEN WERE NICE ENOUGH TO INVITE ME BACKSTAGE.
TIN HORN SYMPHO
AND NOW WE'RE ALL INVITED TO THEIR AFTER PARTY.
REALLY?!!
YESSS!
TALK ABOUT YOUR HAPPY ENDING.

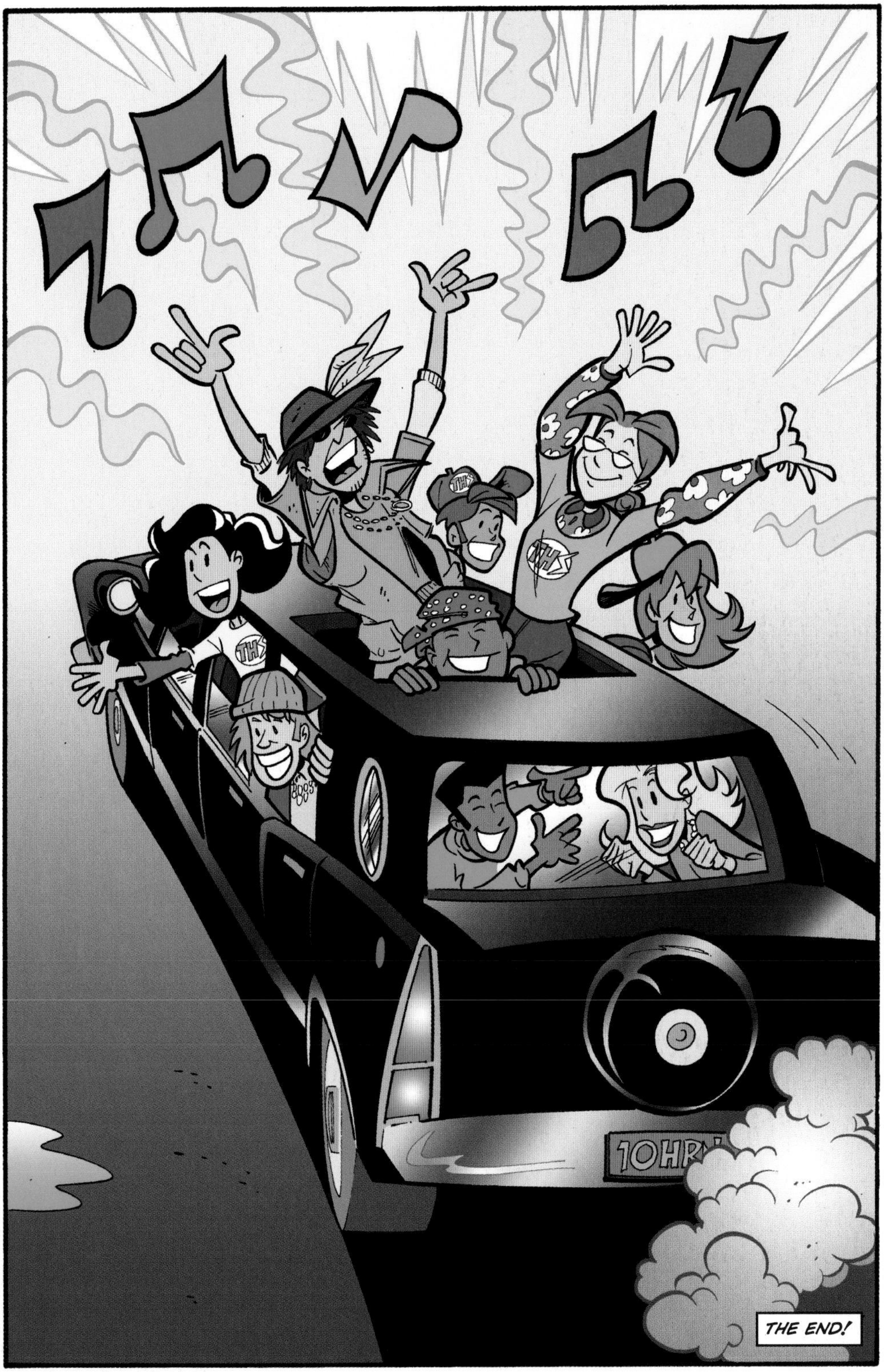
THE END!

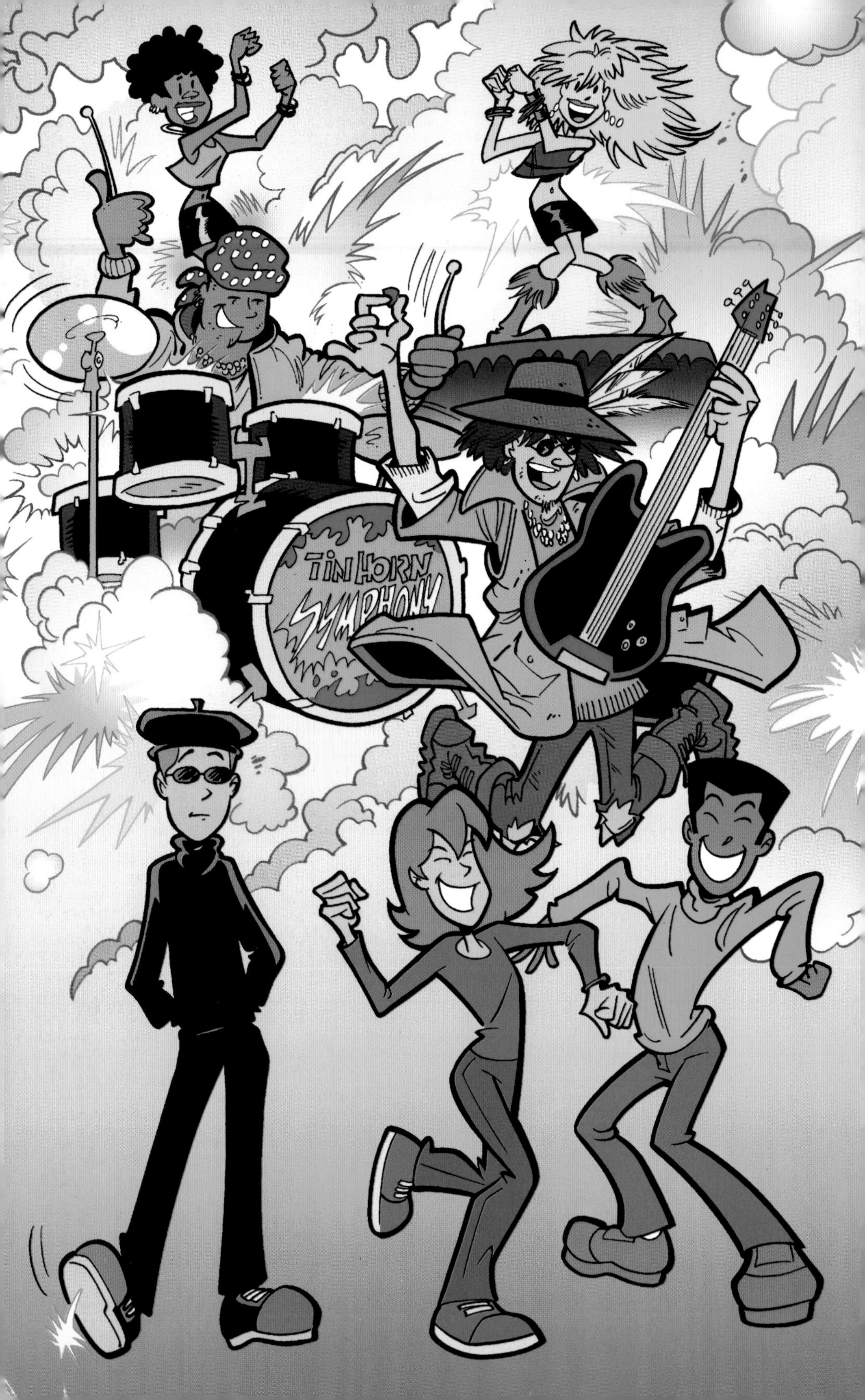
TIN HORN
SYMPHONY

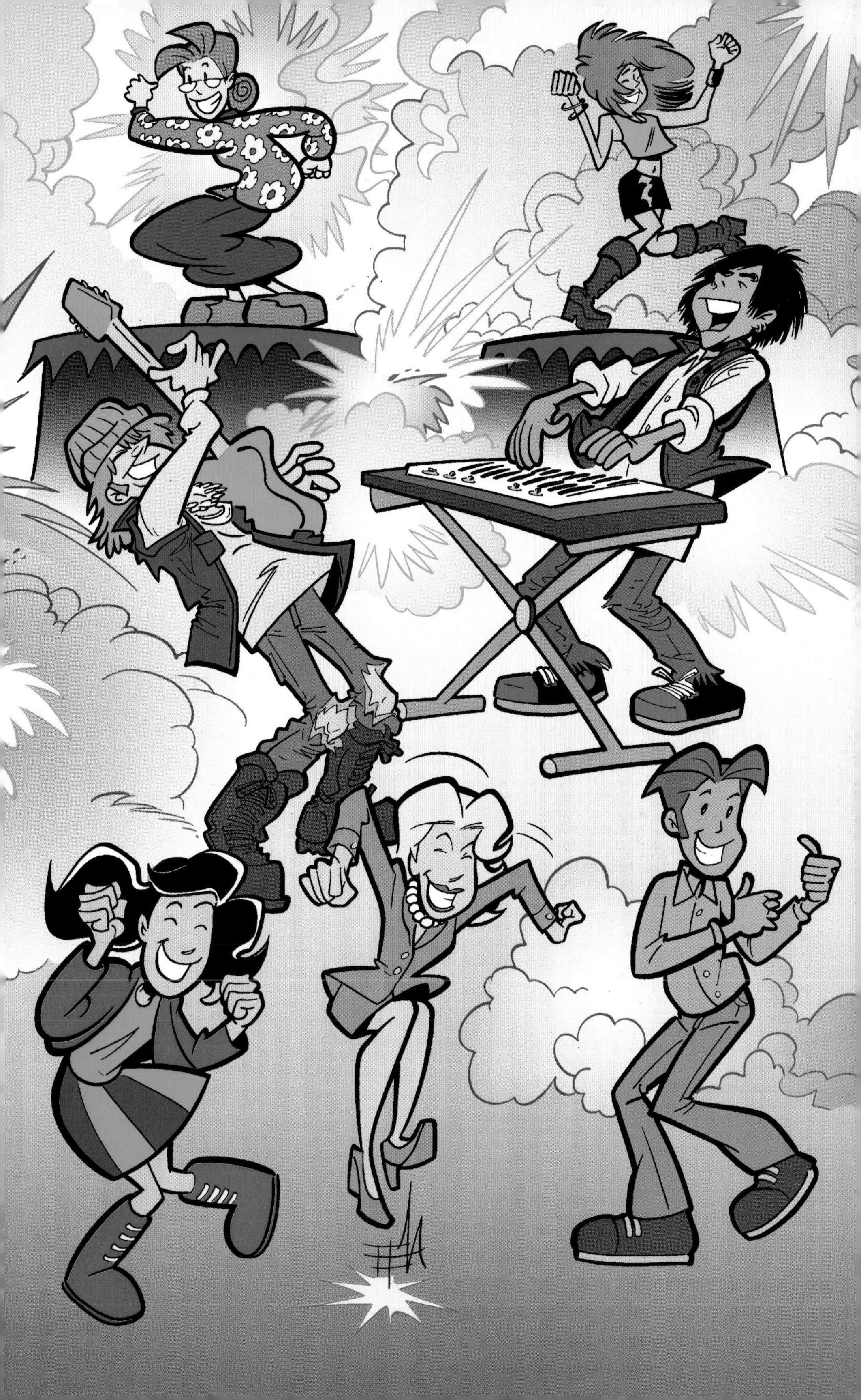

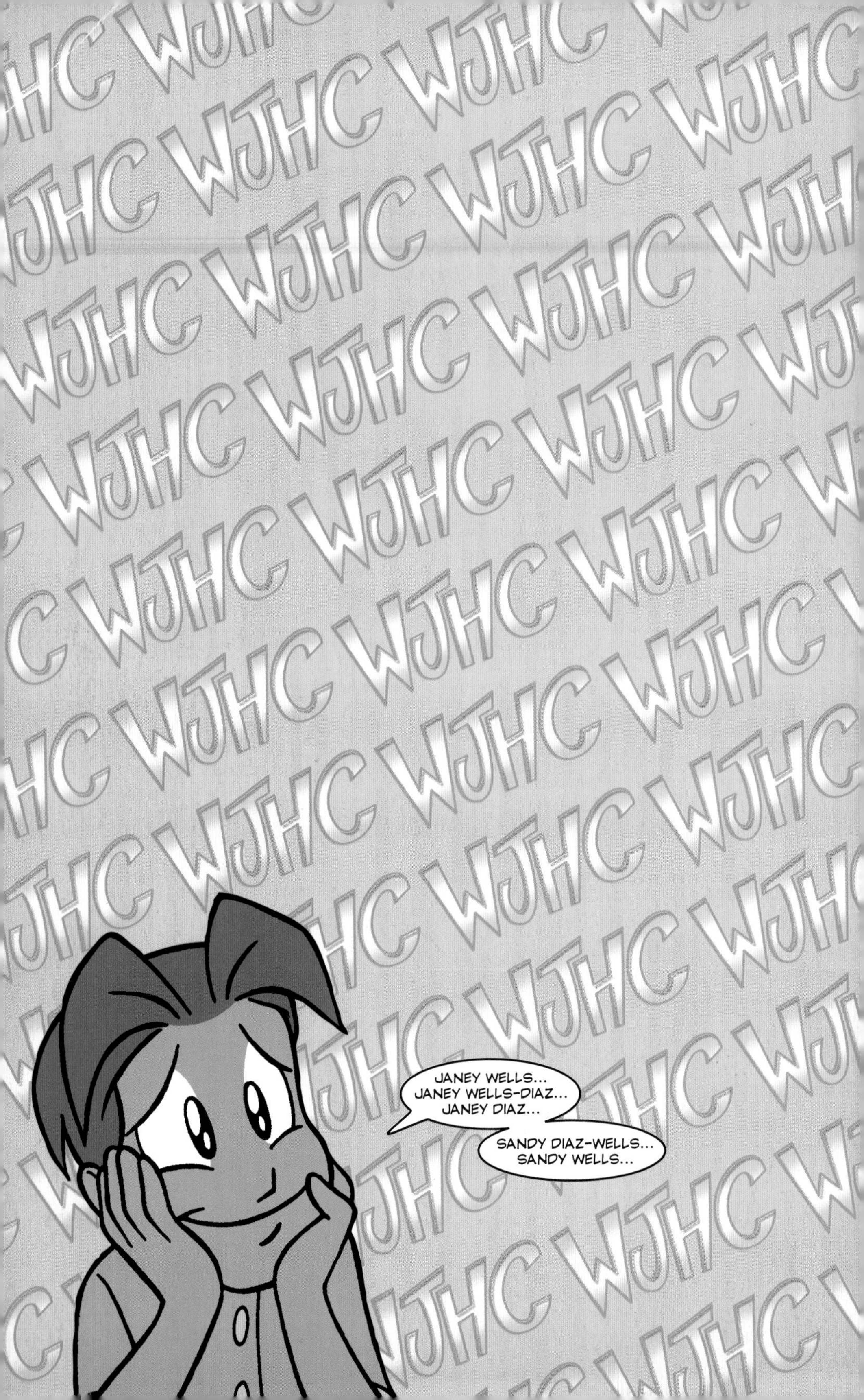
JANEY WELLS...
JANEY WELLS-DIAZ...
JANEY DIAZ...
SANDY DIAZ-WELLS...
SANDY WELLS...

START TO FINISH

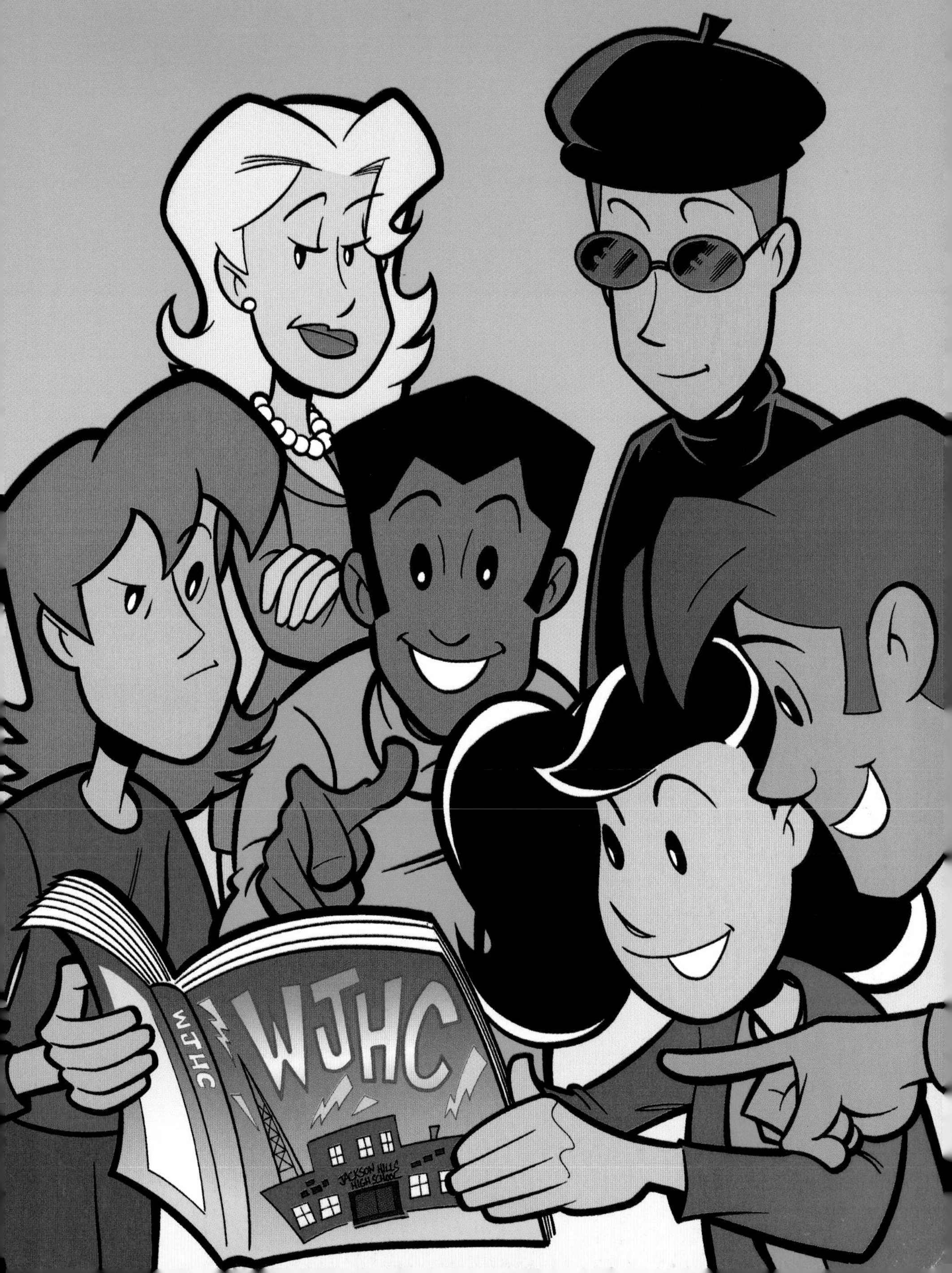
WJHC
WJHC
JACKSON HILLS HIGH SCHOOL

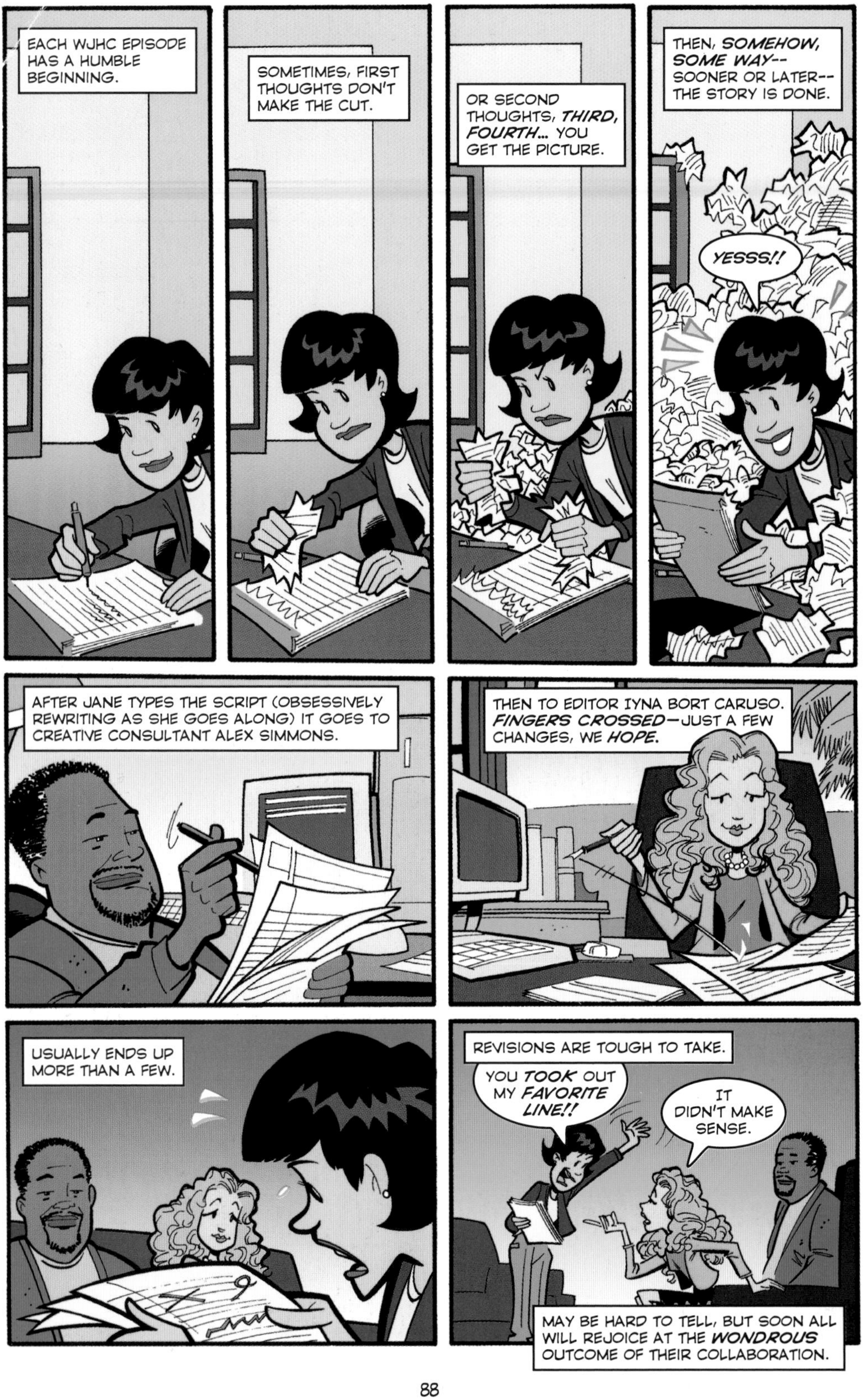
EACH WJHC EPISODE HAS A HUMBLE BEGINNING.
SOMETIMES, FIRST THOUGHTS DON'T MAKE THE CUT.
OR SECOND THOUGHTS, *THIRD, FOURTH...* YOU GET THE PICTURE.
THEN, *SOMEHOW, SOME WAY--* SOONER OR LATER-- THE STORY IS DONE.
YESSS!!
AFTER JANE TYPES THE SCRIPT (OBSESSIVELY REWRITING AS SHE GOES ALONG) IT GOES TO CREATIVE CONSULTANT ALEX SIMMONS.
THEN TO EDITOR IYNA BORT CARUSO. *FINGERS CROSSED*—JUST A FEW CHANGES, WE *HOPE.*
USUALLY ENDS UP MORE THAN A FEW.
REVISIONS ARE TOUGH TO TAKE.
YOU *TOOK* OUT MY *FAVORITE LINE!!*
IT DIDN'T MAKE SENSE.
MAY BE HARD TO TELL, BUT SOON ALL WILL REJOICE AT THE *WONDROUS* OUTCOME OF THEIR COLLABORATION.

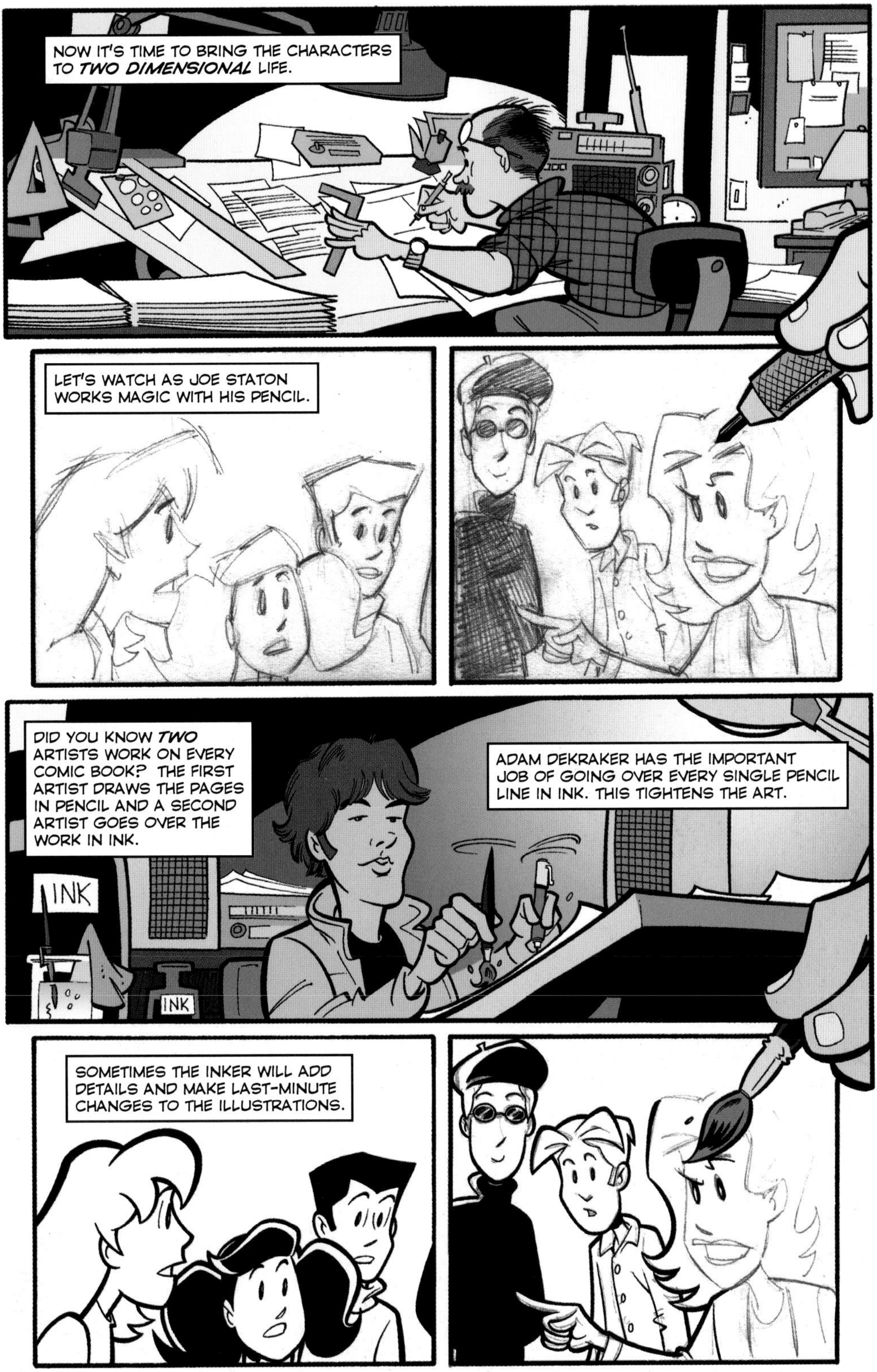
NOW IT'S TIME TO BRING THE CHARACTERS TO *TWO DIMENSIONAL* LIFE.
LET'S WATCH AS JOE STATON WORKS MAGIC WITH HIS PENCIL.
DID YOU KNOW *TWO* ARTISTS WORK ON EVERY COMIC BOOK? THE FIRST ARTIST DRAWS THE PAGES IN PENCIL AND A SECOND ARTIST GOES OVER THE WORK IN INK.
ADAM DEKRAKER HAS THE IMPORTANT JOB OF GOING OVER EVERY SINGLE PENCIL LINE IN INK. THIS TIGHTENS THE ART.
INK
INK
SOMETIMES THE INKER WILL ADD DETAILS AND MAKE LAST-MINUTE CHANGES TO THE ILLUSTRATIONS.

JOHN GREEN IS OUR COLORIST/LETTERER **EXTRAORDINAIRE.**

THE MAN IS THE ORIGINAL **MULTI-TASKER,** WORKING AT LIGHTNING SPEED.

WITH THE CLICK OF A MOUSE JOHN ADDS COLOR...

...AND WORD BALLOONS.

OH **JANEY,** HOW COULD

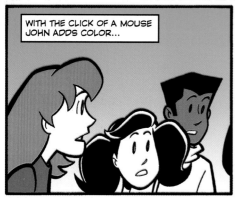

THE FINISHED WORK IS PUT ON A CD AND SENT TO THE PRINTER WHO SENDS A **"PROOF"** SO JANE CAN CHECK FOR MISTAKES...

...AND IYNA CAN CHECK FOR MISTAKES...

...AND HAROLD BUCHHOLZ, PRINT MANAGER, CAN CHECK FOR MISTAKES.

AND THERE'S **ALWAYS** AT LEAST ONE TYPO CAUGHT AT THIS STAGE.

I DON'T **BELIEVE** IT.

AT LEAST WE **CAUGHT** IT.

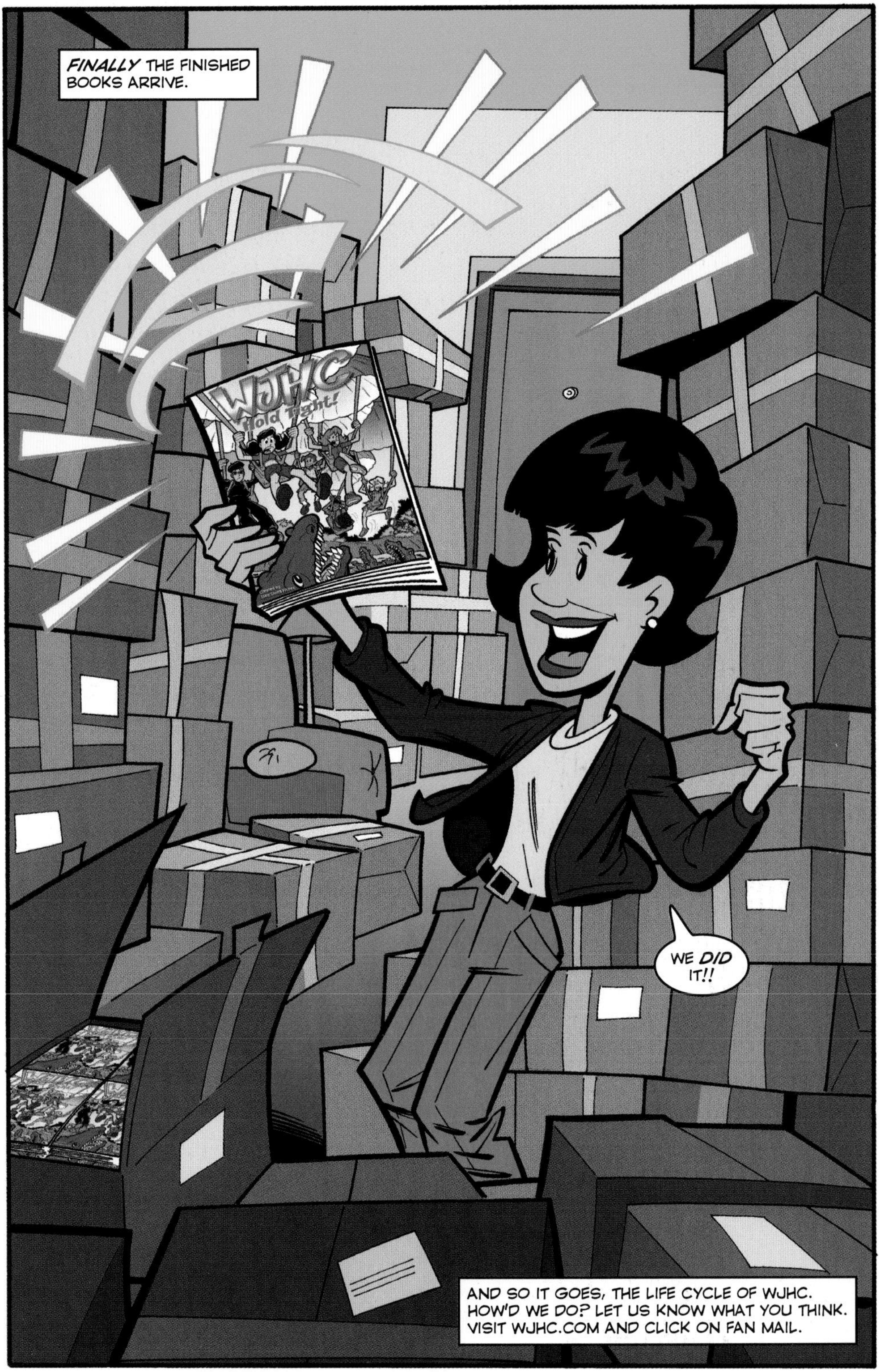
FINALLY THE FINISHED BOOKS ARRIVE.
WJHC Hold Tight!
WE DID IT!!
AND SO IT GOES, THE LIFE CYCLE OF WJHC. HOW'D WE DO? LET US KNOW WHAT YOU THINK. VISIT WJHC.COM AND CLICK ON FAN MAIL.

WJHC inside scoop!

Janey

Rumor has it there's a boy who's sweet on Janey. And we're not talking Sandy Diaz. Stay tuned for details.

Skate

Check this out -- the Skate lost his first five skating competitions. In one he finished downright last. Still, he never gave up. Now, of course he's a statewide champ.

Roland

After Roland saved the team on *Fittest of the Fit* his popularity meter soared. The word is he may even be asked to host the Jackson Hill High Battle of the Bands.

Ciel

Did you know Ciel thought of the radio station call letters, *JHC?* Yep, she did. They stand for *Jackson Hill Crowd.* W is the first letter in all radio station call letters in the eastern part of the U.S.

Tara

At age 11, Tara got the lead role in the sixth grade play. She never saw the stage, however. She quit the play when the leading man was announced, sighting he wasn't her equal in looks and talent.

Sandy

Once again Sandy made the High Honor Roll. Guess that's not much of an inside scoop. There just aren't many surprises in this kid's life.

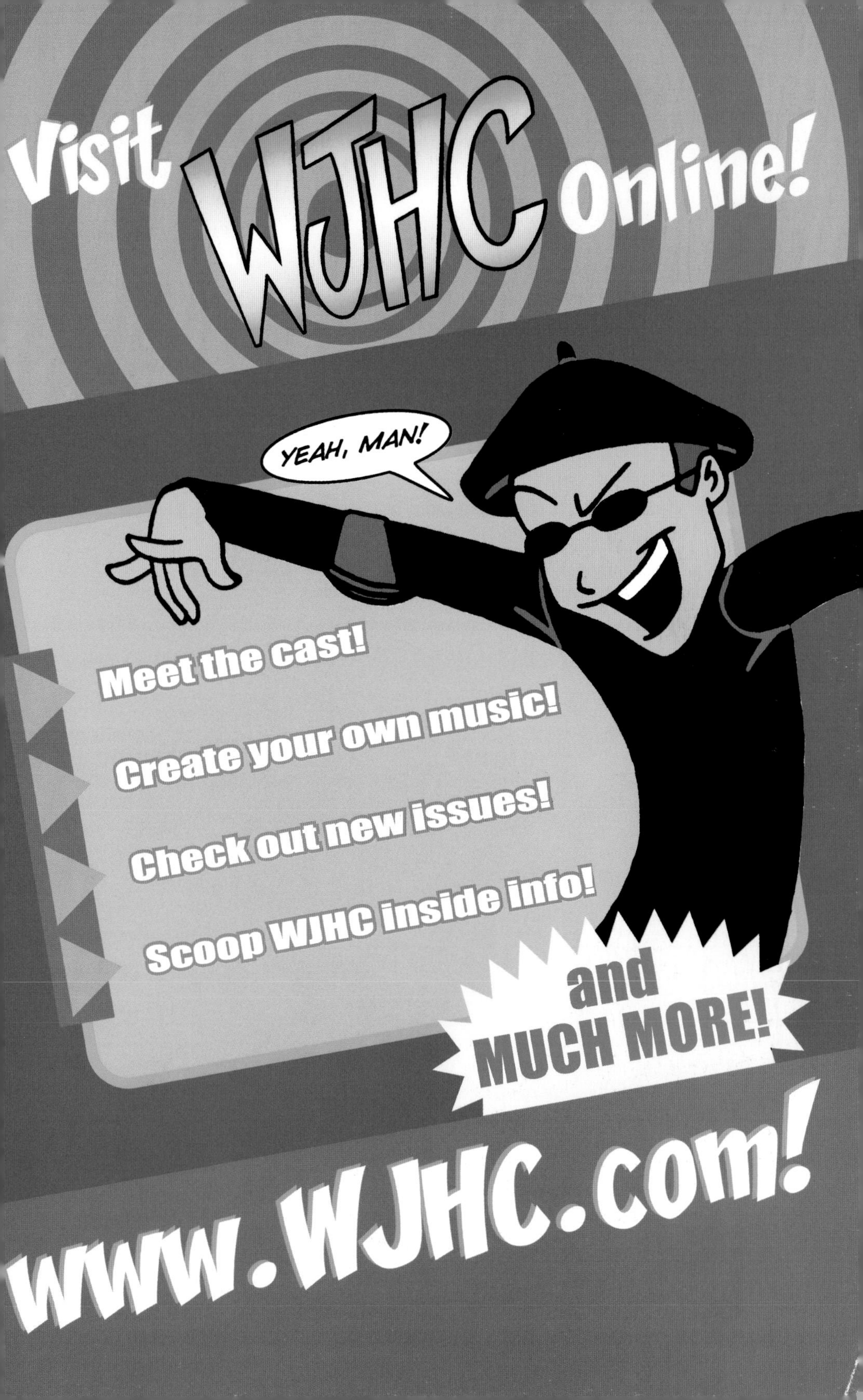
Visit WJHC Online!
YEAH, MAN!
Meet the cast!
Create your own music!
Check out new issues!
Scoop WJHC inside info!
and MUCH MORE!
www.WJHC.com!

On The Dial

We're back -- Jackson Hill's mischief-makers and *me*.

The response to the first book, *WJHC: On the Air!* was terrific. It received wonderful comments from readers and great editorial reviews. I'm so grateful to those who "tuned in." More on that later.

And now the second book. I took a bit of a turn with this one. I like to keep WJHC light and fun, but I felt it would be unrealistic if my characters never faced any teen dilemmas. Plus, I wanted to show different sides of the characters. After all, as Tara pointed out in *Fittest of the Fit,* no one's personality is one dimensional. I'm glad I went this way and very happy the animated art and bright colors kept the stories upbeat. Which leads me to my next paragraph.

You know I can't create my Jackson Hill antics without the WJHC team. Adam's inking, John's color and production – both brilliant! And thank goodness Alex and Iyna continue to pull the creative reigns in on me. We did have one major change in our group. After five years with WJHC, Kirsten Petersen moved on to other artistic pursuits. We all wish her well. We also thank our lucky stars that Joe Staton took her place. That man can work a pencil. Thanks a million to Joe and the whole WJHC team.

Now I'd like to give a special thanks to the library community. It's been a thrill to watch librarians across the country embrace WJHC. Not to mention the library journals and websites that gave WJHC wonderful reviews. Thousands of kids have been introduced to the WJHC series through copies of *WJHC: On the Air,* found on library shelves. In addition, copies of the WJHC library issue, *Between the Stacks,* continue to be distributed to kids by libraries from coast to coast. Truly, the success of WJHC has been in large measure a result of library support. Thank you so much.

Once again I saved the best for last. Many, many thanks to my friends and family for indulging me in my WJHC world. I never take your continued enthusiasm and support for granted. My son, Andrew, continues to soar to new heights, amazing me each day. Of course, he remains my inspiration.

And to you, my readers. I was so grateful when you gave the first WJHC graphic novel a chance. And here you are back with me for the second book. That is really something. It's not that I'm so humble. It's just that your response to the daily foibles of a bunch of wonderful, nutty teens is overwhelming to this everyday girl (with big dreams). See you again, right here in the next edition.

Jane

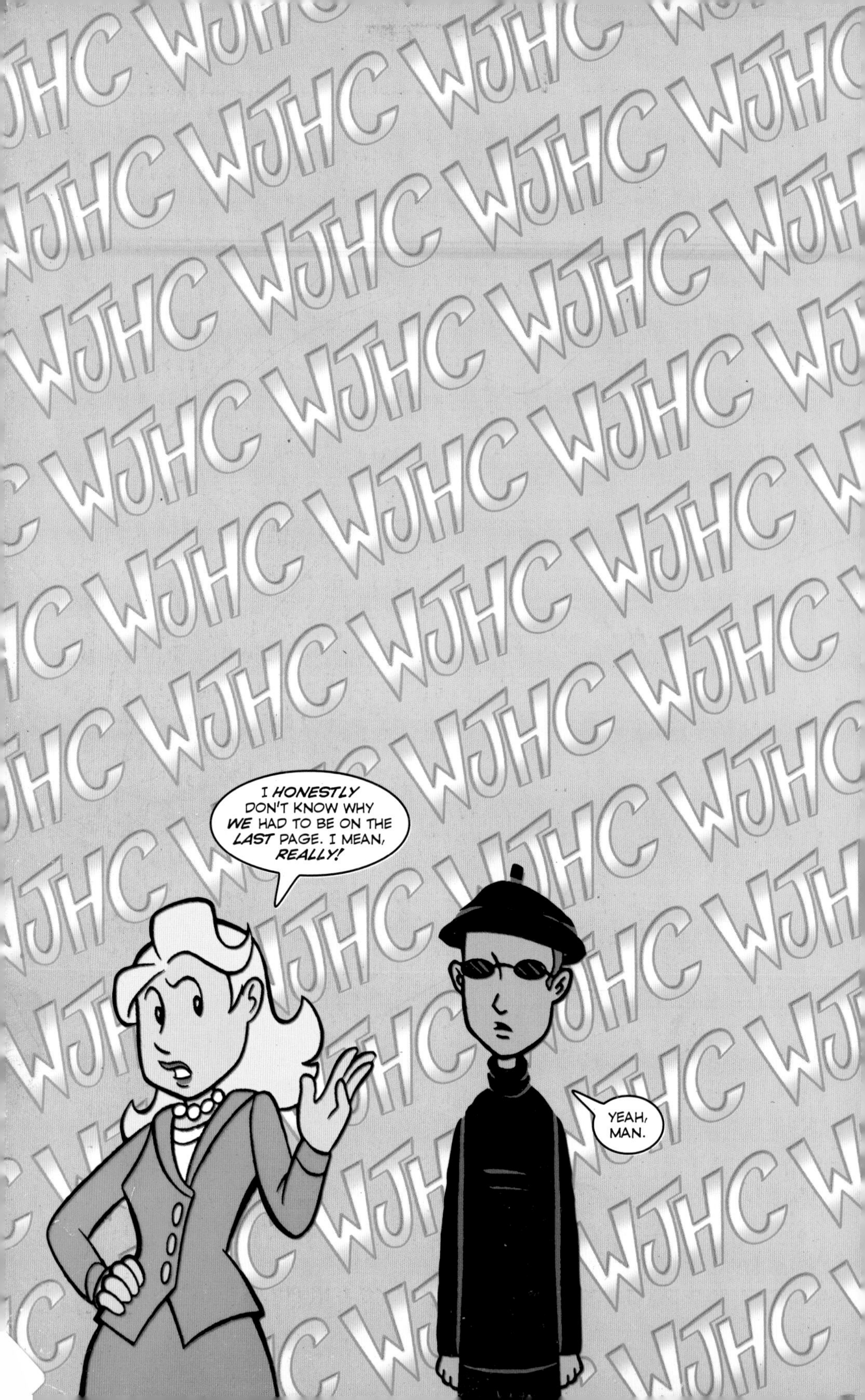
I HONESTLY DON'T KNOW WHY WE HAD TO BE ON THE LAST PAGE. I MEAN, REALLY!
YEAH, MAN.